ARCHITECTURE WALKS

ARCHITECTURE WALKS
The Best Outings near New York City

LUCY D. ROSENFELD
MARINA HARRISON

RIVERGATE BOOKS
An imprint of Rutgers University Press
New Brunswick, New Jersey, and London

Library of Congress Cataloging-in-Publication Data
Rosenfeld, Lucy D., 1939–
Architecture walks : the best outings near New York City /
Lucy D. Rosenfeld and Marina Harrison.
p.   cm.
Includes index.
ISBN 978-0-8135-4734-3 (pbk. : alk. paper)
1. Architecture—New York State—New York (Region)—Guidebooks.
2. New York Region—Guidebooks.   I. Harrison, Marina, 1939– II. Title.
NA735.N5R67 2010
720.974—dc22   2009020403

A British Cataloging-in-Publication record for this book
is available from the British Library.

Visit our Web site: http://rutgerspress.rutgers.edu

Manufactured in the United States of America

CONTENTS

NEW YORK STATE: LOWER HUDSON VALLEY, EAST

NEW YORK STATE:
MID-HUDSON VALLEY, EAST

NEW YORK STATE: WEST OF THE HUDSON

NEW YORK STATE: LONG ISLAND

NEW JERSEY

DELAWARE AND PENNSYLVANIA

PREFACE

Welcome to the fascinating world of architecture—from both the historic past and the thoroughly up-to-date! Readers do not need to be knowledgeable about architecture in order to take pleasure in the wonderful sites described in this book.

From reflections of three hundred years of history to expressions of the most contemporary design, you will find these examples inspiring, informative, and aesthetically intriguing. They range from the earliest colonial saltboxes to some as-yet-unfinished contemporary structures on college campuses, from nineteenth-century follies to Gilded Age palaces, from lighthouses to windmills to romantic ruins. This region is filled with treasures to explore.

We have chosen to include sites within two hours' driving time (more or less) around New York City, so that you may have a comfortable one-day outing. We recommend that before leaving home, you check an institution's visiting hours, as such information can change. The region includes parts of Connecticut, New York, New Jersey, the eastern edge of Pennsylvania, and one site in Delaware. New York City, with its abundant collection of architectural wonders, is for another book, as are the other large cities in this area. We have included, however, college campuses, small villages, planned and utopian communities, National Historic Sites, castles and forts, churches and temples of architectural interest, and a Buddhist monastery (but note that we have not included any private residences, despite their architectural merit, as we are mindful of their owners' privacy). Each site has its own fascination.

We recommend that you check the hours for interior visits before leaving home, as such information can change.

At the end of the book, you will find descriptions of architectural styles, as well as suggestions on how to choose an outing of interest to you, with listings of outings by architect or designer, by architectural style, and by particular types of sites. Whether you are an explorer or an armchair adventurer, we are sure you will find something to capture your interest in the nearly one hundred sites we have included.

We would like to express our appreciation to a number of people who have been very helpful in guiding us to the many architectural pleasures in this area. Special thanks go to Margaret Brooks, Bill and Lisa Westheimer, Jeannie Boose, Don Mallow, Sophie Rosenfeld, Bob and Sue Rodgers, Robert Fertitta, Karen C. Pierce, John Franzen, Iris Levin, Alvin First, Robert L. Harrison, and Harrison Hunt.

We hope you will enjoy the outings as much as we have. Many of these sites were discovered by word of mouth, and we always appreciate hearing from readers about new places to visit for future editions.

CONNECTICUT

1 ·
ICONIC MODERNISM

The Glass House of Philip Johnson, New Canaan

✾ DIRECTIONS

From the Merritt Parkway (Route 15) take exit 36 (Route 106). Go north on Route 106 to the center of New Canaan. The Glass House Visitor Center is located at 199 Elm Street, directly opposite the Metro-North train station. From there you will be taken to the Glass House site via minibus for your guided tour.

✾ INFORMATION

The Glass House is open for tours daily except Tuesdays, from April through October. Tickets must be purchased in advance; as of this writing there is a one-year waiting list because each tour group can accommodate only ten people at most. Tours (not recommended for children under ten) leave from the Visitor Center at 199 Elm Street, directly opposite the Metro-North train station. You can purchase tickets by telephone at 866-811-4111 or online at www.philipjohnsonglasshouse.org. For more information, visit the Web site.

✾ The Glass House, one of architect Philip Johnson's most celebrated creations, has been an object of wonder and fascination ever since it was built in 1949. The concept of living in a transparent house with no apparent walls separating you from the natural world is certainly appealing in theory; but how does it work at the practical level? How can a virtually all-glass house be viable as a private dwelling? These days you can answer these questions for yourself by actually seeing the house in person. Since the summer of 2007 it has been open to the public on a carefully controlled and limited basis, through prearranged guided tours for small groups of people at any given time.

A visit to this remarkable site is a memorable experience on many levels, from the architectural and aesthetic to the naturalistic and environmental. You find yourself gazing at one-of-a-kind architecture while surrounded by

3

The Glass House (Philip Johnson), New Canaan

rolling lawns and fields, ponds, and woodlands. And the breathtaking views are inspiring, as they certainly were for Philip Johnson.

For many years Johnson lived in this bucolic setting with his longtime partner, David Whitney, an art collector and curator. In 1945, when Johnson first came here, he bought just five acres on which to create this rural retreat; he placed the house on a rocky bluff, overlooking the grounds. During the next fifty years he acquired more land and, inevitably, created new buildings. The present forty-seven-acre estate includes not only the legendary Glass House but also thirteen additional structures (some of which are included on the tour) that enhance the landscape in their own distinctive ways.

These original structures are all different from one another: from the surprisingly small, simple, but sybaritic glass box to the brick guesthouse, bunkerlike painting gallery, airy sculpture pavilion, and eccentric follies appearing here and there. Reflecting Johnson's eclectic architectural tastes and desire to try new things, they range from his vision of classical and traditional forms to the modern and postmodern. According to him, "architecture should move you, amuse you, inspire you," which is what these buildings do—one way or the other.

Philip Cortelyou Johnson (1906–2005) was undoubtedly one of the most creative and energetic architects of the twentieth century. From 1930 he was at the very center of American architecture, designing residences, museums, office towers, and religious institutions; serving as director of architecture at the Museum of Modern Art; collecting and donating works of art; supporting the work of younger architects; and curating shows and writing articles.

He was a great admirer of the modernist Ludwig Mies van der Rohe and in fact collaborated with him, notably on the Seagram Building in New York City. Johnson's Glass House was inspired by Mies's Farnsworth House, even though it was actually built one year earlier. Johnson's penchant for experimentation resulted in a turn in his career path, when he built the controversial AT&T Building in New York City. With its curious "Chippendale" top, it was the very reverse of what he had designed before and was seen as a travesty of the principles of modern architecture. But Johnson was undaunted and carried on with his phalanx of supporters. His last building on the Glass House site, the quirky "Da Monsta," is a testament to his continuing need to challenge and be challenged: located near the austere front entrance gate, it appears as an oddly shaped, brilliantly colored sculpture—the complete opposite of the serene Glass House.

Toward the end of his long life Johnson donated the property to the National Trust for Historic Preservation, which operates the site today, offering tours, educating the public, preserving modern architecture, and raising funds to sustain the property. The comprehensive tours (lasting from ninety minutes to about two hours) will give you a good sense of Johnson the architect, collector, curator, critic, and socialite—an American original.

A tour of Johnson's unusual buildings here is unlike any other; the acres are a naturally beautiful setting for a number of extraordinary architectural statements, with many homages to an eclectic mix of ancient and modern designs. As you visit them on your guided tour, you will find the pathway punctuated with contemporary sculptures as well.

The tour begins at a decidedly imposing entrance gate (c. 1980). "Referencing medieval gates" is how the estate characterizes these two twenty-foot-tall slabs of plum-brown concrete, with an elaborate system of electronic pulleys and a big aluminum bar. Described as "ceremonial," the gate makes a strong preliminary statement.

Just inside the gate is **Da Monsta** (c. 1995), a startlingly asymmetrical building of gunnite in the International style. In fact, it is much more expressionist in style than the more geometric rectilinear forms of many of the other (earlier) buildings on the property. Johnson was influenced by

German Expressionism and by contemporary sculpture in its design of curving walls and warped, "torqued" forms. In fact, Da Monsta appears to be a large sculpture itself, but there is also an interior space, which is just as oddly shaped.

As you walk down the hillside path, you'll find the library/study on the left. This is a one-room building, described by Johnson as "an event." Made up of basic geometric forms (square rectangles and a conical tower with skylight), this small building resembles a construction made of children's blocks; it was a favorite place for the architect to sit and read.

Further down the path is the pièce de résistance, the **Glass House**, and its companion, the Brick House. The Glass House, one of the best known architectural statements of the mid-twentieth century, was built in 1949. A low, horizontal, glass-and-painted-steel building, it is notable for its rectilinear elegance, its transparency (the lovely landscape is visible both around and through it), and its amazingly reductionist simplicity—both inside and out. The Glass House ushered in the International Style to residential architecture in the United States; Johnson lived here from 1949 to his death in 2000, and it became an iconic example of what we know of today as "modern architecture."

You'll be amazed at how simple the interior is, reducing the necessaries of daily life to a minimum, so that the design and exterior landscape are paramount. Note the prominent place of sculpture (Elie Nadelman) and painting (a Nicolas Poussin landscape) and the few elegant furnishings by Mies Van der Rohe.

Just across the path is the **Brick House** (also 1949), built as a counterpart to the Glass House. It is of a similar size; whereas the Glass House is all about transparency, the Brick House seems impermeable. The almost completely windowless house (it has skylights and a few round windows at the rear) was an homage to the Renaissance master architect Filippo Bruneleschi's Duomo in Florence. The Brick House contains the support systems for the Glass House, as well as guest rooms and a library.

Down the incline from the promontory on which the Glass House is built is a small lake, and at its edge is another Johnson construction. Known as the **Lake Pavilion**, this concrete folly has a gold-leaf ceiling and an ancient-seeming series of arches and columns set on a flat surface at water's s edge. It was an exercise in size and perspective that reportedly influenced Johnson's design for the New York State Theater at Lincoln Center.

Two of the major buildings on the tour are devoted to Johnson's and his friends' interest in contemporary art. First on the continuing walk is the **Painting Gallery** (1955), housing the architect's extensive collection of large-scale contemporary paintings, including works by Frank Stella, Robert Rauschenberg, and Andy Warhol, among others. This unreal building appears as a grass-covered mound, topped by a parapet with a large stone entrance with deep red walls. It was modeled on an ancient Greek temple (the Treasury of Atreus, c. 1250 B.C.) and is made up of three adjoining circles within. There are ingenious rotating walls within the circles, so that the exhibitions can be changed easily; any six of these forty-two large works can be shown at one time.

The **Sculpture Gallery**, over a narrow bridge from the Painting Gallery, is the last major building on the tour. Completed in 1970, it is white-painted brick and is composed of a series of squares punctuated by stairways. A glass ceiling is supported by steel rafters. There is light everywhere and a wonderful interplay of shadows throughout the interior, which houses all kinds of contemporary sculptural pieces by renowned artists. This extraordinary gallery is a perfect setting for the abstract forms of sculpture by artists ranging from George Segal to Frank Stella and Bruce Nauman, among others.

2 ·
THREE EIGHTEENTH-CENTURY ARCHITECTURAL TREASURES ON THE CONNECTICUT SHORE

Bush-Holley House, Cos Cob; Ogden House, Fairfield; and Judson House, Stratford

❈ DIRECTIONS

Bush-Holley House: *39 Strickland Road, Cos Cob. From I-95 (Connecticut Turnpike) take exit 4, then take Indian Field Road north to Route 1 (East Putnam Avenue) and make a right. Then take a right on Strickland Avenue, to number 39.*

Ogden House: *1520 Bronson Road, Fairfield. From I-95 take exit 21, then make a left onto Mill Plain Road; bear left on Sturges Road; at the stop sign turn right onto Bronson Road. Ogden House is about a mile ahead, on the right.*

Judson House: *967 Academy Hill, Stratford. From I-95 take exit 32, then take Route 1 east to Ferry Boulevard, toward the American Shakespeare Festival. Academy Hill is just beyond the Festival, near the water.*

❈ INFORMATION

Bush-Holley House: Open Saturday and Sunday, 12 to 4 P.M., January and February; Tuesday through Sunday, 12 to 4 P.M., March through December; or by special appointment. Guided tours (about forty-five minutes) are offered. Telephone: 203-869-6899.

Ogden House: Open 1 to 4 P.M. on Sunday, June through September, and by special appointment. Telephone: 203-259-6356

Judson House: Open 11 A.M. to 4 P.M. mid-April through October on Wednesday, Saturday, and Sunday. Telephone: 203-378-0630.

❈ Connecticut certainly has its share of historic houses with architectural merit. In the southwest corner, along the shoreline, there are three eighteenth-century examples that stand out. They are geographically close enough to make for an interesting day's tour. (Of course, if you prefer a more leisurely experience, you can see them on separate days, too.) You'll find that the houses are relatively close to one another and are easily accessible from the turnpike. Note that you must take a guided tour in order to visit; so be sure to check hours, as each house has its own schedule.

The **Bush-Holley House**, built around 1738, presents itself as an eclectic mix of architectural styles, reflecting its unusual history. It began as a simple farmhouse with the typical parlor, dining room, kitchen, and small bedrooms surrounding a central chimney. As the family expanded to include ten children, two wings were added to accommodate them all. The next owner enlarged the house further, with the addition of a second-floor porch and Victorian windows.

Soon after Edward P. Holley bought the house in 1882, it took on a new mission. The Impressionist painter John Henry Twachtman persuaded Holley to open the house to his art students, as a place to gather and gain inspiration. Thus, it became an informal "art colony"—maybe the first of its kind in the area—attracting a long list of distinguished artists over several generations: among them, painters J. Alden Weir and Frederick Childe Hassam, as well as writers Willa Cather and Lincoln Steffens. In the 1950s the Historical Society of Greenwich took charge of the house, turning it into a museum.

The grounds surrounding the house include a nineteenth-century barn, wash house, and shed. Nearby you'll see an 1805 house, which was the post office of Cos Cob in the early twentieth century.

The **Ogden House**, a modest saltbox-style house built for David Ogden and his bride, Jane Sturges, around 1750, gives you a sense of what life was like for a family of well-off—but far from wealthy—mid-eighteenth-century farmers. This typical farmhouse was home to the Ogden family for some 125 years. Some of the furnishings are original, in accordance with David Ogden's 1774 farm dwellings; the kitchen is centered around a giant fireplace (five feet high by ten feet in width), which was certainly the family's favorite gathering place on those cold New England winter nights.

Ogden House, listed on the National Register of Historic Places, is beautifully situated overlooking a picturesque brook. Behind the house is a charming eighteenth-century-style kitchen garden with symmetrical raised beds; carefully maintained by the Fairfield Garden Club, it features herbs like those used at the time.

The last place to visit on this odyssey is the **Judson House** in Stratford. Like the Ogden House, it dates to the middle of the eighteenth century and was the dwelling of a farmer, but one who also happened to be a very active community leader. Its architectural style is also Colonial saltbox, with an enormous central chimney, but with some Georgian features; as such, it represents a transition between the two styles.

Judson House was the home of Captain David Judson, whose descendants occupied it until the late 1880s; its subsequent owners willed it to the Stratford Historical Society, which oversaw its authentic restoration. The house is listed on the Park Service's Register of Historic Places.

Throughout the building you'll discover items that reflect the sophistication of the household, from the 1760 piano (which belonged to William Samuel Johnson, a signer of the Constitution and later president of Columbia University) to the elegant dining-room table set with antique china from Canton and the many period furnishings. Features that make this house quite distinctive include its original front door with bull's-eye glass (which is thick at the center), the curved pediment of the doorway, and the wide overhangs of the gable.

If you have time, walk through the **Catherine Bunnell Mitchell Museum** just behind Judson House, which features items relating to Stratford's history.

3 ·

TWO ARCHITECTURAL ECCENTRICITIES

Gillette Castle and Goodspeed Opera House, East Haddam

❀ **DIRECTIONS**

Gillette Castle State Park: *From I-95 (Connecticut Turnpike) take exit 69 and go north on Route 9 (near Old Saybrook) to Route 148 east, past Chester. Follow signs to the ferry. As you cross the river, you will see the castle directly in front of you, its unmistakable silhouette looming above. The Castle is located on River Road.*

Goodspeed Opera House: *The opera house is about two and a half miles from Gillette Castle, at 6 Main Street in East Haddam: continue on River Road and turn left at Route 82 and then left again on Norwich Road, to Main Street.*

❀ **INFORMATION**

Gillette Castle: Castle hours are 10 A.M. to 5 P.M. daily, from Memorial Day to late November (the fourth weekend after Thanksgiving); park hours are 8 A.M. to dusk, year-round. You can visit the castle on your own or by guided tour; there is an entrance fee. Telephone: 860-526-2336. Web site: www.ct.gov.

Goodspeed Opera House: The theater season itself usually goes from late April through early fall, when Saturday tours of the building are offered. Of course, you are always free to walk around the opera house at any time of the year. For information call 860-873-8664. Web site: www.goodspeed.org.

The Chester-Hadlyme car ferry, off Route 148, operates from early morning until sunset, April to November. (There are year-round river crossings at Route 82 between Haddam and East Haddam and between Old Saybrook and Old Lyme, from I-95.)

❀ If you have a taste for architecture on the eccentric side, you won't want to miss the picturesque river town of East Haddam, where two such sites stand out: Gillette Castle and the Goodspeed Opera House. Both are

Gillette Castle, East Haddam. Photo by Michael Melford.

delightfully offbeat and amusing to visit. And the fact that they are also accessible by ferry—a pleasant five-minute boat ride to the east side of the river—adds a touch of romance to this adventure.

Gillette Castle, perched high atop one of seven hills overlooking the scenic Connecticut River and surrounded by 122 acres of woodland, appears as a grandiose folly from a bygone era. The craggy, hand-built fieldstone castle, terraced gardens, high walls, woodsy pathways connected by suspended bridges, and the remnants of a private outdoor railroad all paint a picture of unusual imagination and whimsy.

The creator of this unique place was William Hooker Gillette, an actor and playwright whose portrayal of Sherlock Holmes in the early 1900s had finally brought him fame and fortune. In 1913, while looking for the ideal site to build his dream home, he was taken by this captivating riverfront location and its sweeping views.

Gillette himself designed the twenty-four-room castle, with its thick granite walls (in the style of a medieval fortress) and its eclectic interior. The house is full of fanciful and original ideas—for example, each of the forty-seven oak doors is different from the next; doorstops and mantels are shaped like cats (Gillette had a particular fondness for them and kept as many as fifteen at any given time); and hanging light fixtures appear as garlands of colored glass salvaged from old bottles. Gillette was something of an amateur locksmith and made most of the castle's locks himself. He also had an aversion to metal: no nails were to be exposed, and his light switches were actually made of wood. In fact, there is so much wood in the house that for fire protection a sprinkler system was installed, something unheard of at the time.

It took five years, from 1914 to 1919, to complete construction. And it took at least a million dollars, an extraordinary sum in those days. Gillette also developed the surrounding grounds. A train and locomotive enthusiast, he built for himself and his friends a human-size railroad that began at the castle and wound around through the forest, making a three-mile loop. You can still see the remnants of the railroad track. He also created a number of intricate walking paths, arched stone bridges, wooden trestles, and a goldfish pond, and many of these oddities still exist.

Gillette's will, reflecting his eccentricities, stipulated that the property should not "fall into the hands of some blithering saphead who has no conception of where he is or with what surrounded." So after his death, it was acquired by the state and in 1943 officially became Gillette Castle State Park. Over the years the site has welcomed thousands of visitors, adults and children alike, who inevitably take delight in the many things to discover here.

The **Goodspeed Opera House**, just two and a half miles away, is also a one-of-a-kind landmark, set high above the river. In its eclectic Victorian style, the theater looks like a delicious confection, all fluff and whimsy. It's impossible to miss this imposing structure: standing proudly at six stories, it is the tallest building on the river for miles.

The opera house was built in 1876 by William Henry Goodspeed, an entrepreneur in finance and shipping who had a special fondness for the theater, and it opened on October 1877 to great public acclaim; it presented musical theater for many years. Patrons and actors who arrived by boat used its steamboat terminal. After Goodspeed's death the opera house suffered a decline, threatening its future existence. The building was even used as a militia base during World War I, then as a storage depot. Fortunately, in the late 1950s local preservationists saved and restored the building to its former magnificence. Since 1963 it has presented a vast repertoire of musical theater—from Cole Porter revivals to the latest, often untested, musicals —gaining quite an international reputation for its excellence.

Goodspeed Opera House, East Haddam. Photo by Robert Benson.

The interior of the building is definitely worth seeing. We recommend either attending a performance—to really get into the spirit of the place —or taking a guided tour, available on Saturdays in season. You can always walk around on your own, but check with the office first. Not surprisingly, you'll find the décor quite lavish, reminiscent of nineteenth-century steamboat saloons, with polished brass surfaces, shiny walnut banisters, and glittering chandeliers. Highlights include the stage area, Victorian bar, sitting room, and drinking parlor—all beautifully restored. Don't miss the collection of photographs (especially views of Goodspeed from the bridge over the river) and the hand-painted backdrop of a river steamer.

4 • A BUSTLING, CAREFULLY PRESERVED COLONIAL VILLAGE

Litchfield

❁ DIRECTIONS

From the west side of Manhattan take the Saw Mill River Parkway to the Cross County Parkway to the Hutchinson River Parkway to I-684 north to I-84 east. Take exit 17 and go north on Route 63 to Litchfield. From the east side of Manhattan take FDR Drive to the Major Deegan Expressway to the Saw Mill River Parkway, and then follow the same directions above.

❁ INFORMATION

The annual tour of selected historic houses occurs on the second Saturday of July (for a small fee). Call the chamber of commerce at 860-482-6586 for details.

The **Litchfield Historical Society and Museum** (860-567-5862) in the Noyes Memorial Building exhibits Revolutionary-period paintings, including those of Ralph Earl, as well as some furniture and law books, in an uncluttered and inviting setting. Open April through December, Tuesday through Sunday, from 11 A.M. to 5 P.M. **Tapping Reeve House and Law School** is open May through October, 11 A.M. to 5 P.M.

Wolcott Memorial Library, South Street, exhibits paintings, sculptures, and photography. Though the main library is new, it is attached to a 1799 house built by Oliver Wolcott Jr., son of one of the signers of the Declaration of Independence. Open year-round, Tuesday through Saturday.

❁ This is a trip to a rare, unspoiled New England town. Litchfield is a village that has managed to retain its colonial character for over three hundred years. The visitor arriving here is astonished by the seemingly endless rows of perfect eighteenth-century white houses, the elegant Congregational church poised above the town green, the cobblestone courtyards of shops. But Litchfield is not a reconstruction or a self-conscious preservation effort;

it has been able to retain its architectural integrity by vigilant citizen effort and through accidents of geography and history. Yet it is a bustling town with lots to see within a relatively concentrated area.

Litchfield has an illustrious history for such a small place. It was home to the nation's first law school and the first seminary for girls, and the eighteenth-century home of Connecticut's chief justice is found here, as is the 1787 parsonage where Harriet Beecher Stowe's father lived. Litchfield was a small but well-to-do colonial and federalist settlement, as can be seen from the grandeur of its early homes.

In 1719 Litchfield was incorporated in the Connecticut Assembly, divided into sixty homesteads, each of fifteen acres. Some of these can still be visited. The colony prospered, and soon Litchfield became an important stagecoach stop between Boston and New York and between Albany and New Haven. In 1751 it was chosen to be the county seat. By the time of the Revolution, Litchfield, strongly on the patriot side, provided as many as five hundred men to the effort. Among the Revolutionary tales is one describing how an equestrian statue of George III was toppled in New York City and dragged all the way to Oliver Wolcott's woodshed on South Street in Litchfield, where it was melted down into bullets by the local ladies. And, we should add, both Lafayette and Washington slept here— many times.

Litchfield citizens became prominent in several fields. Tapping Reeve (not an original landowner) started the nation's first law school in 1774; among its students were Aaron Burr (Reeve's brother-in-law), twenty-eight senators, three Supreme Court justices, and more than a hundred congressmen. Here Sarah Pierce opened her Female Academy, the first school for young ladies' higher education in the country.

By the 1850s, when railroads brought people and prosperity to towns along their lines, Litchfield was left behind. In 1859 it was still the only four-horse stagecoach stop on the Naugatuck Road. As it escaped industrialization, it became a haven for retired people, summer visitors, and eventually for commuters attracted by the quiet charms of the village and surrounding hills. In 1913 the White Memorial Foundation incorporated to preserve the area, including Bantam Lake; some five thousand acres are devoted to a bird sanctuary, wild gardens, and recreational facilities. And in 1959 Litchfield itself was designated a historic area. Tapping Reeve's law school and the village green, as well as areas of both North and South streets, are registered National Historic Sites.

Pick up a walking tour at the town hall near the village green for a detailed description and guide to each house. You may want to find a pictorial guide to colonial architecture that identifies such details as eaves, roof lines, and fall windows.

The historic district lies right in the center of town along the green and North and South streets, which are each about half a mile long. You will walk past stately Colonial homes, uniformly white with black shutters, that have been occupied by governors, justices, and senators through the years, as well as the birthplaces of Ethan Allen, Henry Ward Beecher, and Harriet Beecher Stowe.

Your walk should begin with the church at the green. The First Congregational Church is a fine example of the double-octagon steeple design. Built in 1829, it was moved in the 1870s; after functioning as a meeting place and movie house (with its steeple removed), it was returned in 1929 to its proper site on the green and fully restored. The church is open daily.

Also on the town green are the parsonage (built in 1784), several small shops built in the 1780s, the Litchfield Historical Society Museum, and the much admired Court House.

Along North Street you'll find a number of beautiful Colonial homes, Sheldon's Tavern (where George Washington actually slept), the bank, and the antique jail.

On the other side of the green take South Street for additional architectural pleasures that epitomize the late eighteenth-century New England style. Here is the first law school in the United States; it was located inside the house. You'll see a wonderful wood-paneled room with stenciling from the eighteenth century inside. Next to it is the one-room law office where Judge Tapping Reeve founded the law school in 1784. (Among its illustrious graduates were John C. Calhoun, Aaron Burr, over one hundred senators and representatives, and three U.S. Supreme Court justices.) There are fine antique furnishings, handwritten ledgers, and sundry historical mementoes to be seen.

Other noteworthy buildings on South Street include the Seymour House (1819), the Moses Seymour House (1807), the Oliver Wolcott House (adjacent to the library; 1799), the Ethan Allen House (1786), the Kirby House (1772), another Wolcott House (1780), the Hanks House (1780), and a fine 1819–1820 building called "The Sanctum." For details on each of these buildings—and their illustrious owners—consult the Historical Society Museum, which also has a nice collection of portraits.

5·
A MODERNIST CHURCH
IN THE SHAPE OF A FISH

First Presbyterian Church, Stamford

✿ DIRECTIONS

Take the Merritt Parkway to exit 34. Take Long Ridge Road to downtown Stamford. Make a right on Summer Street, a left on Bedford Street, and then another left on Bedford Street to number 1101.

✿ INFORMATION

Tours are available upon request. Church is open daily. Telephone: 203-324-9522. Web site: www.fishchurch.org.

✿ Certainly one of the most unusual and eye-catching of churches, the First Presbyterian Church of Stamford is worth a visit from anyone with an interest in architecture, new religious buildings, stained glass, or simply eccentric design. This is an extraordinary melding of symbolism and modernism, as the shaping of the building to resemble a fish refers to early Christian symbolism: forbidden to practice their religion, early Christians drew a fish in the sand to direct worshipers to their meeting places. Designed by Wallace K. Harrison (the architect of Rockefeller Center, Lincoln Center, and the United Nations), it was completed in 1958.

In addition to the striking design of the building, a carillon tower, which at 260 feet is the largest in New England and which has fifty-six bells and unusually transparent construction, adds immeasurably to the overall design. The church is set in spacious grounds, easily visible from a variety of angles.

In using the fish symbol for the building's plan, Harrison chose to create a two-sectioned shape, suggesting the body and tail of the fish, and to cover it with small pieces of Vermont slate to represent the scales. This unique shape has few traditional elements (no flying buttresses, for example); instead, a modernist "space construction" supports the soaring interior space.

In fact, it is the sanctuary itself (open to visitors) that most catches one's attention. Although the exterior is certainly different and symbolic, it is perhaps hard to describe it as beautiful. But the interior, with its twenty thousand small jewel-like pieces of stained glass in abstract designs, can truly be described as beautiful. Varieties of blue and reds and greens, these faceted pieces are juxtaposed in great sections, which change with the light outdoors.

The glass pieces were made, according to the architect's design, in Chartres, by Gabriel Loire, an acclaimed glass maker. There are eighty-six different colors of glass, each set in a kind of epoxy and refracted to reflect the light.

If you study the glass design carefully, you can discern crosses (white glass) and a variety of scenes, representing the Crucifixion, but the windows can also appear abstract.

The roof tilts at ten different angels. There is also a chapel with a lovely stained-glass window behind the altar and a wall with over one hundred stones that come from foreign soil and trace the roots of Christianity.

Although virtually nothing is "Gothic" about this church, it does create the atmosphere of the great Gothic cathedrals, with its soaring spaces and jeweled light. Even the interior furnishings are remarkable. You can pick up an informational sheet at the church that details the origins of the pulpit, lectern, altar, and the like. Among the most unusual features is the thirty-two-foot-high wood cross, which came from the Canterbury Cathedral library, after the church was damaged by bombing in World War II.

Although many of the modernist buildings described in this book have appropriated traditional design and historical symbolism, perhaps none has so strikingly combined the past and the present into a cohesive aesthetic statement.

6·
FROM McKIM, MEAD & WHITE TO CESAR PELLI

The Architects of Waterbury

❀ **DIRECTIONS**

From New York City take the Saw Mill River Parkway to the Cross County Parkway to the Hutchinson River Parkway to I-684 north to I-84 east. Take exit 21 and go north on South Main Street to Tourist Information (on your left between Grand and Center streets). Continue to East Main Street and go left along the green.

❀ **INFORMATION**

Mattatuck Museum, 144 West Main Street: Tuesday through Saturday, 10 A.M. to 5 P.M.; Sunday, noon to 5 P.M. Telephone: 203-753-0381

Saint John's Episcopal Church, 16 Church Street: Telephone: 203-754-3116

Except for the Mattatuck Museum and the churches, the following walking tour is for exterior viewing only.

❀ Waterbury, like so many other small New England manufacturing cities, had its heyday many years ago. With thriving factories and a strategic location in southern Connecticut, it was home to a brass industry (the largest in the United States), a button industry (largest in the world), and clock manufacturing, in addition to numerous other enterprises. Not surprisingly, a strong civic presence accompanied this thriving environment; an entire municipal center complex was designed and built by leading architects, engaged by public-spirited citizens determined to create a fine New England city. Despite the desecration of the area brought about (as in so many small American cities) by the construction of a huge highway, architectural pleasures from that long-forgotten prosperity remain to be seen today. Waterbury came on hard times, but there has been a turnaround, with revitalization efforts that include conserving and refurbishing historic buildings.

A good place to start your architectural tour is the **Mattatuck Museum**, at 144 West Main Street. The museum, one of the oldest in the state, is dedicated to Connecticut history, displaying fine and decorative arts and artifacts. One of the museum's more unusual permanent exhibits features a formidable collection of buttons (ten thousand of them!). At the museum entrance you can get information and brochures, and the staff is very helpful. You can also purchase the museum's guide to the Hillside Historic District, a useful item to carry along if you plan on driving through there later to see that elegant Victorian neighborhood (discussed later on this tour).

The museum was formerly situated in the historic Kendrick House across the green; it was relocated here in 1986, in a 1912 stone building that had been a Masonic Temple. The original thirty-five-thousand-foot L-shaped temple, which has since been renovated, has four stories attached to a new seventy-six-hundred-square-foot addition by the Argentinean-born architect Cesar Pelli. This sleek addition comprises a new light and airy entrance, a gift shop, and an "orientation gallery," as well as a small sculpture court featuring a giant Alexander Calder sculpture of a bright red creature.

You will have noticed by now that Waterbury has an unusually large number of churches for its size. Steeples seem to appear everywhere you look. One of the most impressive is the imposing **Church of the Immaculate Conception**, at 74 West Main Street, opposite the green right near the museum. Its façade will remind you of an Italian Renaissance church; in fact, it was modeled after Rome's beloved Santa Maria Maggiore. Waterbury's version, also a basilica with a cross-shaped floor plan, was completed in 1928; it is made of limestone, with interior columns, marble floors, and mosaics.

Across the green, at 16 Church Street, is another church worth noting, **Saint John's Episcopal Church**. Originally built in 1737, then destroyed by fire, the present church dates from 1873. This Gothic Revival structure is made of granite, with stone arches, tracery, and trimmings. Don't miss the five Tiffany stained-glass windows.

Walk to 3899 Meadow Street (corner of Grand) to the **Union Station Clock Tower**. This is the city's most well-known landmark. Designed by McKim, Mead & White in 1909, it is patterned after the Torre del Mangia at the Palazzo Publico in Siena, Italy. The tower itself is 240 feet high and has eight gargoyles in the form of she-wolves, a reference to the story of Romulus and Remus. This unusual building houses the local newspaper offices.

The grandest plans for Waterbury's downtown involve a civic center. Two Waterbury brothers, Harry S. and Frederick S. Chase, who headed an industrial empire including brass and button works, decided to redo the city's downtown; their plans called for five buildings to house municipal offices and banking centers. But they didn't want ordinary functional buildings; their aim was to make a grand, artistic center of the downtown, with monumental buildings, sculpture, stained glass, and ornamental ceilings.

The Chase twenty-year plan focused on Grand Street, which the brothers saw as central to the complex. They hired the renowned landscape designer Frederick Law Olmsted to create a park at the station end of Grand Street. Then they invited Cass Gilbert (1859–1934) to design the municipal complex. Gilbert was already well known as the architect of landmark buildings, including the Supreme Court Building in Washington, D.C., and the Woolworth Building in New York City. He was known for grand edifices with elegant architectural detail on all four façades; despite the traditional styles of most of his buildings, he made many innovations that influenced modernist architects of the next generation.

There were to be five major buildings along Grand Street; they are easily spotted today. First we come to 235 Grand Street, the **Municipal Building** itself (1913–1915). Note over the entrance the words "Cass Gilbert's Municipal Building; Quid Aere Perennius," the Latin meaning "What is more lasting than brass" and so apparently an allusion to the Chase brass fortune. The building is a Georgian or Colonial Revival building on fittingly grand scale. The circular entranceway and stairway are marble, behind what the architect called an "entourage," a large landscaped area in front of the building. The huge building (203 feet long) has three façade levels with crowning balustrade. The first level is marble with arched windows; each corner is slightly recessed, and in their center there is a shallow pavilion. The second and third levels are brick. The arched windows are set within bays and are delineated with fluted pilasters. Note the narrow terra-cotta decoration with geometric patterns.

Across the street is 236 Grand, the **Chase Building** headquarters for the company and its welfare and social activities. More than a block long, this 1917–1919 building echoes the municipal building's design, emphasizing the façade planes by reversing them. Here bay windows project from the wall plane. There is a striking center enhanced with bronze lanterns and grilled windows beneath four "Temple of the Winds" columns that support entablature and a roof balustrade around three sides. Notice that the cornice caps have friezes decorated with rosettes.

Further along the block at 95 Grand Street (on the corner of Field Street) is the **Waterbury National Bank/Citytrust Building**. Made entirely of limestone, with round arches and six sectioned windows, this Renaissance Revival structure has two matching street façades. A vertical wave pattern (matching that of the Municipal Building) covers wooden panels on the façade. There are bronze doors and Corinthian pilasters separating the second the third levels.

Our next Cass Gilbert building is at 43 Grand, the **Chase Dispensary**. (You can see the architect's name on the entryway impost blocks.) This two-story building is a Georgian Revival structure made of brick accented with marble. Note the marble balustrade atop the building and the entrance stairway.

Walk back to your car and head up the hill on Willow Street to the Hillside Historic District, where the city's most prosperous industrialists once lived. This area was carefully planned to set off the grand old houses. The houses, built between the mid-1800s and the 1920s, represent a wide variety of architectural styles, from Queen Anne and Arts and Crafts to Colonial and Tudor Revival. As you drive along streets named Hillside, Pine, Buckingham, or Woodlawn Terrace, you will see some of the best examples (without even having to get out of your car). Here are just a few of the ones we found most striking:

32 Hillside Avenue: This very large Queen Anne–style "cottage" (1879) is one of the most fanciful houses in the neighborhood, with its projecting gables and chimneys. Surrounded by greenhouses and gardens, it sits grandly on top of the hillside.

168 Buckingham Street (1910) is one of the only Arts and Craft houses here; note details such as the splayed eaves on the second story, with its half-timbered façade.

176 Buckingham Street (c. 1904) is a fine example of the Queen Anne style, with stained-glass transoms, third-story half-timbering, and gabled dormer.

70 Hillside Avenue (1902), an example of Baroque Revival, also shows influences of the Georgian style (see the main entryway) with English Tudor (in its large plastered chimneys). In front is a decorative granite terrace that leads to the gardens below.

63 Prospect Street (1852) is a picturesque house in the "cottage" style; note its distinctive red color (recently repainted to match the original).

270 West Main Street (c. 1910), on the edge of the neighborhood, is one of the largest Colonial Revival houses we've seen anywhere; note the distinctive circular porches supported by different types of columns.

❈ ALSO IN WATERBURY

Holy Land U.S.A. (*Slocum Avenue, on top of Pine Hill*)

DIRECTIONS: *From Main Street East turn onto Baldwin (crossing over the highway); take a left at Pleasant to the end and continue up the hill, following the signs.*

After your architecture drive, you might welcome a completely different, offbeat experience. Holy Land U.S.A., a miniature village representing the Bible lands of Jerusalem and Bethlehem, is a short drive uphill to the very top of Waterbury. (As you've driven on I-84 over the years, you've no doubt noticed a large cross overlooking the city, which signals this site.) Though the village is (and has been for some years) officially closed to the public and has since been vandalized and is in sad condition, it is among the oddest curiosities we've discovered and is still worth a quick look.

The site, which includes the remains of more than two hundred tiny buildings and decapitated statues amid weedy rubble and broken-down pathways, dates to the mid-1950s. It was the brainchild of a local eccentric named John Greco. For many years it was an important tourist attraction, boasting as many as fifty thousand visitors a year. Seeing it in its present neglected state makes it hard to imagine how it once looked, when so many people came in droves to explore on their own or take guided tours. (There were even catacombs to poke through.)

Today there is talk that this landmark may be brought back to life. Meanwhile, if you plan to walk around and explore (obviously at your own risk), we recommend you wear good, stout shoes. And be very careful as you go!

❈ IN THE VICINITY

Woodbury

DIRECTIONS: *From Waterbury take I-84 west to exit 15 and go north on Route 6 to Woodbury.*

As you enter town you can't help but note the striking Masonic Headquarters known as **King Solomon's Temple**. Set on the top of a rocky hillside, this Greek-style temple has columns and classical proportions and grandeur.

While in Woodbury, note two additional sites:

The **First Congregational Church** at Main Street and Judson Avenue: This is a classic white-frame Colonial church dating to 1819.

Glebe House and Gertrude Jekyll Garden on Hollow Road: The house, built in 1690, is both architecturally and historically interesting; it was the birthplace of the American Episcopal Church and the setting for famous gardens designed by the distinguished landscape architect Gertrude Jekyll. The house itself is one of the oldest and loveliest preserved buildings in the area.

Continue north on Route 6 for a few miles toward Minortown. Right on this road you'll see an eccentric structure known as the **Stone House**, with a combination of curious homemade designs by a character known as "Cadillac Joe." It resembles a Roman temple, a stone lodge, or even a house of worship, and it fits into no known category of architecture.

7·
A WALK THROUGH THE "JEWEL OF LONG ISLAND SOUND"

Southport

❀ DIRECTIONS

From I-95 (Connecticut Turnpike) take exit 19 and follow signs to Southport.

❀ INFORMATION

Southport is a pleasure to visit at any time of the year.

❀ If you enjoy strolling through lanes of graceful old houses with widow's walks amid gentle seaside breezes, you'll like this walk. A history of Southport called *Walking through History* is available at the Fairfield Historic Society in Fairfield; there is also a cassette describing each historic building, available at the library.

For a fairly short stroll through this picturesque and architecturally fascinating town, follow the path described below.

We start at the library itself, a pink granite Victorian located at the intersection of Westway and Pequot avenues, about one block from the seafront of town. Designed by a protégé of H. H. Richardson named Robert H. Robertson, it was built around 1887 in the Romanesque style.

Walk east on Westway to Willow Street and make a right. At 14 Willow you'll see an early-1800s house built by Lott Oakley, a sea captain. Like many of the local houses, it is white clapboard with green shutters, which are closed during hot or buggy weather.

Westway, across the street from the library, has several interesting buildings. At 89 Westway is another captain's house, built in 1837 by Captain Edwin Sherwood. It is a graciously proportioned example of its period. At 67 Westway, a house built by Captain Sherwood's son in 1884 is in the Queen Anne style. At 45 Westway, Captain Henry Perry built a gracious Greek Revival mansion. Dating from 1832, it features tall Ionic columns and fan windows. At 25 Westway an 1857 Italianate-style house has a decorative porch;

this house illustrates the tremendous stylistic changes from decade to decade in nineteenth-century American architecture.

Turn right onto Harbor Road. One of the oldest houses in town is located here, at number 824. A "vernacular farm house," the house is shingled (rather than clapboard), to withstand salty ocean gales. It is an example of a "three quarters house," meaning that there are four bay windows in the front, instead of the usual five.

Old storehouses (early nineteenth century) at 789 and 825 Harbor Road have been converted to residences. Number 789 was also used as a clubhouse for the Pequot Yacht club.

Gurdon Perry House (c. 1830) at 780 Harbor Road belonged to a wealthy merchant in the early part of the nineteenth century. An unpretentious house, it is simpler in style than many later homes built for merchants.

Austin Perry House (c. 1830) at 712 Harbor Road is particularly interesting for its portico, which is considered one of the finest of its kind, probably dating from the 1840s.

Pequot Yacht Club (c. 1835) at 669 Harbor Road was a warehouse during the port's commercial peak.

Jennings Store Building (c. 1834 and later) at 668–670 Harbor Road included the town's general store and post office. Sections were added during the Victorian period, when the second floor was used as a reading room before Pequot Library was built.

Walk north on Harbor Road to Main Street. **South National Bank** (1833) at 227 Main Street is now a private residence. Note its Greek Revival style.

The buildings at 244 and 252 Main Street were once tenements that housed stores and offices. They were converted into apartments in 1950s.

Southport Savings Bank (1865) at 226 Main Street was built to resemble the roof pitch of the Episcopal Church.

Oliver Bulkley House (1859) at 176 Main Street is a wonderful example of early Gothic architecture. For years this house was called the Pequot Inn and was used by summer boarders in the 1920s, until it was converted into a private home. Note its lovely grounds.

Charles M. Gilman House (1873) at 139 Main Street is an interesting combination of Italianate and Gothic styles.

Old Academy (1827) at 95 Main Street has served in many capacities. First a private school, it then held church services and finally became a private home in the late nineteenth century.

You will now be near the corner of Center Street and Pequot Avenue. Here you'll find a particularly fine example of a church built in 1862 in the

Carpenter Gothic style after its original structure (virtually identical) was destroyed by a tornado. The church has a lovely slender spire that can be seen for miles.

We also recommend strolling around the causeway at the edge of the harbor (take Rose Hill Road toward the water). Notice, as you cross the causeway to see the houses opposite town, a wonderful old brown structure now housing architects' offices.

We know of no other town with such an architectural variety—each an interesting example of its time—in such a beautiful natural setting.

8·
TRADITION MEETS
THE CONTEMPORARY
Yale University Architecture, New Haven

❀ DIRECTIONS

From I-95 (Connecticut Turnpike) take exit 48 and take Route 34 into New Haven to Church Street. Turn right on Church Street to Chapel Street. Park in the vicinity of the New Haven Green (there are both metered street parking and a parking garage on College Street).

❀ INFORMATION

Call 203-432-2700 or visit Yale University Information Center at 149 Elm Street (which borders the New Haven Green). Web site: www.yaleuniversity.edu.

❀ Yale is, of course, one of this country's premier universities, with a reputation for excellence in many fields. Perhaps less well known is its quite spectacular collection of buildings, architectural statements that range from the most traditional collegiate (patterned on the campuses of Cambridge and Oxford universities in England) to the most contemporary of structures, including a building known as the "The Whale" for its unusual profile. New Haven is a more urban environment than that of many American colleges, and it is dotted with Yale's buildings—many quite recent. In fact, as universities have become settings for signature buildings by the most famous architects, institutions such as Yale have become the most eye-catching architectural venues in the country.

We should mention, too, that among academic institutions, Yale has become one of the chief proponents of "sustainable" or "green" architecture in its concern for the environment and its role in fostering conservation. In the past few years the university has, among its many initiatives, developed programs to make the campus greener, for both existing and new buildings. Quite a number of older buildings are being renovated, while new structures are being designed and built according to the latest guidelines for sustainability. On this walk you will see several examples of these new additions.

This is a fairly big university, covering many blocks of downtown New Haven. There are pockets of green with trees and grass here and there in quads surrounded by lovely buildings, but essentially the university occupies city streets. The notable sites are mostly within a walkable distance from one another, so we have devised an architectural walking tour to take you from one to the next of the most interesting examples of the various styles and eras.

We begin at the New Haven Green, where three old churches remind us of the early days of New Haven's storied history and its development around nine squares: Center Church, United Church, and Trinity Church. Center Church still has a Puritan graveyard behind it, but all three churches, built at about the same time at the beginning of the nineteenth century, reflect both early attempts at town planning and competition between Episcopal and Congregational parishes. **Center Church** (1810–1815), at 250 Temple Street, was the design of Asher Benjamin and Ithiel Town; based on the design of St. Martin's-in-the-Fields in England, it is a graceful, traditional four-columned building with a pointed spire and an ornate roof balustrade decorated with urns and elaborate pediment carving. Just to its north is **United Congregational Church** (1812–1815) by Ebenezer Johnson and David Hoadley; it is similar in style to Center Church: both have domed vaults, columns, and high steeples. (Hoadley also designed the Philosophical Building at Yale.) **Trinity Church** (1812–1814) was built by the same Ithiel Town; it has an embellished steeple and an octagonal lantern tower, and it is in the Gothic Revival style. The three churches look out on the green on either side.

Begin your Yale walk at **Phelps Gate**, at the corner of College and Elm streets, known as the heart of Yale. Phelps Gate is a Tudor-style stone gateway; it was built in 1895 by Charles Haight as an entrance to what is called the "Old Campus." As you walk into the Old Campus you'll see Connecticut Hall on your left and **Dwight Hall** (the Old Library). Dwight is an 1840s Gothic Revival building designed by Henry Austin (1804–1891). This dark brownstone building has a distinctive outline with two narrow decorative towers and an overall Gothic look. It introduces the visitor to the campus of old; just beyond it is one of the university's green quads. Also through Phelps Gate is Yale's second-oldest building, Dwight Chapel, designed as well by Henry Austin.

Near the corner of Chapel and High streets note the windowless building of one of the university's storied secret societies, Skull and Bones. Designed in 1856, this building is Greek Revival in style and is one of several such society edifices on the campus.

Walk to your right to the **Old Arts Building**, with its Romanesque arches (1928); it has great Tiffany windows. Adjoining it is the picturesque "Bridge of Sighs," over the street, with castlelike towers and crenellation.

Continue along Chapel Street to the **Yale University Art Gallery** (1953), designed by Louis Kahn (1901–1974) and renovated in 2006 by Polshek. This first "modern" structure on the campus was the subject of some controversy with its blank, four-story brick façade and interior open concrete work. It represented a departure from the historical styling of traditional college buildings; today it is one of the many modernist structures at the university.

Directly across the street is the more recent Louis Kahn building, the **Yale Center for British Art** at 100 Chapel Street. (It is also known as the Mellon Center.) Kahn was a consultant to Yale's architecture program for many years; his buildings made an indelible impression on the campus. Built in 1977, this distinguished art museum houses a fine collection of British art within an architectural work of art. Considered the "best" building at Yale by many critics, Kahn's structure (which was built several years after his death) is a rectangular, four-story building with a flat roof and many skylights. Its outer cladding is subtly graded in color, allowing reflections of sky and light, and the interior is airy, bright, and spacious. Its façade is divided into numerous rectangles of brushed metal. Kahn's building integrated shops with its street façade—an unusual gesture to the urban streetscape. Although the building may be described as "functional" architecture for its unadorned geometric form, it uses its modernity to reference the other art buildings on the Yale campus. Kahn described his efforts as combining "silence and light," an attempt to explore the expressive powers of simple forms with reference to historical styles.

Continue on Chapel Street to the corner of York Street. The **Art and Architecture Building** (180 York Street) is our next stop. Designed by the architect Paul Rudolph, it was built in 1963 and is another example of modernism on the urban campus. Rudolph (1918–1997) was the first chairman of Yale's Architectural Department. The A&A building, as it is known, has been the subject of controversy since its dedication; even a major fire in the building in 1969 was viewed with suspicion. In fact, it seemed a typically grand modernist gesture in rough concrete, composed of a wide variety of rectangles; it was described critically as "architecture as art" and has been plagued with many technical problems. It has now been renovated by Gwathmey Siegel, who have also constructed a new adjacent building.

Turn right on York Street and walk to Broadway (corner of Elm Street). A short block on Broadway will bring you to a 1961 complex by Eero Saarinen (1910–1961), one of the best-known twentieth-century architects. The **Morse and Stiles Colleges** are residential buildings surrounding green spaces; though built in the 1960s, they make an attempt to relate their modernity to the traditional Yale "Gothic" look. Made of randomly shaped stones set into tan-colored cement, each building shares a common wall with another, adding to the sense of collegiate community, which resembles a Tuscan or Greek village. The David S. Ingalls Rink (see below) is another Saarinen building nearby.

Retrace your steps on Broadway to Elm Street; here, between York and High streets you'll find an important center of the university campus, **Sterling Library**. Built by James Gamble Rogers (the architect of many of Yale's colleges) in 1930, this quintessential Yale building appears to be Gothic in style. But Rogers built a masterpiece of functional and mechanical design, so that modernists can hardly criticize the complex, with its two courtyards and innumerable sections within—each with its own personality and function. The granite exterior is joined by an imaginative "fairy-tale castle" roofline, as one critic described it, and there are all kinds of ornaments and historical references. We recommend going inside this building to see a truly fascinating library. Don't miss the recent additions within: the **Gilmore Music Library** (1993), designed by Shepley Bulfinch Richardson & Abbott, and the most recent addition (2008), **New Cross Campus Library**, designed by Thomas Beeby.

Directly in front of Sterling Library is the distinctive 1993 monument by Maya Lin that honors women at Yale. Called *The Women's Table*, this flat, elliptical granite table with trickling water suggests both the chronological and dynamic future for women.

Walk past the Law School on High Street to the corner of Wall Street and the **Beinecke Rare Book and Manuscript Library**. This striking building is the design of Gordon Bunshaft of Skidmore, Owings & Merrill (1963). Bunshaft (1909–1990) set the building on a granite plaza, where it rises to six stories aboveground. He combined granite, bronze, glass, and thin, translucent Vermont-marble walls to create this light-sensitive library; the walls change color and transmit light according to the outdoor atmosphere. This elegant modernist building makes little attempt to fit in with the Beaux Arts style of the neighborhood's colonnaded Bicentennial Buildings, built at the turn of the twentieth century by Carrère & Hastings. But the juxtaposition only adds to the complexity and variety of Yale's many different architectural configurations.

From the Beinecke Rare Book Library continue on High Street to Grove Street, where you will see the imposing entrance to the **Grove Street Cemetery**. A brownstone Egyptian Revival structure, it was designed in 1845 by Henry Austin, architect of several public buildings in New Haven, including Dwight Hall (see above) and City Hall, located on Church Street. The gate is a massive trapezoid-like structure resting on two large columns; above is the solemn inscription, "The Dead Shall Be Raised." Austin (who is buried here) worked in a variety of styles popular at the time, among them Gothic, Italianate, and the more exotic Moorish Revival. This historic cemetery is one of the earliest American examples of burial grounds used exclusively for family plots.

Turn right on Grove Street and then turn left on Prospect Street for the next stop, the **Becton Laboratory and Applied Science Center**. Dating from 1970, it was the creation of the Bauhaus designer Marcel Breuer (1902–1981), also known for his tubular metal furniture (especially his signature "Wassily chair"). This building, a hefty rectangular mass, is characteristic of Breuer's architectural style, with its precast concrete panels and sculptural concrete base piers.

Continue on Prospect until you reach Trumbull Street. On your right you'll find Yale's **Engineering Research Building**, also known as the Malone Center, one of the newest and "greenest" buildings on campus. Designed by Cesar Pelli and completed in 2005, this 64,700-square-foot laboratory building is, as of this writing, still being improved on to be even more ecological. Its many sustainable features are impressive: building materials are recyclable; most of the woodwork comes from sustainably managed forest; maintenance is minimal (for example, no harsh chemicals are needed to clean the polished concrete floors); occupants breathe completely filtered outdoor air; all storm water is retained and filtered on-site; most of the workspaces have direct views to the outdoors (where the landscape has been carefully designed to feature native species, to eliminate the need for irrigation); the roof is made of reflecting materials to reduce the amount of heat trapped inside. Aesthetically, the building is sleek and elegant, with slightly curved glass walls.

Continue walking up Prospect until you come to Sachem Street. On your left you can't miss the spectacular **David S. Ingalls Rink**, otherwise known as the "Yale Whale" (you could see it as a giant sea creature about

Malone Center (Cesar Pelli), Yale University. Photo by Margaret Brooks.

to leap out of the water). Created by Eero Saarinen in 1958, this exuberant modern building is all swooping, playful lines. Its central arch, from which roof-support cables are hung, is reminiscent of Saarinen's landmark arch in St. Louis, which marks the gateway to the West. This ice-skating rink holds at least three thousand spectators and has been the scene of many campus events.

Kroon Hall, the Yale School of Forestry and Environmental Studies, is farther up, at 195 Prospect Street. Appropriately—given its dedication to the environment—it is considered to be Yale's greenest building to date. (As of this writing, it is still being completed.) Designed by the London architect Michael Hopkins (whose firm, Hopkins Architects, is known for its low-impact and environmentally friendly designs), it is a long, four-story concrete and wood structure with a rounded roofline. Kroon Hall's comprehensive list of sustainable features is impressive; one innovative element is an underground connection between it and other nearby buildings to minimize the general footprint. We were also interested to learn that the building's electricity needs are to be met through the use of solar power, as well as wind and other alternative sources. And this in cold New England!

Continue on Prospect to **Kline Biology Tower** at number 219. This strikingly tall 1964 building was designed by Philip Johnson (1906–2005) and is considered to be an important example of postmodernism. Its stone and brick work is said to make reference to the fortified medieval cathedral of Albi in France. Situated atop Science Hill, it forms a trio with two other science buildings (the nearby **Kline Chemistry Lab** is also by Johnson). Note the chunky round columns, which appear in all three buildings, and cantilevered colonnade.

The last stop on this tour is best reached by car. Return to your car either by retracing your steps or, for variety's sake, by walking down Prospect a couple of blocks, turning left on Trumbull, then taking a right on Temple Street. (Temple goes all the way to New Haven Green.)

For a brief detour en route to our last stop, you might enjoy a tour through a neighborhood of great houses of the past on a street called St. Ronan Street. It represents a panoply of domestic American architecture. To reach St. Ronan Street, drive north on Whitney Avenue to the corner of Edwards Street, where you turn left. The next right is St. Ronan; drive on it to Armory Street, where you turn right and then right again on Whitney; then park at the **Whitney Water Purification Facility**.

This one-of-a-kind complex site includes the structure itself, 90 percent of which is buried beneath the surface, and the park above it. This imaginative solution for what could have been an unsightly plant and storage warehouse is the result of a brilliant collaboration between the architect Steven Holl and landscape designer Michael Van Valkenburgh. This is among the greenest structures we've seen anywhere—in fact, the building was recently voted one of the top-ten green projects nationwide. What you see is just the administration building (an example of the "deconstructivist modern" style, it is shaped like an upside-down water drop) with the park serving as its green roof. Holl and Van Valkenburgh are both known to be great innovators in sustainable architecture. Holl's building leaves a minimal footprint and is cooled and heated by geothermal wells; the six-section park is, at thirty thousand square feet, the largest green roof in the state. Another interesting correlation between the structure and the roof garden: each garden section is designed to illustrate the water purification process that goes on below ground level. Walk around these remarkable grounds and enjoy, among other things, the wildflowers carefully sequenced by season. You'll be fascinated!

9·
EXUBERANT VICTORIANA
The Lockwood-Mathews Mansion, Norwalk

❀ **DIRECTIONS**

The Lookwood-Mathews Mansion is located at 295 West Avenue, Norwalk. From I-95 (Connecticut Turnpike) take exit 15, then Route 7 north (for a short distance) to West Avenue.

❀ **INFORMATION**

The business office of the Lockwood-Mathews Mansion is open Monday through Friday, 9:30 A.M. to 4:30 P.M., year-round. Hourly tours are given Wednesday through Sunday at noon, 1, 2, and 3 P.M. Telephone: 203-838-9799. Web site: http://www .mta.info/mnr.

❀ The Lockwood-Mathews Mansion, an elegant example of Victorian exuberance, is a very grand place. Built in 1864 by the architect Detlef Lienau for Ann Louisa and LeGrand Lockwood, its eclectic style was drawn from the sixteenth-century French château, with Gothic, Renaissance, Second Empire, and Victorian elements thrown in. The result, known as the "chateauesque" style, became the inspiration for the fabled mansions of Newport years later.

In building this fifty-room mansion, it looks as though Lockwood, a self-made man who became treasurer of the New York Stock Exchange, spared no expense. He brought in the best craftsmen from Europe to hand-cut the granite exterior and create the elaborate parquet floors, paneled walls, frescoes, and carved woodwork, which you still see today, all beautifully restored. A giant forty-two-foot octagonal rotunda, surrounded with a second-floor balcony with skylights is a central element in the design; it is here that the Lockwoods received their guests. They also used it as an exhibition hall for their impressive art collection.

You might wonder where the "Mathews" part of the story comes in. Ironically, barely a year after moving into his dream mansion, Lockwood precipitously lost his entire fortune, when the price of gold suddenly and unexpectedly plummeted on September 24, 1869. Within two years, he had

Lockwood-Mathews Mansion, Norwalk. Photo by Robert Gregson.

died (of pneumonia), and his widow was obliged to sell the estate. The new owners, Charles and Rebecca Mathews, lived here (quite lavishly, we are told) for many years, as did their descendants, until the late 1930s. The mansion has since been renamed, restored, and opened to the public.

The tour will take you through its labyrinth of rooms, including the library, dining rooms (decorated with columns, pediments, chandeliers, and frescoes), music room (though no one in either the Lockwood or Mathews families ever played an instrument), conservatory, and the "Moorish" room, with its horseshoe configuration and diamond-shaped tiles—a favored touch of exotica in the High Victorian style. We are told there were once bowling alleys on the bottom floor, too!

On the outside of the building you'll note conical, pointed roofed towers, steeply pitched gables, and turrets; the grounds, apparently designed by Frederick Law Olmsted, include some thirty acres, with stables, carriage house, and various cottages.

10·
EXCEPTIONAL STAINED GLASS, BOTH TRADITIONAL AND MODERN

Bethel, Bridgeport, Fairfield, Greenwich, Old Greenwich, Stamford, and Waterbury

❀ INFORMATION

To find out when you can visit a particular church that interests you, we recommend phoning in the morning, when church offices are usually open.

❀ Ever since the Middle Ages the art of stained glass has been an integral part of the design of churches. By the tenth century, Venice had become the center of stained-glass making, but the art spread widely and became a beloved characteristic of great ecclesiastical buildings around the world.

Stained-glass windows are, in fact, a major element of the spiritual and aesthetic ambience of church interiors, whether as realistic images of saints and Bible scenes or as more abstract designs. From traditional rose windows to modern geometric compositions, the filtering of light into a large interior space—always a major consideration of architects—is dramatically enhanced by the bright color of the windows. In both pictorial and abstract windows, these deep, shining tones and the darkly outlined shapes and configurations of the glass add immeasurably to the architectural layout of the interior.

Connecticut has numerous examples of churches with unusual stained-glass windows, some made by famous designers, some anonymous. We have chosen a few of the most interesting churches for a tour of this beautiful element of design in architecture.

Bethel

Saint Thomas Episcopal Church: 95 Greenwood Avenue, 203-743-1494. In this church, dating from the early 1900s, you'll find several Tiffany windows, including one with a particularly striking image of Jesus with open arms, and two smaller angel windows on either side of the altar.

The more recent (1970s) windows were mostly the work of L. Ysbrend Leopold, artist of Stained Glass and Allied Arts.

Bridgeport

Saint John's Episcopal Church: 768 Fairfield Avenue, 203-335-2528, www.saint johnbridgeport.org. This grand, Gothic Revival church, located on the corner of Fairfield and Park avenues in the western section of the city, has a large collection of stained-glass windows. Most are elegant Victorian windows in deep colors. Their images are expressive and rich with embellishments, typical of the Romantic era. The rose windows are also worth noting; for a great view of them, you can climb up a spiral staircase. In addition, the church has modern windows, with simpler and more geometric designs.

Art lovers should know that here are two important works by the famed sculptor Gutzon Borglum: a beautiful white altarpiece and a statue depicting Christ the Shepherd, surrounded by three stained-glass windows depicting the patron saint of this parish.

Fairfield

First Church Congregational: 148 Beach Road, 203-259-8396, www.firstchurch fairfield.org. In this old parish (the current building dates from 1892 but is the sixth to occupy this site) you will find Tiffany windows, made by the master himself, as well as by his studio. A detailed booklet describing these and many fine additional windows is available at the church.

If stained glass is your interest, you won't want to miss this collection.

Greenwich

Christ Episcopal Church: 254 East Putnam Avenue, 203-869-6600, www.christ churchgreenwich.org. Three fine Tiffany windows—including a particularly nice angel in a field of lilies—grace this church. Made in the late nineteenth century, they were supplemented in the first two decades of the twentieth century by windows designed by the Gorham company (c. 1910), Heaton,

First Congregational Church of Greenwich. Photo by
Robert Fertitta.

Butler & Bayne (1910 and 1915), and the Mayer company (1910). The church
has available a booklet about its outstanding windows.

Saint Paul's Roman Catholic Church: 84 Sherwood Avenue, 203-531-8466.
The Willet Stained Glass Studios of Philadelphia made the attractive windows at this church. Divided into semiabstract patterns of bright tones,
they were created in 1962 and enhance the circular design of the building.

Old Greenwich

First Congregational Church of Greenwich: 108 South Beach Avenue, 203-
637-1791. The stained glass in this lovely old stone church dates from the late
nineteenth and twentieth centuries. The chancel window, one of the most
spectacular here, was created by the Willet studios in the 1960s and features
brilliant glass of deep blues and reds. It includes one of our favorite images,
on the middle panel, showing Christ on a donkey entering Jerusalem on
Palm Sunday.

The north transept window (near the right of the congregation) is said to include the work of John Singer Sargent. Dating from the 1890s, these windows were made of opalescent glass at Lamb Studios in Tenafly, New Jersey.

Besides religious themes, other windows of the church depict historical events relating to the town of Greenwich and beyond and are of interest to the history buff too.

Stamford

You won't want to miss the strikingly modern, jewel-like designs of the stained-glass windows designed by French glass artist Gabriel Loire at the **First Presbyterian Church** in Stamford (see Connecticut, outing 5).

Waterbury

Holy Trinity Greek Orthodox Church: 937 Chase Parkway, 203-754-5189. The windows in this church were made by Willet Hanser. These stained-glass icons are graced with beautifully rich colors, typical of the Eastern Orthodox tradition. In that liturgy there is great emphasis in iconography, including stained glass. The symbolism of the church is extended to its architecture, which features a rotunda supported by twelve columns, representing the disciples of Christ. For further information on the windows call 1-800-533-3960.

First Congregational Church: 222 West Main Street, 203-757-0331, www.first church-stby.org. Once again, the stained-glass windows seen here were created by the Willet Stained Glass Studios, circa 1965. Note their bright, fragmented, quite modern designs.

11·
HISTORIC SITES IN A COASTAL COMMUNITY
Guilford

❀ DIRECTIONS

From I-95 (Connecticut Turnpike) take exit 58 and follow signs to the center of town.

❀ INFORMATION

Guilford Chamber of Commerce, 51 Whitfield Street: Telephone: 203-453-9677.

Henry Whitfield State Museum, 248 Old Whitfield Street (corner of Stone House Lane): Telephone: 203-453-2457.

Hyland House, 84 Boston Street: Open daily (except Mondays), June through Labor Day, 10 A.M. to 4:30 P.M., and weekends from Labor Day to Columbus Day. Telephone: 203-453-9477.

Thomas Griswold House, 171 Boston Street (corner of Lovers Lane): Open from mid-June to mid-September, daily (except Mondays), 11 A.M. to 4 P.M. Telephone: 203-453-3176.

❀ A quintessential New England village on the Connecticut shore just east of New Haven, Guilford is filled with architectural and historical delights in a picture-perfect setting. Serenely situated in the center of town is the beautiful town green; considered to be one of the best in the region, it is surrounded by seventeenth-, eighteenth-, and nineteenth-century houses, churches, art galleries, and shops. You can't resist walking around this bustling town and exploring its many offerings.

Before your walk, stop at the Chamber of Commerce to purchase tickets to the historic houses and museums you plan to visit. Start with the nearby **Henry Whitfield State Museum**, where you can take your own self-guided tour through the three-story house and gardens. This antique house, built in 1639 for the Reverend Henry Whitfield (a founder of Guilford), has the rare distinction of being the oldest stone house in all of New England, as well as the oldest house in Connecticut.

The Colonial Revival house has undergone several changes since its days as the Whitfield home, including a major renovation in the early 1900s. Its massive stone walls (three feet thick) attest to its former role as a fort to protect the community. In addition to thick walls, it has imposing chimneys, a steeply pitched roof, and casement windows. Inside is an impressive collection of seventeenth-, eighteenth-, and nineteenth-century furnishings.

Hyland House, once the home of the Hyland family and now a museum featuring colonial life and architecture, dates from the late 1600s. This red, saltbox frame house features leaded glass casement windows, hand-split clapboards, and wide-board floors. Don't miss the unusually beautiful wood paneling, walk-in fireplace, and eclectic collection of artifacts that appear everywhere. As you walk through the rooms you get a real sense of what life was like for these eighteenth-century townsfolk. Especially inviting is the wonderful kitchen (added in 1720); well equipped with basins, boards, and bowls, it also includes an intriguing "gossip wheel," a spinning wheel where two women could work while catching up on the latest news. Outside is a delightful flower and herb garden.

Just a few doors east, on the same street, is the **Thomas Griswold House**, a picturesque 1774 saltbox. The home of generations of Griswolds, the house has been extensively restored (it recently went back to its original shape). Listed on the National Register of Historic Places, it features, among other architectural details, a ten-foot-wide fireplace with two beehive ovens. And, as you might expect, this house, too, is filled with period furnishings, implements, and objects of various degrees of interest. The grounds are expansive enough to accommodate an annual Civil War encampment, usually held in late July.

12·
CONTRASTING ARCHITECTURAL NEIGHBORS

Bridgeport

❀ DIRECTIONS

To reach downtown Bridgeport take I-95 (Connecticut Turnpike) to exit 27, following signs for Main Street.

❀ INFORMATION

Barnum Museum, 820 Main Street: Open daily, year-round, except Monday. Telephone: 203-331-1104. Web site: www.barnum-museum.org.

People's United Bank, 850 Main Street: Open daily, during banking hours. Telephone: 1-800-894-0300.

Playhouse on the Green, 177 State Street: Telephone: 203-333-3666. Web site: www.playhouseonthegreen.org.

❀ Bridgeport, an industrial city with a long history, has several buildings of architectural interest. Elegant period structures attest to the city's more prosperous past, and brand-new ones add sparkle to its downtown appearance.

Not to be missed is the **Barnum Museum**. This fanciful, one-of-a-kind building dates to 1891. It presents the legacy of Phineas Taylor Barnum, the father of the Barnum & Bailey Circus and also a mayor of Bridgeport. Barnum began his famous circus in 1871, performing before a crowd of ten thousand in Brooklyn. The pink-toned structure is quite eclectic, with Romanesque domes, towers, and curving details and a bit of Gothic and Byzantine thrown in for good measure. Among the museum's offerings is a gallery featuring four well-known mansions of the city, focusing on the architecture, character, and fate of each one. On the third floor is an exhibit that will fascinate everyone, including children: a huge moving scale model

Barnum Museum, Bridgeport. Photo courtesy Barnum Museum.

of the three-ring circus. It has more than five hundred thousand pieces all carved by hand (over a period of sixty years!).

In sharp contrast and directly next door—in fact, wrapping itself around the old Barnum Building—is a bright new edifice. The **People's United Bank** was designed in the late 1980s by the eminent modernist Richard Meier. Its exterior is brilliant white with glass; you can walk into the spacious interior lobby to see his familiar white balustrades, skylights, and expansive spatial design.

One of Bridgeport's most successful renovations, the **Playhouse on the Green** is an elegant 1911 building in the Greek Revival style, with stately columns, marble walls, gold-leaf trim, and brass light fixtures. Once a bank, since 1999 it has been an intimate and elegant home to the Playhouse, known for its eclectic variety of stage entertainment.

AND KEEP IN MIND . . .

13 ⋆ Berlin Historic District

DIRECTIONS: *Take I-95 (Connecticut Turnpike) to I-91 north to exit 20 (Route 9) north to Berlin.*

The smallish town of Berlin has a distinctive history and flavor. In the 1800s it was the center of Connecticut's famous "Yankee peddlers," door-to-door salesmen who sold everything from guns to hats, silk to bricks. The idea originated in Berlin with Edward and William Pattison, who in 1740 began the first tin-ware manufactory here and began selling tin, in town and then all over the Northeast. Today, the more than fifty buildings from both the eighteenth and nineteenth centuries encompass the Berlin Historic District and attest to the thriving past of this town.

14 ⋆ Two Forts near New Haven

DIRECTIONS: *From I-95 (Connecticut Turnpike) take exit 50; make a right turn to Woodward Avenue. Follow signs for Black Rock Fort and Fort Nathan Hale.*

INFORMATION: Open daily from Memorial Day to Labor Day from 10 A.M. to 4 P.M. Free. Telephone: 203-946-6970 or 203-946-8027. Web site: fort-nathan-hale.org.

These two reconstructed historic sites remind us of Connecticut's role in American military history. They have the requisite ramparts, bunkers, moats, and bridges—all the fortifications we associate with forts, in fact. These are two great sites for kids to visit. Both forts have been well restored and are open to visitors with self-guided tours.

Black Rock Fort was built in 1776 to protect New Haven from the British; it did not succeed and was captured in 1779 by three thousand enemy troops. However, when the British reached New Haven, they were routed by some three dozen Patriots.

Fort Nathan Hale was built around the time when war was again threatening, before 1812. During that war the Americans at the fort defeated the invaders. The structure was rebuilt in 1863 with new ramparts and a drawbridge and eighteen guns, in preparation for a possible Civil War attack, but it was never used.

15 ◆ Hotchkiss Clock Tower, Sharon

DIRECTIONS: *Take the Taconic State Parkway to Route 44 east to Route 343 to center of Sharon.*

The far northwest corner of Connecticut has several lovely towns to visit, including Lakeville, West Cornwall (which has a covered bridge), and Sharon, which boasts an unusual clock tower. Constructed in 1885, this four-story tower with a pointed top is at the end of Main Street. It was built of red and gray granite, with a rough-hewn Norman look.

16 ◆ Milford's Wharf Lane Complex

DIRECTIONS: *From I-95 (Connecticut Turnpike) take exit 37 to High Street. Wharf Lane Complex is at 34 High Street.*

INFORMATION: Open Memorial Day to Labor Day on weekends. Call the Milford Historical Society for hours. Telephone: 203-874-2664.

This complex includes three historic eighteenth-century houses brought together as a museum overlooking the Milford harbor. It is a picturesque remnant of the past. The **Eells-Stow House** (1700) has a cove overhang, two chimneys, and wonderful tiny diamond windows common in the Elizabethan Age. If you go inside, note the dog-leg staircase.

The **Clark Stockade house** (1780) was constructed from the beams and framework of an earlier structure and moved to this site in the 1980s. In the interior there is a rare built-in bookcase, original beams, and chimney stones.

The **Bryan Downs House** (c. 1785) is barn red in Colonial style (reassembled after several years in storage). It houses a well-known Native American collection of artifacts as well as a "general store."

NEW YORK STATE
Lower Hudson Valley, East

1 ·
SUNNYSIDE

One of America's Favorite Houses, Irvington

❀ DIRECTIONS

From New York City take the New York State Thruway (I-87) north to I-287 east; take an immediate turn onto Route 9 south and follow signs.

❀ INFORMATION

The house is open daily except Tuesday, 10 A.M. to 4 P.M., from April 1 to October 28; off-season, open only on weekends. Guided tours are offered regularly. Telephone: 914-591-8763. Web site: www.hudsonvalley.org.

❀ Washington Irving (1783–1859) was one of the literary lions of nineteenth-century America, called, in fact, "The First American Man of Letters." His richly written and imaginative combination of Romanticism and Americana made him a respected and beloved figure. His "Legend of Sleepy Hollow" (the "headless horseman"), his characters Rip Van Winkle and Ichabod Crane, his storytelling skills, his descriptions of the beautiful Hudson River Valley, and his understanding of the American character all contributed to his tremendous success as an indigenous voice of the land.

In 1835 Irving decided to settle on the banks of the Hudson. He had traveled widely, spending years in Spain, and had chosen the magnificent site with care. "My idea," he wrote, "having purchased a small farmhouse on a parcel of land along the river, is to make a little rookery somewhat in the Dutch style, quaint, but unpretending. It will be of stone. The cost will not be much."

Sunnyside, which became known as one of the favorite houses in America, was more than a quaint stone house in the Dutch style. With Irving's collaboration, architect George Harvey (1800–1878) designed the mansion that to this day is revered for its blend of architectural styles and its overall Romantic ambience. Sunnyside reflects Irving's interests in Spanish, Dutch, and Scottish history, as well as in the house's American locale. Dutch parapet gables echo those of early Dutch Manhattan, and Irving's own Scots

Sunnyside, Irvington. Photo courtesy Historic Hudson.

heritage and his visits to Sir Walter Scott in his Gothic and Tudor Revival setting in Scotland also influenced him.

Typical of the Scottish architecture were the steeply pitched rooflines, cross-gable configurations, many chimneys, stepped gables, and cut stone. Irving himself described the romantic dwelling of Sunnyside as "made of gable ends . . . full of angles and corners as an old cocked hat."

Even Spanish design contributed to the architectural mélange that became Sunnyside. In 1847 Irving added a tower, which was influenced by Spanish monasteries (though it was known as "the pagoda" at the time). He had spent many years in Spain and had written "The Alhambra," as well as other works relating to Spanish history and culture.

But for all Sunnyside's many architectural influences, the house became a felicitous example of nineteenth-century America's confidence and Romanticism. Like the Hudson River painters of the time, Irving chose to celebrate art and nature and the Hudson Valley with his eccentric but inviting home, exemplifying what became known as the "American Cottage." The house epitomized the ideal American home, appearing in prints and ads and magazines and even on plates and sheet music. Oliver Wendell Holmes called it "the best known and most cherished house in the land, next to Mt. Vernon."

A visit to Sunnyside is a treat for the tourist. The house and grounds are appealingly unspoiled and well kept, and the architectural details are easy to see and just as distinctive today as some 170 years ago. You can go inside to see Irving's very armchair and bookshelves, his sketches, and so much more. Anyone with an interest in nineteenth-century literary history, as well as in the wonderful mélange of architectural styles that embodied the ideal mid-nineteenth-century American home, should not miss this visit.

2·
FRANK LLOYD WRIGHT'S "USONIA"

A Planned Community, Pleasantville

❀ DIRECTIONS

From New York City take the Henry Hudson Parkway to the Saw Mill River Parkway to Hawthorne Circle. Take Route 141 north to Pleasantville. Turn right on Lake Street and then right again on Bear Ridge Road to the intersection with Usonia Road.

❀ INFORMATION

You can visit Usonia either on your own, by following the self-guided walk described below, or by taking a guided tour (on which you will be able to visit the inside of at least one house). For general information or to book a guided tour, contact Justin Ferate's Tours of the City at 212-223-2777 or jferatetours@earthlink. net. Web site: www.justinsnewyork.com.

❀ Usonia is no ordinary community. Nestled in rural Pleasantville, in the rolling hills of Westchester County, this unique enclave of some forty-eight modern houses set amid nearly one hundred acres of wooded land is distinctive in its architecture and philosophic raison d'être. The creative spirit behind Usonia was the great architect Frank Lloyd Wright, who designed its site plan, as well as three of its homes. To visit this community is to enter the fascinating world of this twentieth-century master and to see firsthand a realization of his aesthetic ideals and philosophical concepts. A walk in this pretty area is also very pleasant, with hilly, wooded roads throughout. The name "Usonia"—an acronym of United States of North America (with an added "i" for euphony)—was used by Wright to describe architecture for the "average U.S. citizen."

The term "Usonian house" applies not only to the specific houses in Usonia but to a type of house Wright designed in the 1930s and 1940s; it was meant for the average middle-income American. Intended to be simple in construction and proportion and, therefore, affordable, it was nonetheless anything but average. Rooted in Wright's radical concept of organic unity, a Usonian house was totally linked to its environment. It was to be "a natural performance, one that is integral to site, to environment, to the life of the inhabitant. Into this new integrity, once there," wrote Wright, "those who live in it will take root and grow." Houses were made of natural materials —usually wood and stone—with large expanses of glass to relate the out-doors with the indoors; structures were low, with cantilevered rooflines, so they would blend in better with their natural surroundings.

In 1944 a group of Wright's admirers, seeking affordable housing in a co-operative setup in the country, retained Wright to design Usonia. The main instigator of the project was David Henken, a mechanical engineer who had seen an exhibit of Wright's, a project called Broadacre City, at the Museum of Modern Art. Henken had been so impressed that he then went to study with Wright for two years at his headquarters in Taliesin, Wisconsin. The idealistic Henken envisioned a Utopian community where responsibility and costs would be shared, where ownership of property would be communal, and where everyone would live in harmony. (This utopian ideal has a long history in the United States, particularly in the nineteenth century, but Uso-nia was unusual for its time—the 1940s and 1950s—when individual rather than communal ownership was a goal of the "American dream.") Henken organized a nucleus of twelve families, all enthusiastic about the idea of cooperative living in the country. They pooled their financial resources—at first, ten dollars a week from each family for the cooperative. They found the ideal piece of land in Pleasantville for a mere twenty-three thousand dollars. Wright—who had agreed to build only five of the proposed fifty-five houses plus the community buildings—began drawing up the site plans for Usonia. In the end, he built only three houses (in the late 1940s and early 1950s): the Serlin, Reisley, and Friedman houses, all of which can still be seen. Other architects with similar aesthetic ideas were engaged to design the remaining houses: Ulrich Franzen, Kaneji Domoto, Aaron Resnick, Ted Bower, and David Henken himself.

Wright designed circular, rather than traditional, rectangular, site plans. In this way there would be common land between each one-acre circle, and the land would flow freely without the arbitrary divisions usually imposed in a traditional subdivision. There were to be no backyards or front yards, and the houses were sited so that they would blend into the surrounding landscape, rather than disturb the natural beauty of the area. The shapes of the houses were odd and irregular (the Friedman house is circular) to ac-commodate their surroundings. Even though there was a common theme that united the houses in Usonia and they were to be built in groups and not individually, each was designed to be distinctive.

By the early 1950s practical problems plagued the cooperative. More money was needed to finance additional houses (a total of fourteen houses were built cooperatively), but banks were unwilling to grant mortgages to such a nontraditional group. There were also the inevitable problems concerning materials, schedules, and prices (the homes ended up costing more money than anticipated). Tensions and disagreements arose within the community. By 1955 individual owners—rather than the cooperative—had taken possession of their own homes, and only the forty or so acres of recreational land were left for cooperative control. A similar fate befell most of the other cooperative communities that had preceded this one, indicating perhaps that human nature may be more idealistic in the abstract.

Today the cooperative continues to maintain the roads, water system, and tennis court, and there is still a very strong feeling of community (few of the original owners have moved away or sold their homes). The original utopian dream may have faded, but its legacy lives on, as you will see on your walk through Usonia. Though you will find only three houses that Frank Lloyd Wright designed himself, all forty-seven structures adhere to Wrightian architectural ideas, and each is interesting in its variations on the Wrightian plan. This is a moderately hilly walk through lovely rock- and tree-filled terrain, which would be enjoyable even without the added interest of the architecture. The site chosen for Usonia has a natural beauty all its own, like many Hudson Valley areas, and it has remained totally unspoiled.

If you decide to follow the self-guided walk described below (which will take you past the major houses and sites but not inside them), rather than the official guided tour, leave your car just off Bear Ridge Road at the intersection with Usonia Road.

As you begin your walk heading up Usonia Road you will see a modernish white house in what Wrightians somewhat satirically call the "international style" on a hill to your right. (It is not a Wright house.) But as you continue along Usonia Road, you will overlook to your left several contemporary homes below the road level. These are Usonia tract homes, though not of specific Wright design. If they interest you enough for you to want a closer look, take Tulip Tree Road, the first left you will come to, and walk down before returning to Usonia Road.

Continue along Usonia Road, where it overlooks a lovely valley, and turn left on Orchard Brook Drive. Very soon you will spot a distinctive house wonderfully set on a hilly overlook. It is unmistakably by Frank Lloyd

Wright. The master's touch is evident in the round portion of the structure and its distinctive interaction with the natural beauty surrounding the building. This is the **Friedman house**, one of three original designs for the site. Mr. Friedman was a toymaker, and Wright decided to design an appropriately playful house for him. (He later called it "House for a Toymaker.") You can take a detour here to see it from another angle if you wish, by walking along the road to its end.

The Friedman house is in the vein of Wright's prairie-style houses, characterized by horizontal wood siding, deep eaves, and a great deal of stone and glass. But it is particularly innovative in its use of round forms. The structure is designed on a plan of two intersecting circles, on which building cylinders rise and are capped by hat-shaped roofs. The view is unobscured by solid walls; the generous use of glass brings sky and forest to view throughout the house. Even the low stone wall surrounding the house is part of the design, creating a level for the cylinders to sit on. Wright described the Friedman house himself: "There will probably never be another Friedman house nor any closely resembling it. It is of the hill not on it, and I believe the Friedmans are loving it more and more."

If you continue along this road, bearing somewhat to the right, at the very end you will find the second Wright house of Usonia, the **Serlin house**. This one is less easily seen from the road, though you can view it from beyond the driveway without intruding on the privacy of its owners. The Serlin house is even more clearly based on the prairie-house design, being low and horizontal. It too is set on a knoll with a wonderful view of surrounding hillsides and forest. Its rectangular forms, divided by areas of glass and horizontal wood siding, deep eaves, and the acute angles associated with Wright's designs make it a quite typical example.

Retrace your steps back to Usonia Road, passing some less spectacular, but nonetheless interesting, Usonia houses. Back on Usonia Road you will soon come to Wright's Way, a right-hand turn. At a short distance on this little road is David Henken's own complex of houses and studios. The Henken family still uses this intricate compound of buildings. Though Hanken designed this group, it seems thoroughly Wrightian. One of Henken's children, who grew up in one of these houses in Usonia, recalled the tremendous amount of glass and light: "In winter, I used to lie on the warm floor and look outside to the birds in the sun. . . . The light coming in, with all the different angles in the house, was always shifting." It seemed to be the perfect setting for a creative family compound.

Back on Usonia Road you will pass several other Usonia houses before coming to Bayberry Road. Turn right onto this road to make a loop, passing by several interesting houses. Soon you will come back to Usonia Road near its end. Here you should turn left and reverse your direction on the main road. On your right almost at once you will find what is often considered Wright's best Usonia house.

The **Reisley house**, designed by Wright and partially completed by 1953, was quintessentially Wrightian both inside and out. It should be viewed from several angles. Your first look at it will be from below as the road rises up the hill. Keep walking up the road to get another, quite different, impression. It too was designed as a prairie house, with low, rectangular forms and acute angles. It has the combination of fieldstone and wood that Wright preferred and small cabinlike windows along the horizontal wing.

Like the other Wright homes, the Reisley house was designed to blend in with nature; for example, its low stone walls look like a natural rocky ledge. Among its features are a balcony overlooking the wooded terrain and a twenty-foot cantilevered living room. Some of the furniture was designed by Wright and was built-in. The interior contains a dramatic, irregularly shaped central room with lovely views of the hillside, and small angled bedrooms. A stone fireplace, also set at an angle, is the centerpiece of the living room.

As you walk back toward your car, you will have a new sight of each contemporary house along the way. You also will spot the amusing metal sculpture garden of one artist along Usonia Road (just to the left after the Reisley house).

If you have found the Usonia idea intriguing and want more information on it, you might be interested in picking up a copy of *Usonia, New York: Building a Community with Frank Lloyd Wright,* by Roland Reisley and John Timpane. You can also look up a 1958 exhibition catalog devoted to Usonia at the Hudson Museum in Yonkers, New York (telephone: 914-963-4550). In addition, some of Wright's ideas for utopian communities were expressed in his exhibition for Broadacre City (a 1940 exhibition at the Museum of Modern Art); the catalog can be found in a good library.

3·
BUDDHIST SYMBOLS AND INFLUENCES IN RURAL PUTNAM COUNTY

Chuang Yen Monastery, Carmel

❀ **DIRECTIONS**

The Chuang Yen Monastery is located ten miles east of Cold Spring, on Route 301. From New York City take the Henry Hudson Parkway north to the Saw Mill River Parkway to the Taconic State Parkway to Route 301 east toward Carmel; go 1.7 miles to the entrance on the left, at 2020 Route 301.

❀ **INFORMATION**

Visitors are welcome, but check hours and events before going. Telephone: 718-884-9111 or 718-884-7894. Web site: www.bays.com.

❀ You may be surprised to discover, as we were, an extraordinary edifice hidden in the tree- and lake-filled wilds of Putnam County. In fact, a visit to Chuang Yen Monastery makes one think of a movie set, perhaps built specifically for a dramatic scene. The main building—the Great Buddha Hall—is brightly colored, imposingly set, obviously Asian in concept, and dramatically, overwhelmingly huge. It epitomizes a modern grandeur—a somewhat startling concept for a religious site in this day and age—but it is interesting precisely because its designers have used both contemporary and traditional architecture in creating it.

The Great Buddha Hall is described as being in the style of the Tang Dynasty (618–907 A.D.), with its stepped rooflines and huge, unsupported, empty hall space—except for the giant Buddha, reported to be the largest in North or South America. The Tang Dynasty—a golden age in Chinese culture—is known for its architectural innovation. The former style of projecting eaves supported by rows of pillars in major buildings gave way, during the Tang period, to shadowing eaves, unsupported by pillars and turning

Chang Yen Monastery, Carmel

upward in the style now traditionally considered typically Chinese. Such temples in China were populated by thousands of monks, so that grand spaces became a familiar aspect.

This complex, which includes numerous additional buildings, was completed in the 1980s. The main hall, with twenty-four thousand square feet of space, can accommodate two thousand people. The building is eighty-four feet tall and sits imposingly on a hill, with a wide path to its entrance. Along this walkway are eighteen statues of disciples and two elephants. Within the building are some ten thousand small Buddhas, a lotus terrace, and numerous other features, including a huge mural. Everything is very grand, with orange predominating, and quite symmetrical. Two matching open edifices flank the stairway: one has a huge drum; the other, a bell.

The picturesque lake, Seven Jewel Lake, that is part of the enclave, is a serene setting with a ten-foot-high statue of Buddha at one end. A library, terraces, dining hall, living quarters, and other buildings dot the more than one hundred acres of the complex. But it is the center—the Great Buddha Hall—that is of architectural interest, not as contemporary innovation or historical example but as a blend of the vaguely Chinese and grandiose American version of an ancient culture.

4·
BOSCOBEL

A Hudson River Estate in the
Federal Style, Garrison

❀ **DIRECTIONS**

Boscobel is located on Route 9D. From New York City take the George Washington Bridge to the Palisades Parkway to its end. Cross the Bear Mountain Bridge and turn left (north) onto Route 9D. Boscobel will be on your left.

❀ **INFORMATION**

Boscobel is open daily, except Tuesday, from April to October, 9:30 A.M. to 5 P.M.; March, November, and December, 9:30 A.M. to 4 P.M.; closed January and February, as well as on Thanksgiving and Christmas Day. Tours (lasting about forty-five minutes) are offered daily. Telephone: 845-265-3638.

❀ Boscobel, an elegant, historic estate high above the Hudson River, is regarded as one of the finest examples of Federal architecture not only in our region but in the entire country. For those readers who are seeking a spot for a walk that is scenic, in addition to being of great architectural merit, this is a place to see. We were entranced by the combination of artistic perfection of the house—both inside and out—and the enchanting flower gardens (yes, there are those, too!) overlooking the river and the surrounding orchards and woods.

The house, majestically set on a wide expanse of sloping lawn with sweeping views extending for miles (West Point can be seen just across the river) is considered to have the most beautiful interior décor of any of the Hudson River villas. But its outward appearance is a delight to the eye, too. With yellow-ochre walls and slender, creamy white columns and carved wooden swags, it embodies the grace of another era.

Boscobel ("beautiful woods" in Italian) was conceived by States Dyckman and his wife, Elizabeth. Completed in 1808—two years after Dyckman's death—it was modeled after a pattern by the great Robert Adam.

Surprisingly, it is not known who the actual architect was, though the Dyck-mans were certainly involved in much of the planning. The estate remained in the family until late in the century, when the family fell on hard times. By the mid-1950s the estate's very existence was threatened, and demolition plans were under way. Happily for us all, the philanthropist Lila Acheson Wallace came to the rescue; the house was saved, relocated a few miles north to its present spectacular site, and completely refurbished. In 1961 it was opened to the public.

In keeping with the house's architectural style, the interior contains one of the country's most important collections of furniture and decorative arts of the New York Federal period, approximately 1780–1820. When you first enter the house you see the great hall, with a magnificent central staircase; after the landing it gracefully divides into two, leading to the second floor. The rooms are impeccably proportioned, and throughout the house you'll find elegant details: Palladian windows, ivory-colored columns, arches, a beautifully carved mantelpiece, vintage wallpaper, and hand-painted floors (based on a late-eighteenth-century pattern). In the bedrooms and parlors are several pieces of furniture by the great cabinetmaker Duncan Phyfe, as well as family portraits by Benjamin West and other prominent artists. And from just about every room you can enjoy spectacular river views—es-pecially the library/sitting room upstairs, which has floor-length windows opening onto a balcony.

You won't want to miss the basement, now a wonderful exhibition space featuring family documents, original housewares, and other items of inter-est. Nor will you want to skip a walk through the beautiful gardens (fif-teen of the estate's forty-five acres are devoted to them), including herb, boxwood, rose, and English gardens. On the grounds are also a charming orangerie filled with fruit-bearing citrus trees, a small pond, wildflowers, and an apple orchard. And, again, from almost every spot you can glimpse the great river below.

5·
MANITOGA/THE RUSSELL WRIGHT CENTER

Unique Architecture by a Prominent Twentieth-Century Designer of Decorative Arts, Garrison

❀ DIRECTIONS

From New York City take the George Washington Bridge to the Palisades Parkway to its end. Cross the Bear Mountain Bridge and turn left (north) onto Route 9D. The entrance to Manitoga is 2.5 miles from the bridge, on your right.

❀ INFORMATION

Manitoga is open for house and landscape tours from April to October. Daily tours are offered Monday through Friday at 11 A.M., Saturday and Sunday at 11 A.M. and 1:30 P.M. Reserve in advance. You can take self-guided walks in the grounds daily year-round, during daylight hours. Telephone: 845-424-3812. Web site: www.russell wrightcenter.org.

❀ Manitoga/The Russell Wright Design Center is a unique site unto itself. Situated on the edge of an abandoned quarry on a wooded hillside with giant rocks and rushing water, the barely visible house and studio of the great industrial designer are perfectly integrated into the surrounding forest. The seamless union between the constructed and the natural make this rustic woodland retreat appear almost timeless, as if it has always been here. But, in fact, Manitoga (or "Place of the Great Spirit" in Algonquin) was carefully designed down to the last detail (including the landscape) and conceived and fashioned over a period of many years. The site is a fascinating combination of architecture, interior design, and landscape architecture, all in one.

Russell Wright, one of the most important American designers of decorative arts during the 1930s, 1940s, and 1950s, created this unusual place. He first discovered the property in 1942, then ravaged by years of quarrying and lumbering. Over the next three decades he slowly and deliberately transformed it into his domain. He built "Dragon Rock," the house and studio, atop a dramatic rocky cliff overlooking the quarry; reconfigured the surrounding seventy-five acres with trees, mosses, ferns, mountain laurel, and wildflowers; moved giant boulders to create dramatic effects; redirected the waterfall so its bubbly sounds could be heard near the house; and designed more than four miles of paths winding through the woods. The result is as beautiful a setting as any artist could ask for and a most inviting place to visit.

It is not surprising that this one-of-a-kind masterpiece is listed on the National Register of Historic Places. (Wright considered it his best work of all.) It represents, however, the exception to Wright's creative output: he was known as a designer of objects for the home, rather than as an architect or landscapist. In fact, he has even been called the Martha Stewart of his generation! His sophisticated yet inexpensive designs—including furniture, dishes, glassware, table linens, pottery, and what have you—were so popular at the time that they were mass produced in the millions and had a profound impact on the American home. Many of his designs are still collector's items.

Dragon Rock, the only twentieth-century modern home open to the public in New York State, is a fascinating place to visit, combining architecture, landscape, products, archives, and even philosophy. To see it you must take a guided tour (see the Information section above for details), which begins at Mary's Meadow (named after Wright's wife); meanders along, past the former quarry, with amusing diversions along the way (we leave you to discover these yourself!); and finally culminates with a visit to the house itself. (Be sure to wear sturdy shoes, as you'll be walking on uneven terrain, across a log bridge and up massive stone steps to the house.)

Though the blue-gray house may seem small on the outside, it is actually on eleven levels and is filled with original and unexpected touches that make it a delight to walk through. A committed naturalist, Wright literally brought the outside into the house; you will find boulders, trees (including an uncut floor-to-ceiling cedar trunk supporting the main part of the roof), flagstone flooring extending onto the terrace, and laminated leaves and grasses used for decoration. In the studio—Wright's favorite retreat—pocket windows actually slip down into the walls, so that you are practically outside, enjoying the sounds and fragrance of nature.

Throughout you will see examples of industrial and domestic design that Wright pioneered. Furniture and housewares are carefully crafted in organic shapes and materials: for example, a ceiling light fixture is made with—of all unexpected things—burlap.

A champion of democracy, Wright claimed, "Good design is for everyone." His legacy lives on in his many clever and original creations, epitomized in the rustic and down-to-earth sophistication that is Manitoga.

6·
PHILIPSBURG MANOR

Northern Plantation Style, Tarrytown

❀ DIRECTIONS

From New York City take the Henry Hudson Parkway to Route 9 north to Tarrytown. The site is two miles north of the Tappan Zee Bridge.

❀ INFORMATION

Philipsburg Manor is open daily except Tuesday, 10 A.M. to 5 P.M., from April to December. In March it is open only on weekends, and it is closed during January and February, as well as on Thanksgiving and Christmas Day. Demonstrations are offered, as are hands-on tours for children (on weekends). Telephone: 914-631-8200. Web site: www.hudsonvalley.org.

❀ Philipsburg Manor is among the most picturesque sites you'll find in the Hudson Valley. This rural property was once a vast plantation dating back to the late seventeenth century; now, much reduced, it is centered around a restored manor house and working gristmill, with surrounding greenery, including a small vegetable/herb garden. The buildings are both delightful examples of rural colonial architecture, history, and life on the plantation (plenty of information is offered on these subjects, with costumed guides on hand to answer questions).

Once a bustling place with a large population of farmhands (including enslaved Africans), Philipsburg Manor was the first industrial complex in the thirteen original states. At its height, the mill produced so much flour and meal that much of it was shipped overseas. The ninety-thousand-acre property included not only the present manor but also the private residence of the Philipse family (located in what is now Yonkers; see below). The Philipse family operated this flourishing enterprise until after the Revolutionary War, when, because of their loyalist sentiments, they were forced to flee to London. Many years later and in disrepair, the manor was purchased by the Rockefeller family, restored, and eventually opened to the public. It is now operated by Historic Hudson Valley, along with several other nearby sites.

Philipsburg Manor, Tarrytown. Photo by Mike Hales/Historic Hudson.

You can visit the house and mill on your own, following a self-guided tour. The whitewashed fieldstone manor house with its gambrel roof is relatively small, though it is double the original size (it was added to in the 1750s). It was set up more as a place of business than an actual home, with space for work, office, living, and storage. Most of the furnishings (some are authentic to the period, though not necessarily original to the site, and others are reproductions) are fine eighteenth-century examples of Dutch and regional pieces.

The highlight at Philipsburg is certainly the mill, everyone's favorite (including children, who also are likely to be intrigued by the costumed miller's demonstrations of its workings). The romantic image of the mill with its wooden waterwheel, reminiscent of a Currier and Ives print, is one that is most captivating to visitors. The mill was completely restored—it was no longer functioning by the late nineteenth century and had even been moved—after archaeological excavations during the 1950s revealed its exact footprint.

A nearby site relating to Philipsburg is also worth a stop: **Philipse Manor Hall**, where the Philipse family actually lived, is just a few miles south, at Warburton Avenue and Dock Street in Yonkers. This broad, brick, Georgian-style house was built after the manor house, in the beginning of the eighteenth century. When the Philipse family fled, the house and surrounding lands were sold to local farmers. The structure has not been restored; here you can see a remarkable Rococo ceiling—one of the best in the country—and decorative woodwork and plaster from the 1750s. (Telephone: 914-965-4027.)

7·
LYNDHURST

A Romantic Castle, Tarrytown

❀ DIRECTIONS

From New York City take the Henry Hudson Parkway to Route 9 north to Tarrytown; Lyndhurst will be on your left. From locations west of the Hudson River take I-87/287 and cross the Tappan Zee Bridge; take the first exit (Route 9) and go south for about half a mile, following the signs for Lyndhurst.

❀ INFORMATION

Lyndhurst is located at 635 South Broadway, Tarrytown. Open May through October, Tuesday through Sunday, 10 A.M. to 5 P.M.; November through April, Saturday and Sunday, 10 A.M. to 5 P.M.. Telephone: 914-631-4481. Web site: www.lyndhurst.org.

❀ The words *grand* and *spacious* immediately come to mind in describing Lyndhurst. As you enter the gates of this sixty-seven-acre Hudson River villa, you drive through a parklike landscape dominated by broad lawns with giant specimen trees. Finally you reach the mansion, considered to be possibly the finest surviving example of the Gothic Revival style in the United States. Looming dramatically on the horizon as in a romantic novel, it commands sweeping views of the river. Around it are majestic copper beeches, lindens, sycamores, chestnuts, and maples.

The imposing stone castle, with its landmark turrets, tower, spires, oriels, high-arched doors, vaulted ceilings, bay windows, and Tiffany glass, represented the full American flowering of the neo-Gothic style. Known as "English collegiate," this style loosely followed the architecture of the colleges at Oxford and Cambridge. Its romantic allure and rural charms were quintessential elements of the "picturesque," an aesthetic that was popular in England at the time. Lyndhurst was built in the late 1830s for William Paulding, a former mayor of New York City. It was the first of a series of picturesque Hudson Valley estates designed by Alexander Jackson Davis, perhaps America's greatest architect of the mid-nineteenth century, and undoubtedly Lyndhurst is his best. Each of its subsequent owners added his own imprint.

The first owner, the merchant George Merritt, doubled the size of the original white marble villa, adding—among other things—the dramatic four-story tower. According to an account of the time, "The Tower surpasses any construction of the kind in America, and is not excelled in England." Merritt also turned Paulding's library into a billiard room (it remains as such today). The plan of the house was modified to become more asymmetrical, reflecting the surrounding Hudson Valley landscape. The enterprising Merritt built the first greenhouse on the property; he expanded the grounds, creating an English-inspired romantic landscape to complement the house. After Merritt's death, the house passed into the hands of railroad tycoon Jay Gould, its most famous occupant.

Gould purchased Lyndhurst as a summer home in 1880. In addition to changing the house and gardens to suit his own taste, he decided to rebuild the greenhouse, which had been destroyed by fire. He commissioned John William Walter, a designer of ecclesiastical architecture, to create an imposing Gothic-style conservatory in keeping with the aura of the mansion. Once the largest in the country, today it appears as a glassless and ghostly structure, awaiting renovation.

After Gould's death in 1892, the house went to his daughter Helen, who created the magnificent rose garden, which remains one of the loveliest spots on the grounds. In 1964 Lyndhurst was bequeathed to the National Trust for Historic Preservation.

If you are interested in learning more about the life of a bygone era in American history—in addition to architectural details—you can take one of the regular guided tours (or a self-guided audio tour) of the mansion. You will walk through many sumptuous rooms, many of them decorated with "faux" materials, made to look like something else. Note the intricate interior woodwork and elegant Gothic furniture, much of it designed by the architect.

After your tour, you won't want to miss a walk through the magnificent grounds, which you can do on your own and at your own leisure (or, again, on a self-guided audio tour). It comes as quite a surprise to discover, in the midst of this imposing setting, the unusually intimate and charming rose garden. Circular in design, the garden is built around arched trellises surrounding a graceful Victorian gazebo. In the garden are rosebushes and climbing roses in all shades and varieties (some are well over a century old!). Nearby you'll find what remains of the conservatory. You should also see the Victorian fern garden near the entrance gate; the Rose Cottage, a children's playhouse; and the Carriage House, where in summertime you can enjoy a light lunch.

8·

KYKUIT

Palatial Glamour in a
Classical Revival Estate,
Pocantico Hills

❀ DIRECTIONS

To Philipsburg Manor, where you will leave your car: From New York City take the Henry
Hudson Parkway to Route 9 north to Tarrytown. The site is two miles north of the Tappan
Zee Bridge. Follow signs to Philipsburg Manor and Kykuit Visitors Center.

❀ INFORMATION

Tours are required for a visit to Kykuit, and there are numerous different kinds
to choose from: modern art, outdoor sculpture, gardens, interiors, and so on. You
must have a reservation, made well in advance of your visit. There is a small fee.
All tours begin at Philipsburg Manor and are available every day except Tuesday,
May through November. Call for hours, which vary. Telephone: 914-631-8200 x618.
Web site: www.hudsonvalley.org.

❀ If you like palatial estates—in this case, one with a spectacular art collection both indoors and out—Kykuit is well worth a visit. This was the
home of four generations of Rockefellers, and it is indeed a testament to
the wealth and taste of the founder John D. Rockefeller (Kykuit was the
only house he ever built) and his heirs. His grandson, Nelson Rockefeller,
assembled most of the art here, much of it from his own impressive collection.

Kykuit is a six-story Classical Revival mansion with elegant gardens designed by William Welles Bosworth, a colleague of Frederick Law Olmsted. Filled with outstanding sculpture amid well-tended greenery, the gardens offer magnificent panoramic views of the Hudson River. The house
itself, though perhaps more reserved than certain other Gilded Age estates
(such as the Vanderbilt estate), appears today as a more elaborate version of the original house built in 1908. Over the years several architects,

Kykuit, Pocantico Hills. Photo courtesy Historic Hudson.

including the interior designer Ogden Codman, have made changes and embellishments in style and decoration. Among the architectural features to note are the ornate stone carvings on the mansion's façade, sweeping staircases, and balconies. Whether your interest is in architecture, art, or gardens, a visit to this remarkable site will transport you to another—more elegant—era.

AND KEEP IN MIND . . .

9· The Old Dutch Church of Sleepy Hollow:
A Very Early House of Worship, North Tarrytown

DIRECTIONS: *From New York City take the Henry Hudson Parkway to Route 9 north to Tarrytown. The church is located at 42 North Broadway (Route 9), just north of Tarrytown's center.*

INFORMATION: Open from Memorial Day through October. Tours are offered on Sundays at 2 P.M. You can also walk in during the church's open season. Note that the old cemetery adjacent (where Washington Irving is buried) is also open to visitors. Telephone: 914-631-1123. Web site: www.olddutchburyingground.org.

The Old Dutch Church is one of the oldest churches in the state still in use today. It dates to 1685, when the Dutch Lord of the Manor of Philipsburg built it. The church is architecturally interesting not only for its antiquity but also for its unusual gambrel roof and stone walls that are over two feet thick and made of yellowish brick brought over from Holland. Note the octagonal belfry (with the original bell still inside it). In its intimate interior you'll experience a general sense of serenity.

10· Union Church of Pocantico Hills:
Where Chagall and Architecture Meet

DIRECTIONS: *From New York City take the New York State Thruway (I-87) north to exit 9; go north on Route 9 to Route 448 (Bedford Road) and turn right. Go up the hill to Union Church on your right.*

INFORMATION: Open April through December, weekdays except Tuesday, 11 A.M. to 5 P.M.; Saturday, 10 A.M. to 5 P.M.; Sunday, 2 to 5 P.M. Guided or self-guided tours are available. There is an admission fee. Telephone: 914-332-6659. Web site: www.hudson valley.org.

This delightful spot is a special place to visit. Here in a rural setting is a small stone church that features exquisitely colored stained-glass windows by Henri Matisse and Marc Chagall. Commissioned by the Rockefeller family and dedicated in 1956, they are the only cycle of stained-glass church windows completed by Chagall and the last completed work of Matisse (he died just two days after completing its design). Finding these brilliant windows in this unpretentious setting is a particular treat, as the windows are the pièce de résistance.

The beautiful rose window is by Matisse; its free-form abstract design was created by using cut-out paper shapes. The glorious side and rear windows are by Chagall and depict scenes from the Bible. (Pick up a flyer in the lobby for a full description.) The church itself is a small traditional stone building, which makes the treasure trove within all the more astounding.

11 • Van Cortlandt Manor: An Example of a Dutch Patent House, Croton-on-Hudson

DIRECTIONS: *Van Cortlandt Manor is located on South Riverside Avenue in the river village of Croton-on-Hudson, a few miles north of the Tappan Zee Bridge. Take Route 9 north to the Croton Point exit and follow signs.*

INFORMATION: The house is open daily except Tuesday, 10 A.M. to 5 P.M. Tours are offered every half hour, starting at 10:30 A.M. (last tour starts at 4 P.M.). Telephone: 914-271-8981. Web site: www.vancortlandt.org.

This very symmetrical, white-porched Dutch patent house (and its grounds) was restored by John D. Rockefeller Jr. in 1953, but the original house dates from the 1680s. The stone structure has a gambrel roof, double chimneys, and matching staircases to the veranda. Many history-oriented events are held here.

Van Cortlandt Manor, Croton-on-Hudson. Photo courtesy Historic Hudson.

NEW YORK STATE
Mid-Hudson Valley, East

1 ·
THE ITALIANATE STYLE OF
AMERICA'S RENAISSANCE MAN

Samuel F. B Morse's Locust Grove, Poughkeepsie

✿ DIRECTIONS

From New York City take the Henry Hudson Parkway north to the Saw Mill River Parkway to the Taconic State Parkway. Take the exit for Poughkeepsie (Route 55) and go west for several miles, almost to the Mid Hudson Bridge, then take Route 9 south for about two miles. The entrance to Locust Grove is on your right.

✿ INFORMATION

Locust Grove is located at 2683 South Road (U.S. 9), Poughkeepsie. The gardens and grounds are open dawn to dusk year-round; house tours are offered daily May through November from 10 A.M. to 3 P.M. Admission is charged. Telephone: 845-454-4500. Web site: www.morsehistoricsite.org.

✿ Locust Grove was the home and studio of one of the nineteenth century's most talented Americans. He was both a fine painter and the inventor of Morse code, among his many accomplishments, and this National Historic Site should not be missed.

The house with its Tuscan-style tower is architecturally delightful and has long been a landmark among the many villas of the Hudson Valley. You can visit the charming grounds, as well as the interior of the house (with frequent tours).

A visit to Locust Grove is unique because it combines Morse's interests in new technology with his consummate skill as a painter. The Morse code and the machine for telegraphing it, known as the "invention of the century," caused him to be called the "American Leonardo." You can see a replica of this machine at the visitor center. There you'll also find sculptures and numerous paintings—mostly portraits but also landscapes—as well as collections relating to his life at Locust Grove.

Surrounding this beautifully set house are 150 acres of trees, spacious

lawns, and gardens, with three miles of walking trails and a looping carriage roadway. The grounds are scenically dramatic, with river views from
the bluff (in Morse's time there were fewer trees to block the view of the
majestic Hudson). Pick up a self-guided tour brochure, which will introduce
you to the sites to visit, including the dog cemetery!

Morse was the founder of the National Academy of Design (in 1825) and
taught "literature of the art of design" at New York University. His finely
drawn paintings established him as a preeminent artist of the American Romantic school, but when he became famous for his invention, he abandoned
painting and was able to enjoy a life of ease, as this villa and its grounds
testify. Morse is known as an important painter of his era and as a major
inventor; a visit here will introduce you to both aspects of this unusual dual
career.

Like many villas of the era, Locust Grove began as a more conventional
building. The original farmhouse that belonged to the Livingston family
was replaced by a Federal-style mansion in 1830, with grand views from
atop the steep bluff. When Morse bought the property in 1847 he decided—
like many midcentury villa owners—to redesign the house in keeping with
more up-to-date styles.

Morse had made a painting tour of Italy in 1829, and he decided to make
Locust Grove into an Italianate mansion—complete with Tuscan tower. He
made numerous sketches himself, as well as hiring the architect Alexander
Jackson Davis. (Their collaboration can be compared with that of another
artist, Frederick Church, who designed Olana with the help of Calvert
Vaux, an important architect, some time later.) Davis had known Morse at
the National Academy of Design in New York.

Davis decided to devote himself to designing villas, producing a book
called *Rural Residences*. His designs and those of several colleagues in midcentury often updated the formal Georgian or Federal-style houses built in
the past fifty years; they added towers, and verandas, porte cochères, and
bay windows.

At Locust Grove, Morse and Davis changed its simple Federal formality
into a more imaginative, Romantic building, borrowing ideas from other
times and settings. Thus, the house boasts a Tuscan tower and bay windows
overlooking the river view, balconies and a veranda framed by pilasters and
decorative lattice work, in addition to lovely gardens laid out by Morse himself. All of this can be seen today. (After Morse's death other alterations
were made as well; the original octagonal north wing was demolished and
modern amenities were added.)

In the interior, you'll find collections of Chippendale, Federal, and Empire-style furnishings, art by other painters, including Dutch landscapes, Hudson River School, and even twentieth-century works, as well as many mementoes of Morse's extraordinary life.

Like Montgomery Place, Sunnyside, and Clermont, Locust Grove is a fine example of how diverse architectural elements can be very successfully and seamlessly melded together.

2 ·
SPECTACULAR CAMPUS
ADDITIONS BY FRANK GEHRY
AND RAFAEL VIÑOLY

Bard College, Annandale-on-Hudson

❀ DIRECTIONS

From New York City take the Henry Hudson Parkway north to the Saw Mill River Parkway to the Taconic State Parkway. Exit at Red Hook/Route 199 and go west ten miles on Route 199 through Red Hook and turn right onto Route 9G, continue for 1.6 miles, and follow signs to Bard.

Or take the New York State Thruway (I-87) north to Kingston (exit 19) and take Route 209 over the Kingston-Rhinecliff Bridge. Turn left onto Route 9G and go north for 3.5 miles to Bard.

❀ INFORMATION

Bard College is open year-round. Guided tours of the campus are offered regularly, Monday through Friday, from 9:30 A.M. to 3:30 P.M.; call in advance: 845-758-7472. Or you can walk around on your own to view the buildings from the outside (inside access is limited, except for special events). Pick up a map of the campus, available at the Admissions Office.

The **Richard B. Fisher Center for the Performing Arts** at Bard College is open all year. You can see the interior by taking a tour or by attending a performance. Telephone: 845-758-7900. Web site: www.fishercenter.bard.edu.

Gabrielle H. Reem and Herbert J. Kayden Center for Science and Computation: All events and programs are free and open to the public. For information, visit the Web site: http://science.bard.edu/reem-kayden/.

❀ These days it seems that some of the most striking contemporary architecture is springing up on college campuses. A good example is Bard College, which has become an unusually dynamic institution, with major new buildings by internationally acclaimed architects. Among them are two that are in themselves works of art and worth a trip: the Richard B. Fisher Center for the Performing Arts (designed by Frank Gehry) and the Gabrielle H. Reem and Herbert J. Kayden Center for Science and Computation (designed by Rafael Viñoly).

Bard, founded in 1860 on the site of two historic riverfront estates (Blithewood and Ward Manor), is a small liberal arts college situated high on a bluff overlooking the Hudson. The 550-acre grounds are unusually scenic, with meadows, dense woods, an arboretum and gardens, wetlands, and exceptional views of the river and mountains beyond (the Catskills can be glimpsed across the river). The campus features an eclectic collection of buildings that, despite differences in eras and styles, seem well integrated. A walk (or drive, as the distances from one part of the campus to the other are considerable) will reveal all types of interesting structures, from nineteenth-century stone houses to modern and contemporary examples.

The dazzling new **Center for the Performing Arts**, standing apart from the other buildings on campus, is one of Frank O. Gehry's great masterpieces. This iconic architect needs no introduction. He has designed buildings all over the world that have become huge tourist attractions. (For example, the extraordinary Guggenheim Museum in Bilbao, Spain, has brought a record number of visitors to that relatively obscure city since 1997.) His massive, unconventional shapes seem to come from another planet; they

Bard College, Annandale-on-Hudson: Richard B. Fisher Center for the Performing Arts (Frank Gehry). Photo by Peter Aaron/Esto.

Bard College: The Gabrielle H. Reem and Herbert J. Kayden Center for Science and Computation (Rafael Viñoly). Photo by Peter Aaron/Esto.

appear as twisted, billowing forms in corrugated metal, titanium, even chain link. Though Gehry's iconoclastic projects have also attracted controversy (some think they are overwhelming and impractical and even not "organic" enough), they are always fascinating.

Here at Bard, Gehry's 110,000-square-foot building is beautifully set on the edge of the rural campus, surrounded by greenery. Its dramatic steel and glass exterior is signature Gehry, with bold, untraditional forms on the sides and a massive roof that appears to move like a wave reaching to the sky. The remarkably fluid lines of this breathtaking structure remind us of a giant sculpture shaped by the wind. Be sure to spend enough time to walk around it carefully, noticing the way the shiny silvery surfaces capture the light. And don't miss (if possible) the spacious and elegant interior, which contains state-of-the-art studios, rehearsal halls, and two theaters with exceptional acoustics; performances include orchestral and chamber music, jazz, theater, dance, and opera.

The brand-new **Center for Science and Computation** is by the Uruguayan-born Rafael Viñoly, whose works are also well represented worldwide. His sleek and elegant, often elongated designs are light and airy. Often they are low to the ground—as is the case here at Bard—and seem to belong in their surroundings "organically."

Unlike the Center for Performing Arts, the Center for Science and Computation is set right in the middle of the campus, within a clearing that includes a plaza and walkways. The 49,000-square-foot building is a low and long, gently curving, glass, concrete, and aluminum structure cantilevered over the college walk. Inside are a large atrium, research labs (all facing the woods), high-tech classrooms, and a spacious auditorium. The building is designed to encourage informal interaction among faculty and students, with an open floor plan for maximum flexibility.

The design is also responsive to Bard's natural environment. As Rafael Viñoly says, "It responds to the campus, perhaps not in a stylistic way, but clearly in setting the tone for its future development. It seems to me that it is much more integrated with what makes a campus so interesting, which in my view isn't really the architecture, but the topography, landscaping, and the woods. It is more about the natural quality of the place."

If time allows, you should walk around and explore the campus further. There are many other buildings of interest, including the library with its bright new addition by Robert Venturi and the equally new Center for Curatorial Studies and Art in Contemporary Culture, an exhibition space containing the college's permanent art collection. There is a lot to see here, and you'll find a visit to this campus a rewarding experience.

3·
A McKIM, MEAD & WHITE EXTRAVAGANZA IN THE BEAUX ARTS STYLE

The Vanderbilt Mansion, Hyde Park

❀ DIRECTIONS

The Vanderbilt estate is located about eighty miles north of New York City on the east bank of the Hudson River. Take the Henry Hudson Parkway north to the Saw Mill River Parkway to the Taconic State Parkway. Take Route 55 west to Route 9 north and continue for about six miles. The entrance to the estate is on your left.

Or take the New York State Thruway (I-87) north to Kingston (exit 19) and take Route 209 over the Kingston-Rhinecliff Bridge. Turn left onto Route 9 north.

❀ INFORMATION

The Vanderbilt Mansion is located on Route 9 just north of Hyde Park. The house is open seven days a week throughout the year, from 9 A.M. to 5 P.M. To see the inside of the house you must take a guided tour; tours are offered regularly during the day, the last leaving at 4 P.M. You can walk through the grounds on your own. Telephone: 845-229-9115. Web site: www.nps.gov/vama/.

❀ If you are a first-time visitor to the Vanderbilt estate in Hyde Park on the banks of the Hudson River, you will be astonished by its magnificence. From the fifty-four-room mansion of the Gilded Age to the vast panoramic sweep of the property and its grand river views to the ancient and majestic trees, it is a breathtaking place.

Given its imperial grandeur and spectacular location, it is not surprising that it is one of the premier tourist sites in the nation. "Great house" enthusiasts, history and architecture buffs, high school students studying the railroad monopolies, tourists from abroad—these are among the groups that are very much in evidence amid the gilt and glitter of the house. And with good reason: not only is the house a quintessential example of the Beaux Arts style of architecture popular in the late nineteenth century, but it was also inhabited by one of the nation's wealthiest and most visible families at a particularly flamboyant time in our history.

The Vanderbilts apparently loved to build palatial dwellings (you'll find others in New York City and Long Island, New York; Newport, Rhode Island; and Asheville, North Carolina). You may be surprised to learn that forty-four rooms is actually smaller than most Vanderbilt mansions; this one also happens to be one of the finest, a masterpiece designed by McKim, Mead & White, the most illustrious and successful architectural firm of the time. With its storybook elegance, inside and out, it offers a glimpse of how the ultrarich lived a century ago.

The history of the estate goes back to 1764, when the first house on the site was built. Before the Vanderbilts came on the scene in the late 1800s, there were other owners, including Dr. John Bard and his medical partner, Dr. David Hosack (who had a particular interest in the gardens), and John Jacob Astor (whose son-in-law, Colonel Walter Langdon, built a Neoclassical villa after the original house burned down). Then, in 1895, Frederick Vanderbilt (grandson of the railroad tycoon Cornelius Vanderbilt) happened to see the Langdon mansion—by then abandoned—from the deck of his yacht, as he was sailing up the Hudson. He was completely smitten and purchased it at once.

Actually, Vanderbilt had planned on renovating and expanding the existing structure, rather than building a new one. However, when he hired McKim, Mead & White, it was determined that the house was beyond repair and needed to be razed. In a matter of a few months, new plans were drawn up, and construction began. By 1899, the new house was completed, at a cost of about $3 million, a huge sum then. The architects' work on the six-hundred-acre estate included not only the limestone mansion but also gatehouses, a group of shingled barns, a sixteen-room pavilion (where the family lived during construction), and several guesthouses for friends. Vanderbilt lived here a few months of the year until his death in 1938. Two years later the house was donated to the National Park Service. Today the estate is operated by the Vanderbilt Mansion National Historic Site and remains one of the best estates of the Gilded Age anywhere.

The exterior of the house is imperial and formal, reminiscent of the classical temples of western European palaces (a style favored by McKim, Mead & White at the time). Its symmetrical style is austere and restrained, with monumental Corinthian columns in rows, two-story porches, and smooth, plain, undecorated walls. On three sides are rectangular porches, with a circular porch on the river side, where one could sit and enjoy the views.

The inside is, of course, much more fanciful with its ornate and shining décor. The rooms are grand but more inviting than you might expect, despite their size and imposing furnishings (many in the lavish style of Louis XIV and XV). Ogden Codman, who coauthored *The Decoration of Houses* with Edith Wharton, designed certain rooms, including Mrs. Vanderbilt's exquisite bedroom, meant to evoke that of an eighteenth-century French queen. Here you'll see superb detailing and inset paintings on the wood-paneled walls. Other architects were engaged to design other rooms, including McKim, Mead & White, who were responsible for the beautifully proportioned drawing room, dining room, and hallways.

The estate grounds are as interesting as the house, are far less crowded, and should definitely not be missed. Though you may wonder at the gardens' being so far from the house, you can only be grateful that their quiet charm has survived the crowds visiting the mansion. Here you can stroll on your own, enjoying the Italianate gardens, magnificent trees (over forty species, many labeled), greenhouses, broad lawns, and river views. The formal gardens were of particular interest to Frederick Vanderbilt, who had a degree in horticulture from Yale and a lifelong interest in growing flowers and in farming. But for the most part, the gardens already existed when he purchased the property. In fact, he made only a few changes to the gardens of his predecessors, as the majestic landscape he found suited his taste for the grand.

4 ·
ALEXANDER JACKSON DAVIS AND ANDREW JACKSON DOWNING JOIN FORCES ON A HUDSON RIVER ESTATE

Montgomery Place, Annandale-on-Hudson

❀ DIRECTIONS

Montgomery Place is located on River Road in Annandale-on-Hudson. From New York City take the Henry Hudson Parkway north to the Saw Mill River Parkway to the Taconic State Parkway. Exit at Red Hook/Route 199 and go west ten miles on Route 199 through Red Hook; turn right onto Route 9G and then left onto Annandale Road. Bear left again onto River Road to the entrance.

Or take the New York State Thruway (I-87) north to Kingston (exit 19) and take Route 209 over the Kingston-Rhinecliff Bridge. Turn left onto Route 9G and then follow the directions above.

❀ INFORMATION

As of this writing, the buildings are still closed for restoration, but they can be enjoyed from the outside. Telephone for reopening date. The grounds are open from mid-April through October, Wednesday to Monday, 10 A.M. to 5 P.M.; November, December, and March, Saturday and Sunday only, 10 A.M. to 5 P.M. Telephone: 845-758-5461. Web site: www.hudsonvalley.org.

❀ Montgomery Place is one of the great Hudson River estates, combining romantic, sweeping landscaped lawns, woodlands, and extraordinary views. The 434-acre site includes a nineteenth-century mansion remodeled by Alexander Jackson Davis, one of America's most important nineteenth-century architects, and an idyllic landscape of gardens, ancient trees, expanses of parkland, and walking trails, influenced by the great Andrew Jackson Downing. The fact that Montgomery Place is largely the result of a collaboration between these two masters in architecture and landscape design makes it unique among Hudson villas.

Montgomery Place, Annandale-on-Hudson. Photo courtesy Historic Hudson.

Over the years Montgomery Place has often been regarded as one of the most ravishing of all the estates along the river. In an 1866 guidebook it was described as being "the most perfect in its beauty and arrangements," with "waterfalls, picturesque bridges, romantic glens, groves, a magnificent park, one of the most beautiful of the ornamental gardens in this country, views of the river and the mountains, unsurpassed." It is still viewed in much the same way.

Built in the early 1800s by a branch of the Livingston family (who also owned nearby Clermont), Montgomery Place was part of a 160,000-acre family holding. In the 1840s the Livingstons engaged Davis to transform the original Federal-style house into one that would reflect the elegant lifestyle of the family of the time. (Davis's book *Rural Residences,* published in 1838, had by then made him quite famous.) From 1841 Davis worked on the mansion, making alterations in a highly decorative classical style. He enlarged the house (to twenty-three rooms) and added pavilions, terraces (with urns and pedestals), verandas, and porticoes. (His north portico was regarded as the earliest outdoor room in America.) He embellished new wings with pilasters based on classical Greek designs and ornamented balustrades with laurel wreaths.

Andrew Jackson Downing came on the scene at about this time. Downing was undoubtedly America's first great landscape architect and writer on landscape gardening; he was also a good friend of the distinguished Calvert

Vaux, partner of Frederick Law Olmsted. The family had a special interest in the grounds and started consulting with Downing in 1844, a relationship that lasted for several years (until Downing died tragically in a steamboat accident on the Hudson). Downing and Davis also worked closely together to create a harmonious whole. Soon there were new garden buildings, an arboretum, several gazebos, and a bridge. The splendid romantic sweep of the lawns and curving driveways, the plantings of groves of great trees, and the delightful woodsy trails—these ideas of landscape design were also made with the advice of Downing. (The formal gardens, however, came later.)

The estate stayed in the family's hands throughout the nineteenth century, and the Delafields, descendants of the Livingstons, continued to preserve it. In the 1930s Violetta Delafield, already an amateur botanist and expert horticulturist (with a specialty in mushrooms) created showplace gardens that flourished until her death in 1949. The Delafield family continued to live there until 1986, when the property was taken over by Historic Hudson Valley. The house and garden have been open to the public since 1988.

To visit the house you must take a guided tour (offered regularly). There you will see an invaluable collection of furniture and artworks—most noteworthy is the portrait collection of works by Gilbert Stuart and John Wesley Jarvis. You can walk through the grounds on your own, enjoying the views at every turn.

5·
TOURING THE ARCHITECTURAL HISTORY ON A VENERABLE CAMPUS

Vassar College, Poughkeepsie

❀ **DIRECTIONS**

Take Routes 44/55 from either the New York State Thruway (I-87) or the Taconic State Parkway. Follow signs to Raymond Avenue. Park at the South Parking Lot on Raymond Avenue.

❀ **INFORMATION**

Visit at any time, but to see the museum or other public buildings, visit between 10 A.M. and 5 P.M., Tuesday through Saturday, or 1 P.M. to 5 P.M. on Sunday. As you enter the campus, pick up a map from the guard on duty. Telephone: 845-896-9560. Web site: www.fllac.vassar.edu.

❀ Vassar College was founded in 1861. It is a most interesting campus to visit from an architectural standpoint, with a wonderful variety of building styles from mid-nineteenth century to the present. Many distinguished architects have contributed to this diversity, and a walk around the campus will provide an unusual historical tour of architecture ranging from the 1860s through recent years. We have chosen twelve sites to visit in a loop walk (obviously not in historical order, however) with a thumbnail sketch of each building. (For a more detailed history of each building and its architect take a look at *Vassar College: An Architectural Tour* by Karen Van Lengen and Lisa Reilly. It is available at the college bookshop in Main Building or in Thompson Library.)

1. Frances Lehman Loeb Art Center (Cesar Pelli & Associates, 1994; Balmori Associates, Landscape Design)

Our first stop is just to the right of the entrance to the campus. You won't miss the very contemporary glass-pavilion entranceway into the more traditional-looking art gallery (which, by the way, has a distinguished collection of some sixteen thousand works of art). The all-glass entryway is hexagonal; a glass corridor leads the way from it to Taylor Hall, which has been partially renovated as well. The architect used a variety of materials in the entryway and renovation, matching some to the campuswide aesthetic, such as the pink limestone colonnade at the entrance and the brick façade of the building itself. But overall, the 1994 addition seems modern and new in a traditional setting.

Behind the building (on the Raymond Avenue side) is a charming outdoor sculpture garden, designed by Diana Balmori.

Walk to the next building on your left, the Vassar Chapel.

2. **Vassar Chapel** (*Shepley Rutan & Coolidge*, 1904)

This Norman Revival structure, built of granite with sandstone trim, is huge and imposing with an asymmetrically positioned tower and a series of arched doorways typical of medieval churches. Seating fourteen hundred people, it feels like a European church within, with a high, Gothic, vaulted ceiling of deep-toned wood and fine proportions.

The chapel has two series of excellent stained-glass windows, one group by John La Farge (the west nave windows) and the other series by Louis Comfort Tiffany (the east side of the nave and the unusual rose window of white and pale blues). Their disciple John Leftwich Dodge designed the windows on both sides of the organ.

Walk to your left to see our next stop, the New England Building.

3. **New England Building** (*York & Sawyer Architects*, 1901)

This distinctive building from 1901 (with later renovations) was called the New England Building because alumnae of that region provided the funds for it; a small piece of Plymouth Rock is even ensconced above the door. It was originally designed as a science building—note its large windows, meant to make lab work more clearly visible with natural light. But what catches the eye of today's visitor is the building's pleasing design, typical of the Beaux Arts style popular at many college campuses at the time it was built.

The form of the building is a rectangle, with a notable rounded apse. The brick façade is divided by numerous tall windows with arched tops, and a heavy classical cornice. White pilasters and detailing, as well as decorative ironwork, including a continuous classical-style garland at the edge of the roof and ornate window railings, add to the ornamental details. The interior, today housing lecture halls and a natural history museum, is divided by a grand staircase. The buildings sits proudly alone on a grassy spot—a strong reminder of a felicitous period in American architecture.

Just beyond this building is our next stop: Olmsted Hall.

4. Olmsted Hall (Sherwood Mills & Smith, 1972)

This rather forbidding, functionalist brick building houses the Biology Department. From the outside it resembles a fortress, with repeated forms unbroken by windows or decoration, suggesting the Brutalist period in 1970s architecture. It has mostly cinderblock interior walls and a central atrium within and is particularly known on campus for its wide passageway through to a much cherished view of the southern part of the campus.

Walk back toward the New England Building and head to the next building on your left, Mudd Chemistry Building.

5. Seeley G. Mudd Chemistry Building (Perry Dean Rogers & Partners, 1984)

This postmodern science building combines a variety of design sources into a large, rectangular brick, limestone, and glass-block structure, in a style derived from classical architecture but featuring both technological and design novelties. The use of glass is central to its design, with energy efficiency and sunlight-heated air circulating through the double glass walls. Its exterior is light and airy with horizontal brick bands (in a nod to nearby campus buildings) amid the glass. Walk around to the south side of the building to see the all-glass façade and the glass-block entrance.

The next building to your left is the Center for Drama and Film.

6. Center for Drama and Film (Cesar Pelli & Associates, 2003)

Another Cesar Pelli contribution to the campus is this large, horizontally striped building attached to what remains of the unusual and charming nineteenth-century Avery Hall. The original brick Avery Hall has two matching towers with mansard roofs and decorative white outlines; it is described as being in the "Lombard Romanesque" style, in fashion in the 1860s, and in keeping with other architecture of the early campus. Don't neglect to walk around to see this delightful façade.

The Center for Drama and Film adjoins the old-fashioned Avery Hall without aesthetic compromise. The new building, erected in 2003, is divided from the old by two useful, as well as symbolic, glass-enclosed stairways, marking the transition from past to present. ("The relationship of the old and the new reflects very clearly the state of the performing arts today," said the architect.)

The large, horizontal exterior of the modern center features light- and dark-gray stripes and red masonry blocks that vary in size, with colorful burnt-orange window frames. Its simple blocklike shapes, in contrast with the decorative Avery Hall, are functional and formal in design. The interior houses a theater, a minimalist interior courtyard (designed by Diana Balmori), and state-of-the-art theater and film labs and study centers.

Walk to your left to see Ferry House.

7. Ferry House (Marcel Breuer, 1951; *original landscape design realized in* 1997)

The Dexter M. Ferry Cooperative House is a fine architectural addition to the Vassar landscape, for it not only is an example of the great Marcel Breuer's International style but was the first truly modernist building on campus. Breuer was associated with the Bauhaus style, and the Ferry building has the long, low, geometric design typical of Bauhaus architecture.

The Ferry House architectural vocabulary includes a white painted brick exterior, a second-story wing with innovative sunscreens, floor-to-ceiling sliding glass doors, flagstone floors, and a series of low walls that create a related design for the adjoining landscape. A cooperative living area, Ferry House is furnished with designer pieces by Saarinen, Eames, and Thonet and many interior details by Breuer himself.

Walk around behind Ferry House to see Kautz Admission House.

8. Kautz Admission House (Pilcher & Tachau, 1908; *renovated by* Linda Yowell, 1995)

A fascinating architectural link between old and new is this Arts and Crafts–style stucco house now housing the Admission Office. Its exterior has the low, horizontal look of many houses of the time, as well as a large veranda and projecting eaves, but it is the interior that particularly retains the charm and ambience of the early-twentieth-century Arts and Crafts style.

Note in particular the original details, including the dark-toned, arched woodwork, the tiled fireplace (and the furnishings of the same period) in the living room.

Walk around the cluster of buildings surrounding Kautz Admission House and a short distance to the north edge of the campus to see Noyes House.

9. Noyes House (Eero Saarinen & Associates, 1958)

Part of the master plan for the north side of the campus, Noyes Hall was designed by the noted Finnish/American architect Eero Saarinen. As part of a circular site, the dormitory forms the northeastern edge of the circle with its own outline clearly rounded as well. Like other major Saarinen buildings of the mid-twentieth century, this building uses expressionistic—almost sculptural—forms and is carefully related to its surroundings.

Constructed of repeated vertical brick pillars (in a nod to the surrounding campus architecture) and repeated projecting aluminum-clad glass window bays, the building seems to suggest both the Gothic style of nearby buildings and a sleek modernism. Its light, airy exterior and emphasis on verticality make it seem to float upward.

Noyes Hall houses 156 students and has a sunken lounge, popular in the 1950s and still appealing today.

Continue to your left to see Students' Building.

10. Students' Building (All Campus Dining Center) (McKim, Mead & White, 1913)

Having seen a variety of modernist and postmodern buildings on our walk, it is somewhat startling to come to a traditional college building, complete with white columns and cupola and designed by the great firm of McKim, Mead & White almost one hundred years ago.

This traditional design (now with some additions and renovations) includes a high, columned portico, resembling southern Colonial Revival designs with the red brick and white trim so familiar on American campuses. (The building's architects, of course, were the primary designers of public buildings in their time.) Originally housing a large auditorium with ornate decorations, the building was greatly modified to become an all-campus dining hall in the 1970s. But the traditional exterior still evokes the campus of an earlier time.

Turn back toward the center of the campus to the Main Building.

11. Main Building *(James Renwick Jr., 1865; with later additions by Jean Paul Carlhian of Shepley Bulfinch Richardson & Abbott, 1974–1975 and Sloan Architects PC, 2001)*

The center of the original campus, this giant (five hundred feet wide) Second Empire building was designed by one of America's premier architects, James Renwick Jr. It is a designated National Historic Site. Its grand, rather austere design resembles French architecture (notably the Tuilleries). Built of brick, it has a mansard roof made of slate. It is five stories tall, has arched windows with bluestone trim, and a series of towers. Inside the original building, above the main floor, are carefully decorated rooms opening onto long halls. It is a giant and gracious nineteenth-century building.

However, modern uses have changed a great many things about Main Building. Numerous renovations and additions have created a wing (Thompson Annex) and a variety of other modern additions. The recent entrance is by Cesar Pelli. The first floor and lower level (walk around to the back of the building) are light and airy with lots of glass and skylit courtyards, as well as inviting modern amenities, including the college bookshop and cafeteria.

From the front of the building walk directly ahead to the Thompson Library.

12. Frederick F. Thompson Memorial Library *(Allen & Collins, 1905; Helen Lockwood addition by Hellmuth, Obata & Kassabaum, 1977; Martha Rivers and E. Bronson Ingram addition by Hardy Holzman Pfeiffer, 2001)*

Don't miss the main library on this campus; the original Thompson Memorial Library is just what you may have imagined a traditional college library would look like. (It has been renovated several times, but the atmosphere has been preserved.) The library's two more recent additions provide an architectural counterpoint, as well as a more contemporary update on libraries and acquisition of knowledge in the twenty-first century.

The exterior of the original Thompson Memorial Library is characterized by neo-Gothic elegance with ecclesiastical touches, including a crenellated tower and an ornately carved limestone façade. In the interior, there is an ambience of English Gothic style, with intimate, wood-paneled spaces (fitted with long tables for study with a row of lamps down the center), deep-toned stained glass, clerestory windows providing natural light below, and a dark wood balcony running along both sides of the center under arching overhead beams—a warmly inviting place to study.

On the right side of the building you'll find the new additions. The Lockwood addition is a concrete, modernist design (housing rare books and manuscripts), with strongly rectangular forms and an interplay of voids and overhangs. Its modernist tone is interesting and uncompromising.

Nearby is the large Rivers and Bronson addition: built of brick and limestone to echo the original library materials, it also plays off the Gothic details of the main building, with decorative little towers, a textured façade, and window detailing. Like much postmodernist architecture of our time, it draws on a variety of sources and a high-tech vocabulary for its inspiration.

6·
THE ARTIST'S IMAGINATION IN A DRAMATIC MOORISH PALACE

Olana, Hudson

❈ DIRECTIONS

Take the New York State Thruway (I-87) north to exit 21 in Catskill. Follow signs to Rip Van Winkle Bridge. Turn right and take Route 9G for one mile, following signs to Olana.

❈ INFORMATION

The grounds of Olana are open daily year-round from 8:30 A.M. to sunset. You will find joggers, walkers, and picnickers enjoying the surroundings. The museum is open April 15 through October 31 by guided tour only, Wednesday through Saturday from 10 A.M. to 5 P.M. and Sunday from noon to 5 P.M. (The last tour begins at 4 P.M.) Tours are limited to twelve people, so reservations are recommended, particularly in view of the fact that Olana is a popular place, with some twenty-five thousand visitors to the house annually. Admission is charged. Telephone: 518-828-0135. Web site: www.olana.org.

❈ Olana is often considered the most architecturally interesting villa on the Hudson, where so many extraordinary houses still draw visitors. The Hudson River painter Frederick Edwin Church brought his own romantic vision to Olana, not only to his great landscape paintings but to his home and property as well. Olana, ostensibly designed by an eminent architect, was built to Church's own specifications and fancies. It is a one-of-a-kind house and a marvelous site for a visit.

A spacious 250-acre park surrounds the sixteen-room villa (which is often crowded with tourists). The approach to the house is itself on a grand scale, with a network of roads winding up the hill. The house is at the top, with commanding views that Church captured so beautifully in several of his paintings.

Church was first introduced to the Catskills, which became known as nature's great academy of landscape art, in 1844, when he came to study with Thomas Cole, but it was not until fourteen years later that he decided to live here. By then he had become an international celebrity, having traveled throughout the Americas, from Ecuador to Labrador, as well as in Europe and Asia, to experience firsthand natural wilderness at its most elemental. He had created showpiece landscapes that galvanized the public, who flocked to see them. His *Niagara* (Corcoran Gallery of Art) was hung by itself; it was so popular that it could only be viewed by ticket holders. His *Heart of the Andes* (Metropolitan Museum of Art), a massive five-and-a-half-by-ten-foot canvas that became one of the most celebrated American paintings of the nineteenth century, was actually preached about in pulpits, where ministers extolled Nature's glories.

The Islamic influences (from Moorish to Persian) of Olana's architecture include its towers, patterned brickwork, pointed archways, stenciling (both indoors and out), framed views, and the beautifully laid-out gardens surrounding the ten-acre lake. "I designed the house myself," said Church. "It is Persian in style adapted to the climate and requirements of modern life. The interior decorations and fitting are all in harmony with external architecture."

Whether described as Persian or Moorish, Olana is certainly unlike other villas that dot the Hudson Valley. Like the fairy tales of far-off lands and exotic castles so popular in the nineteenth century, Olana brought a glamorous foreign style to a setting that inspired so many Romantic artists and writers.

7·

THE "PICTURESQUE" IN ARCHITECTURE AND LANDSCAPE DESIGN

Wilderstein, Rhinebeck

❀ DIRECTIONS

Take the New York State Thruway (I-87) north to Kingston (exit 19) and take Route 209 over the Kingston-Rhinecliff Bridge. Turn right onto Route 9G and then right again on Route 9 south through Rhinebeck. Turn right onto Mill Road, go 2.5 miles, and make a right onto Morton Road. Wilderstein is number 330.

❀ INFORMATION

Open May through October, Thursday through Sunday, noon to 4 P.M.; Thanksgiving through December, weekends only. Tours are offered; admission is free. Telephone: 845-876-4818. Web site: www.wilderstein.org.

❀ If you like majestic wood-framed mansions, in the High Victorian style, don't miss this picturesque late-nineteenth-century country house. A redesigned building described as "Queen Anne," it is a many-gabled three-story house with a five-story circular tower (with a conical roof), asymmetrical designs, a porte cochère, a veranda, fanciful colors, and a setting high above the Hudson. Though somewhat worn-out looking, it has had recent coats of paint (striking in color), and its original elegance is easily imagined. (We like the antique look.)

There are some thirty-five rooms that were once lavishly decorated by J. B. Tiffany. The interiors are in Revival and Aesthetic Movement styles, featuring original American furnishings, antiques, and memorabilia relating to the various generations of the owners. Originally built by Thomas Suckley (and redesigned over the years), it stayed in the family for some 150 years, before becoming a Hudson River Historic Site on the National Record of Historic Places.

In keeping with the movement known as the "Picturesque," the landscape around Wilderstein was designed by Calvert Vaux. It is indeed lovely, providing the mansion with a magnificent hillside vista of fields and river, as well as places to walk.

While in Rhinebeck you will want to see several additional sites of interest:

The **Delameter House** on Route 9 (just beyond the traffic light in the center of town) is a modest but elegant 1844 house in the Victorian style, complete with lots of gingerbread decorations. It was designed by Alexander Jackson Davis.

The **Dutch Reformed Church** (on Route 9 at South Street) has an interesting mixture of architectural styles. Built of stone and brick, it features Georgian and Gothic windows; the church dates to 1809.

8·

RICHARD UPJOHN'S VENTURE INTO SECULAR ITALIANATE ARCHITECTURE

Lindenwald, the Martin Van Buren National Historic Site, Kinderhook

❁ **DIRECTIONS**

Lindenwald is located on Route 9H, two miles south of the town of Kinderhook. From New York City take the Henry Hudson Parkway north to the Saw Mill River Parkway to the Taconic State Parkway. Exit at Route 23 and go west to Claverack and then north on Route 9H. Follow signs to the Martin Van Buren National Historic Site.

❁ **INFORMATION**

Open Wednesday through Sunday, 9 A.M. to 4:30 P.M., from mid-May to the end of October. Guided tours are available. Telephone: 518-758-9689. Web site: www.nps .gov/mava.

❁ Lindenwald is interesting both as a historic site—it was the last home of Martin Van Buren, eighth president of the United States—and as a mansion with architectural merit. Located just outside the unspoiled village of Kinderhook, itself a place distinguished for its eighteenth- and nineteenth-century houses, it is an intriguing blend of several styles—Federal, Italianate, and Victorian—reflecting the changes in architectural tastes over time.

But first a bit of history. On this site once stood a stone house, which was replaced in 1797 by a brick, center-hall Georgian, described as "a plain, substantial commodious house" when it was put up for sale in 1839. Enter President Van Buren, who then bought it—along with 137 acres—thinking that he might retire there at some point. (An aside: Van Buren had been raised in nearby Kinderhook and called himself "Old Kinderhook"; one story has it that it is from those initials that "OK" became part of our everyday language.)

Some years later, in 1849, Van Buren's son convinced him to remodel Lindenwald into a style that would reflect the fashion of the day. The architect of the moment, Richard Upjohn (who had just finished building Trinity Church in Lower Manhattan, to great acclaim), was hired to design this transformation, and he turned a simple Georgian house into an elegant, thirty-six-room Italianate villa with a four-story brick tower. Among his dramatic changes was the addition of an elaborate front porch, a combination of Romanesque and Gothic styles.

Lindenwald was to undergo further alterations, though temporary ones. As Victorian styles lost their appeal, there was a renewed interest in early American or Colonial styles. In this spirit, one of Lindenwald's later owners actually added a Neoclassical portico (reminiscent of Mount Vernon) to detract from the house's eclectic Victorian look, which was considered old-fashioned. However, in 1974 the National Park Service bought Lindenwald to create the historic site and appropriately restored it to the way it had looked in Van Buren's time.

The house you see today is a graceful building with double chimneys, arched windows, and shutters. Inside is a beautiful center stairway that winds up through the house; a deep central hall with remarkable French wallpaper (the original) showing hunting scenes; and many comfortable and bright rooms with original furniture, decorative objects, and memorabilia. The surrounding grounds (which have been somewhat restored) are peaceful and rural, befitting the nineteenth-century agricultural property that Van Buren and his family enjoyed.

9·
MILLS MANSION
A McKim, Mead & White Estate, Staatsburg

❀ DIRECTIONS

Take Routes 44/55 from either the New York State Thruway (I-87) or the Taconic State Parkway. Go north on Route 9 to Staatsburg, a few miles south of Rhinebeck.

❀ INFORMATION

Open April through October, Tuesday through Saturday, 10 A.M. to 5 P.M.; Sunday, 11 A.M. to 5 P.M. Closed in November. Tours are available by appointment in December through March. Telephone: 845-889-8851. Web site: www.staatsburgh.org.

❀ This glamorous estate was designed by McKim, Mead & White. The sixty-five-room mansion is in the French Renaissance style—much like a château—or in American terms, the Beaux Arts style. It was built around

Mills Mansion, Staatsburg

an earlier—much smaller—Greek Revival mansion from the 1840s. In 1896 Ruth Livingston Mills, a granddaughter of the original owners, hired White to design a mansion—it might better be called a palace by today's standards —both indoors and out.

The exterior is a grand formal core, including the original rectangular building with two matching wings and, facing the dramatic Hudson view, an elaborate circular staircase and entrance porch. White added two floors, balustrades, bracketed cornices, and fluted Ionic columns, contributing to the mansion's European aura. This palatial building is so imposing and formal that it is hard to believe its residents used it only as an autumn country house—it looks more like the setting for heads of state to sign treaties.

The interior has seventy-nine rooms, and you can take a tour. The mansion has many of the accoutrements of a French palace, from the vast rooms to the elaborate gilded plasterwork, marble fireplaces, oak paneling, pilasters, ornamental stairways, and balustrades to its décor and furnishings in the Louis XIV, XV, and XVI styles. It has paintings by Reynolds, among other great artists, Flemish tapestries, Etruscan pottery and chinoiserie. The dining room is considered the architectural gem of the building.

The setting of this palace overlooking a great sweep of open space and the glistening river below is also spectacular. There are smaller buildings on the estate as well, and the landscaping surrounding one of them—Hoyt House—was designed in the Picturesque style by Calvert Vaux in the 1840s.

AND KEEP IN MIND . . .

10 • Wing's Castle, Millbrook

DIRECTIONS: *Take Route 44 east from Poughkeepsie or from the Taconic State Parkway to Bangall Road and go north to number 717.*

INFORMATION: Open May through October, Wednesday through Sunday, noon to 5 P.M. There is an admission fee. Telephone: 845-677-0085.

If artistic oddities are your pleasure, don't miss Wing's Castle, a work in progress, still being constructed some thirty years after its conception. The artists/owners used salvaged materials from other old buildings and still add the occasional found object to the mix.

Today, though partly covered with greenery and tumbling stones, Wing's Castle is the most romantic of stops on any architecture tour. There are towers and cupolas, the odd birdbath or other found item, and a general aura of antiquity. In fact, events are occasionally held here during the summer, and you can take a tour, too.

11 • Clermont, Germantown

DIRECTIONS: *From the Rhinebeck area take Route 9G north. Clermont Historic Site is just north of the Dutchess County–Columbia County border, on Route 6.*

INFORMATION: Open year-round, April through October, Tuesday through Sunday, 11 A.M. to 5 P.M.; November through March, weekends only, 11 A.M. to 4 P.M. Telephone: 518-537-4240. Web site: www.friendsofclermont.org.

This Hudson River historic site is built on land given to the Livingston family in 1656. The illustrious family built the original Georgian mansion here. (It was burned down by the British but rebuilt on the original foundation.) The present forty-six-room house dates to 1777, and seven generations of Livingstons have lived here. The steeply pitched roof, however, was added, with a nod to the Victorian Hudson River style, in 1874. Thus, Clermont is a Georgian mansion with a nineteenth-century-style roofline—a felicitous combination, as it turns out. The interior, filled with great heirlooms, period furnishings, and decorative details, is well worth a visit. And the setting and grounds are spectacular—some five hundred acres of formal gardens, lawns, trails, and views.

NEW YORK STATE
West of the Hudson

1·
THE STONE HOUSES OF HUGUENOT STREET

New Paltz

❀ DIRECTIONS

Take the New York State Thruway (I-87) north to exit 18; take Route 299 (Main Street) west for 1.3 miles. Take a right on North Front Street, and at the light, turn right on Route 32 north (North Chestnut), then left onto Broadhead Avenue. Parking is on the left; tours begin at the DuBois Fort Visitor Center.

❀ INFORMATION

The historic stone houses are open for tours from May to October, Tuesday through Sunday; tours are offered every hour, 10 A.M. to 4 P.M., at the DuBois Fort Visitor Center. For information call the Huguenot Historical Society (at 18 Broadhead Avenue): 845-255-1889 or 845-255-1660. Web site: www.huguenotstreet.org.

❀ Huguenot Street National Historic District, the oldest street with its original houses in the country, is a site not to be missed by anyone interested in both architecture and history. This quaint little area features seven restored stone houses (the earliest dates to 1705), a reconstructed French church from 1717, an old fort (now the Visitor Center), and a few more recent buildings. As you walk around the tiny community, serene in its simplicity and uniformity, you get a sense of how its inhabitants might have lived some three hundred years ago.

The story of the Huguenots goes back to seventeenth-century France. These French Protestants had left their country even before King Louis XIV had officially banned their religion (in 1685), finding refuge in nearby countries. A more adventuresome group of Huguenot families from the Rhine-Palatinate in Germany arrived in the Hudson Valley as early as 1660. These twelve families bought land from the Native Americans and built log huts. They called their settlement "New Paltz" (from "Die Pfalz," the name of their region in Germany where they had sought refuge from the French).

Huguenot House, New Paltz

Later the huts were replaced with steep-roofed stone houses, and by 1792 the street looked much the same as it does today, with its rows of little stone houses. You might be interested to know that the Huguenot Historical Society, which protects and owns the site, still includes members who are descendants of the original families.

Start at the Visitor Center (DuBois Fort, dating from 1705). Here you can pick up a guided tour. Though you can walk around the community on your own, you must take the tour (which takes about one hour) in order to visit the buildings inside. Make sure to pick up the handy walking guide, which identifies the various buildings to see.

DuBois Fort, originally a smaller structure, was remodeled in the late 1830s. It was never used as a fort, as these early inhabitants of New Paltz never had to seek refuge there. Legend has it that it is haunted by a headless lady!

The stone houses are appealing in their unadorned and genuine simplicity. Originally they were one-room structures, each with a large family kitchen and fireplace. Cupboards displaying pottery and pewter added charm to the plain interior. Many of the buildings still have their original furnishings.

Among the more interesting buildings are the **French Huguenot Church** and the Jean Hasbrouck House. The stone church, actually a 1972 reconstruction of the original 1717 building, is small, square, and features a steep root with cupola (from which worshipers were once summoned by the blowing of a giant conch shell). The church is still used on special occasions.

The **Jean Hasbrouck House** (1721), one of the finest examples of Hudson Valley Dutch architecture in general, is also one of the best-furnished houses on Huguenot Street. But what makes it special is its wonderful, tall brick chimney that is unlike any we've ever seen.

Note also the **Freer House**, dating from the early 1700s, the interior of which has been remodeled to reflect a modern interpretation of colonial living; the **Bevier-Elting House** (early 1700s), once occupied by enslaved Africans, which has been expanded from its original one-room structure; and the **Deyo House**, whose original stone structure has been extended with a Queen Anne–style addition.

Take your time to savor Huguenot Street and its charms. You'll find that the site has been beautifully maintained, with its architectural integrity mostly intact. We can only wish that more historic preservations were as uncommercial as this one!

2·
ROMANTIC CASTLE RUINS ON AN ISLAND

Bannerman's Castle, Pollepel Island

❀ DIRECTIONS

Take the New York State Thruway (I-87) north to exit 17; take Route 17K east into New-burgh, where Route 17K becomes Broadway. Go to the end of Broadway and take a left on Colden Street to the bottom of the hill. You'll find Newburgh Landing, where you take the boat to the island, just beyond the train trestle on the waterfront. Take the "Hudson River Adventures" boat for a quick trip to the island.

❀ INFORMATION

For boat schedules call 845-220-2120 or go online at www.prideofthehudson.com. Boats depart for the island Wednesday through Sunday, May through October. The staff will tell you the schedule of departures and returns. Tours and hard hats are offered. For more information on Bannerman's Castle call 845-234-3204 or visit www.bannermancastle.org.

❀ At the end of a pleasant little boat trip in the beautiful Hudson Valley is a true architectural delight. Anyone with a taste for an eccentric and massive, partly ruined baronial castle perfectly placed in the middle of a river shouldn't miss this outing.

Francis Bannerman VI was an arms merchant who purchased the seven-acre Pollepel Island in 1900 so that he could legally store his tons of munitions there. He also decided to build a bit of a summer getaway on the island, aiming to reproduce the atmospheric manor houses of his native Scotland. He came up with this extraordinary castle complex, which housed both his family and his armaments. Despite a terrible explosion in 1920, his family continued to live in the castle, and it remained a munitions depot until 1967, when it became part of the Hudson Highlands State Park. A fire left it in ruins two years later, and what you see today are the massive remains of a once magnificent building. (Rebuilding it is an idea dogged by controversy, as many tourists prefer their castles in ruins.)

Bannerman's Castle, Pollepel Island

Today you'll find the remains of Bannerman's Castle absolutely fascinating, despite the fact that they are covered with weeds and vines, as well as trees peeking out of windows, since enough of the original castle remains for one to imagine the rest. You can tell there was once a moat, by the engraved stone pillar advising you of it; you can recognize triangles that once outlined formal gardens; and of particular interest, you can still see several massive walls and the corner towers that gave this pseudo-Renaissance castle its particular style.

Much is left, and despite the castle's semidestroyed state, you can easily spy ramparts and ghostly crenellated turrets and rows of windows (with the sky behind them). Elaborate architectural details remain on two sides of the mostly stucco-covered brick building, with a medieval portcullis and grand staircase over the declivity where the moat once was.

Like many eccentric buildings (often known as "follies") Bannerman's Castle reminds us that architecture has long been the art of choice for those individuals who want to create an aura of romance and illusion around themselves: what better way to see oneself as a baronial lord and master than in a massive, almost authentic castle on a very small island?

3·
ENVIRONMENTAL ART— OR ARCHITECTURE

Opus 40, Woodstock

❀ **DIRECTIONS**

Take the New York State Thruway (I-87) north to exit 20 (Saugerties); take Route 212 west toward Woodstock. At fork, take left onto Fish Creek Road to its end. Turn right to Fife Road and follow signs.

❀ **INFORMATION**

Opus 40 is located at 7480 Fite Road, Saugerties. It is open May through October, Friday, Saturday, and Sunday, 11 A.M. to 5 P.M. There is an admission fee to visit Opus 40 and the Quarryman's Museum, but children under twelve are admitted free. Group tours are available. Rubber-soled shoes are recommended. Telephone: 845-246-3400.

❀ In today's ever-changing definition of what constitutes art or architecture we occasionally find a place where such definitions are irrelevant. Opus 40 is such a place: is it an environmental sculpture or an architectural environment? This is a place that truly defies categories.

A visit to Opus 40 will blur the lines not only between the arts but also between art and nature, for the natural and artificial can barely be distinguished from each other here.

Opus 40 is the lifelong enterprise of environmental sculptor Harvey Fite. Fite bought the six-acre site, where bluestone had been quarried, and over a thirty-seven-year period he transformed it into a monumental environmental sculpture. Originally Fite conceived of the quarry as a dramatic sculpture park for his works, but he found the natural surroundings of the abandoned quarry overpowering for his individual carvings. He removed his carvings to the grassy areas bordering the quarry and set to work to make the quarry itself into his major work of art.

Opus 40 is made of thousands of tons of stone laid out into pathways, walls, convex and concave shapes, circular formations around quarry springs and trees, and abstract monuments. You can walk through it and around it, climb on it, enjoy different angles and views of nearby Overlook Mountain, and in general lose yourself within this total environment.

In the center and at the summit of Opus 40 you'll find Fite's monolith, a nine-ton stone column from which the patterns of the sculpture radiate. It is here at the center that some visitors choose to sit and meditate and where jazz and folk music concerts and other events are held on summer afternoons.

In addition to the quarry area, you can also walk on nicely wooded paths around the acreage or loll on the grassy areas where Fite's more traditional sculptures are set. In summer several (nonswimming) pools and fountains that are part of the environmental site are filled with water, making this a pleasant outing on a hot day.

There is also a museum called the **Quarryman's Museum** on the property. Fite built it to house his collection of tools and artifacts used by quarrymen and to honor and explain the tradition of quarrying and stone-working. Hand-forged folk tools and a slide show on the construction of Opus 40 are among the museum's offerings.

Although Opus 40 is certainly not everyone's idea of architecture, we include it in this book because it stretches the ideas of the built environment beyond the traditional and, at the same time, is an eye-opening and fascinating experience for the visitor.

4 ·
A VICTORIAN
WATERFRONT VILLAGE

Historic Rondout, Kingston

❀ DIRECTIONS

The Historic Rondout district of Kingston is located down on the city's waterfront. Take the New York State Thruway (I-87) north to exit 19. At the traffic circle and Route 28, take the second Kingston exit (I-587) to its end (about one mile). At the traffic light, turn left onto Broadway and go for about ten blocks. Bear right and continue to the bottom of the hill, then bear left (you're still on Broadway) for another five blocks to Rondout Waterfront and Mariner's Harbor.

❀ INFORMATION

The **Kingston Heritage Area Visitor Center**, at 20 Broadway, offers self-guided walking tours, maps, regional brochures, and exhibits relating to local architecture and history. Open Monday through Friday year-round, 9 A.M. to 5 P.M.; open on weekends, May through October, 10 A.M. to 5 P.M. Telephone: 800-331-1518 or 800-331-7517. Web site: www.cikings.ton.ny.us. Guided tours of the Rondout Historic District are offered on special occasions (call 845-339-0720).

❀ The Rondout, a hub for maritime activity from the time of seventeenth-century colonial New Netherlands, was once a separate village from Kingston, which is two miles up the hill, one with its own particular story. Whereas Kingston was already an established community by the eighteenth century (as you can see from its architecture), the waterfront village below did not come into its full bloom until well into the nineteenth century. As a result, the architecture you find here reflects the Victorian era rather than earlier styles.

From the launching of the Canal Era in the early 1830s until the end of the century Rondout was regarded as one of the major ports on the Hudson. It was here that the 107-mile-long Delaware & Hudson Canal ended. Barges carrying massive loads of anthracite coal from the Pennsylvania mines unloaded their precious cargo at this very spot; the coal would then

Rondout, Kingston

be shipped to New York City and other locations on different vessels. The scene of these canal boats all crowded together in the narrow Rondout Creek must have been quite chaotic!

For many years the maritime village continued to thrive as home port for freighters and steamers, reaching its peak of prosperity in 1870. Two years later, Kingston and Rondout merged and became known as the City of Kingston.

As railroads took over from canal transportation, Rondout began its steady and inevitable decline. In the 1960s urban-renewal advocates removed the decaying buildings in the east side of Rondout; those on the west side, for some reason, were spared, and some were eventually restored.

Today many of the remaining old buildings have become trendy art galleries, shops, and restaurants; parks have been landscaped and developed along the waterfront, and the old port is again a center for river excursions (plans are under way to restore it further). This waterfront revitalization is largely due to the efforts of the Hudson River Maritime Center Museum, which since its opening in 1980 has been committed to preserving the maritime heritage of the river. (Among its activities, the center offers boat trips, outdoor space for exhibits, and changing shows in its own gallery.)

Despite this ongoing development, the Rondout has retained its unspoiled and genuine quality—and we can only hope it will stay that way! Thus, a walk on the promenade along Rondout Creek is scenic and pleasant, as is a stroll past the picturesque row houses and other buildings along the streets.

Begin your walk by stopping at the Kingston Heritage Area Visitors Center at 20 Broadway. Here you can pick up all the information you will need to explore this delightful waterside community on your own. The center's self-guided walking tour recommends some thirty-five different places of interest. Though most are conveniently located near the water, a few are uphill—but still worth the effort of a somewhat steep climb.

Here are a few architectural and historical highlights:

Hudson River Maritime Museum, at 50 Rondout Landing, features exhibits of the different kinds of boats and tugs once found on these shores. Enter this brick building (more interesting for its contents than for its architecture) to get a real feeling for the maritime life of the community.

Cornell Steamboat Company Boiler Shop (1892) and **Repair Shop** (1901) on East Strand Road are light and airy structures, with their large arched windows opening onto the creek. They are great examples of late-nineteenth-century maritime architecture. The buildings were once used to service tugboats of the Cornell Steamboat Company, one of the most prosperous enterprises here during the late nineteenth century.

West Strand Row (1870), located between 9 and 29 West Strand Street, is a group of seven picturesque Italianate-style buildings, their elegant façades befitting the prosperity of the village at the time. Note the arched windows and cornices typical of this style. The cast-iron columns and lintels you see were locally produced by Rondout Iron Works (the name appears on their bases).

Sampson Opera House, at the corner of West Strand and Broadway, was designed in 1875 by Henry Engelbert, a well-regarded New York City architect. Though its mansard roof and tower are gone (they were destroyed by fire in 1885), the striking building still has its thirty-one cast-iron columns, also a product of Rondout Iron Works (clearly the company was very active in the local construction business!). Apparently only the third and fourth floors were used as performance spaces, with the rest reserved for shopping.

Sampson House, at 16 Abeel Street, home of the owners of the Opera House, was built in 1873–1874. Its style is Second Empire, with its typical mansard roof, tall (two-story) bay windows, and bracketed cornice.

Jacob Forst House, a few houses away at 26 Abeel Street, dates from 1887. This Colonial Revival building was the family home of a German immigrant who created a meat-packing company that became one of Rondout's major economic success stories.

Thomas Burgess House, located at 15 Hone Street, dates to around 1837, making it one of Rondout's oldest existing houses. The Federal-style structure, whose exterior was carefully restored in 1981, features Ionic columns, among other classical details that are part of this elegant style.

Rondout Creek Bridge: Crossing this picturesque old bridge, which connects the mainland to Island Dock, is an experience not to be missed. As you walk across you can see the spot where piles of Pennsylvania coal used to be unloaded before being reshipped to other parts of the coast, and you can imagine what this process must have been like. And, of course, you can also enjoy a bird's-eye view of both shorelines. An interesting detail in the history of this bridge is that the bridge, a 1922 construction, unfortunately required repair before even opening; this work was successfully accomplished by a top electrical welder, who happened to be a woman (an unheard-of rarity at the time).

There are many other places to experience and enjoy, of course. If you have time, take a drive out to nearby **Kingston Point Park**, where scenic beauty, history, and architecture come together. It was here that the British landed in 1777 before their infamous burning of Kingston. Today it is a place of serenity amid beautifully landscaped greenery. The park has a spectacular view of **Rondout Lighthouse**, one of the seven existing Hudson River lighthouses. The yellow 1915 structure—typical of the early-twentieth-century style—is the third built at this scenic location. It is now operated by the **Hudson River Maritime Museum**, which offers regular tours during the summer months. (Note: perhaps the most architecturally appealing lighthouses of the Hudson is nearby **Esopus**, the last of its wooden lighthouses. This delightful structure features trompe l'oeil paintings in the windows, including one of a cat. Unfortunately, Esopus is not presently open to the public, but you can see it from the outside by taking a cruise boat out of Kingston.)

5·
EXPLORING THE
STOCKADE DISTRICT

Kingston

❀ **DIRECTIONS**

Take the New York State Thruway (I-87) north to exit 19. At the traffic circle take Washington Avenue. At the second traffic light turn left onto Schwenk Drive, which curves around and runs into Clinton Avenue. Park on the street near the Visitor Center, at 308 Clinton Avenue.

❀ **INFORMATION**

Before starting your walking tour, whether you are taking a guided tour or exploring the area on your own, stop at the **Kingston Heritage Area Visitor Center** at 308 Clinton Avenue and pick up a self-guided walking guide and map. Open May through October daily, 11 A.M. to 5 P.M. Telephone: 800-331-1518 or 800-331-7517. Web site: www.ci.kingston.ny.us.

Guided tours are given the first Saturday of the month, from May to October, and depart from the nearby **Friends of Historic Kingston Museum**, at 63 Main Street. Telephone: 845-339-0727. Web site: www.fohk.org.

Old Dutch Church Heritage Museum: Open by appointment or during church services. Telephone: 845-334-9355; office: 845-338-6759.

The Senate House: Open mid-April through October, Monday and Wednesday through Saturday, 10 A.M. to 5 P.M.; Sunday, 11 A.M. to 5 P.M. Telephone: 845-338-2786.

❀ If you're a fan of seventeenth- and eighteenth-century American architecture, you won't want to miss a visit to the Stockade District in Kingston, one of the best-kept secrets in the Hudson Valley. This is the oldest section of a historic town that in itself is undiscovered and unspoiled; here, within several blocks in "uptown," high above the river, you'll find more than twenty well-maintained old Dutch limestone houses, a beautiful old church, and the Senate House, a historic site where the first official New York State Senate met. The gray stone houses are the legacy of Ulster

118

County's earliest European (mostly Dutch, though also French Huguenot and English) settlers, who began to migrate here in the 1600s. Kingston was founded in 1652; its original street plan was designed by the provincial governor, Peter Stuyvesant. When the local Algonquin tribe seemed threatening, a simple stockade was built around the settlement for protection, and the name has stuck through the years. In the spring of 1777 Kingston became New York's first capital—but only very briefly; in October of that year the newly formed state government had to flee after learning that the British forces were on their way. In fact, the troops did storm in and succeeded in burning down much of the city. (Reenactments of this event are occasionally held.)

Today the houses of interest include private residences as well as public buildings; some can be visited, but others can only be seen from the outside. Many are surrounded with pretty yards or gardens, too, which add to the pleasure of exploring the area on foot. Most houses are identified with historical plaques that give you all the information you need. You will discover a variety of styles, from early Dutch-style houses (long, low, and one and a half stories) and saltboxes to Federal and Greek Revival structures, or a combination of the above. Most have undergone some form of restoration, and Friends of Historic Kingston keeps a vigilant eye on them all.

Friends of Historic Kingston has also put out a very comprehensive self-guided walking tour (available at the Visitor Center, where you should begin your walk), which points out thirty-three sites to see; these lie within a contained area, along pleasant, tree-lined streets. Though all the structures listed are worth seeing (and many come with interesting or amusing stories), we particularly recommend the following:

The Old Dutch Church, 272 Wall Street, at the corner of Main Street, is not the original church on this site (built in 1661) but was constructed in 1852. This bluestone Renaissance Revival building was designed by Minard Lafever, a popular architect of the time. (He was especially known for his Gothic Revival churches.) The renowned nineteenth-century architect Calvert Vaux considered it "ideally perfect" and a building of "exquisite beauty." Notice its elegantly proportioned steeple that seems to float upward; the bell, apparently cast in Amsterdam in the 1790s (from copper and silver donated by families), has wonderful resonance (and we hope you have the chance to hear it!). The interior includes an 1891 Tiffany window, a handsome vaulted ceiling, and a framed letter by George Washington. Walk around the tree-filled churchyard with its eighteenth-century tombstones (including that of

George Clinton, New York's first governor and the vice president under Jefferson and Madison).

Cornelius Tappen House, at 10 Crown Street, is said to be one of the oldest houses still standing in the Stockade area; it was damaged by the British in 1777 but has kept some of its windows. Here is an example of a "rubble" house, made with rough, irregularly cut stones fitted together. Once a post office (actually, the first in Kingston), it is now a bank.

Judge Lucas Elmendorf House, at 111 Green Street, is an excellent example of an eighteenth-century hip-roofed house on a large scale. This twenty-one-room mansion was built in 1790 by the county's first judge (who was also an associate of Thomas Jefferson's). Note its stylish stone entranceway.

Gerrett Van Keuren House, at 138 Green Street, dates to 1725; it, too, sustained damage when the British burned Kingston and was finally restored in the early 1900s. It represents the quintessential early Dutch-style house, with its long and low structure, only one and a half stories high.

The Four Corners, at John and Crown streets, is an important site here in the Stockade area: it is said to be the only intersection in the country where eighteenth-century houses still stand.

The 1676 Senate House, at 331 Clinton Avenue, is, we are told, the oldest public building in the United States. It was in this private house, then owned by the Van Gaasbeek family, that the first New York State Senate met in September and October 1777, before fleeing the British once again. Fortunately, this venerable old stone house survived the burning of Kingston and still stands proudly before us. Quite modest in size, it is surrounded by an appealing hedged garden. Inside you'll see the kitchen, bedroom, and parlor, where the Senate actually met.

Adjacent to the Senate House is its museum. Though the building itself is fairly recent (1927) and is of no particular architectural interest, its permanent collection of works by John Vanderlyn, the acclaimed early-nineteenth-century landscape painter and portraitist, is impressive. Vanderlyn was a native of Kingston, so it is appropriate that his many paintings, drawings, and papers are displayed here in his hometown.

6·
A RUSTIC VILLAGE OF EARLY DUTCH AND HUGUENOT DESIGN

Hurley

❀ DIRECTIONS

Take the New York State Thruway (I-87) north to exit 19. Go west on Route 28, then take Route 209 south to Hurley.

❀ INFORMATION

Only two of the houses in Hurley are regularly open to visitors, except on Hurley Stone House Day, which is held yearly on the second Saturday in July. For information call **Hurley Patentee Manor** at 845-331-5414 or the **Jan Van Deusen House** at 845-331-8852. But we recommend a walk through this unusual streetscape at any time of year.

❀ Hurley is a small town settled in 1662. Not only is it one of the oldest villages in the state, but it has preserved twenty-five of its wonderful stone houses. Settled by the Dutch and Huguenots, it originally had wood-frame houses along the Esopus Creek (quite a scenic spot).

In the early eighteenth century the stone houses of the village replaced the wooden ones, which were mostly burned down in wars with the Esopus Indians. Hurley has its own historical claim to fame, aside from its beautiful, preserved homes: it briefly served as capital of New York State when the British burned nearby Kingston during the Revolutionary War. Later it became a spot on the Underground Railroad for slaves escaping to Canada. With these historical facts in mind, it is interesting to walk through this town of small, attractive, and sturdy homes. Originally many had only one room, and some also served as tradesmen's shops. Note, for example, the following:

Hurley Patentee Manor was originally a Dutch cottage (1696) before being rebuilt as a Georgian manor house in 1745. Well restored and elegantly furnished, it can be visited. (By the way, don't miss the basement when you go there; it features one of the only indoor animal pens still around.)

More modest, but also noteworthy, is the **Polly Crispell Cottage** (1735), once a blacksmith shop and equipped with a "witch catcher" set into the chimney, to prevent witches (or birds) from flying in. There is a small burial ground behind the house.

The **Jan Van Deusen House** is where the New York State government met during the Revolutionary War; it has a secret room where documents were kept from prying eyes.

The **Drummond House** was used as a prison for a British spy who was eventually hanged from an apple tree across the street.

The **Elmendorf House** is a former tavern built in the 1690s. Behind it is a small, very old burial ground.

Practically every house has a small historical marker identifying it and its historical significance. We recommend strolling down the streets and absorbing the ambience of a three-hundred-year-old American village. It is particularly fascinating to notice the size of everything. Compared to today's sense of proportion and our giant houses, these diminutive buildings with their low door frames and tiny stature tell us of a different understanding of space and home.

7 ·
GOTHIC SPLENDOR AT THE UNITED STATES MILITARY ACADEMY

West Point

❀ DIRECTIONS

From New York City take the George Washington Bridge to the Palisades Parkway to Bear Mountain Circle and Route 9W north. Follow signs to Highland Falls and West Point.

❀ INFORMATION

Almost all buildings are open to visitors between 8:30 A.M. and 4:30 P.M., from April to November. Call for schedule of parades and other events, including tours of the various buildings listed here. Telephone: 845-938-2638. Web site: www.usma.edu.

❀ West Point, the United States Military Academy, has much to see. There are many buildings of interest, as well as historic sites and numerous ongoing events. Go first to the Visitor Center and get a map and information. Walk around to absorb the Gothic-style campus.

Don't miss the following:

The massive **Cadet Chapel** is known for its military Gothic architecture and fine stained-glass windows.

A brand-new building, **Thomas Jefferson Hall**, is a six-story library designed by Price Jepsen. Made of granite quarried in New Hampshire, it has lots of glass, a spectacular open staircase, and panoramic views. It houses one the largest organs in the world, with fifteen thousand pipes.

The **Chapel of the Most Holy Trinity** is built in the Norman Gothic style and is patterned after St. Ethelred's Carthusian Abbey in Essex, England.

The **Old Cadet Chapel** was built in 1837 and moved to its present location.

Warner House is an eighteenth-century house that requires a short boat ride to a small island in the Hudson; it was a strategic site in the Revolutionary War.

AND KEEP IN MIND . . .

8 · The "Cottages" of Elegant Onteora Park, Jewett

DIRECTIONS: *Take the New York State Thruway (I-87) north to exit 21 and go west on Route 23. Follow signs to Jewett.*

Here you'll find a collection of elegant homes that were part of a nineteenth-century summer colony called Onteora Park. Known as "cottages," these imposing homes are good examples of what was known in the nineteenth century as a "retreat," where people of like minds and status spent their leisure time.

Nearby Jewett Center has the exceptional **Saint John the Baptist Ukrainian Church** to see. Complete with onion dome, wooden beams, and carvings, it was built with wooden pins instead of nails. Be sure to see the decorative interior.

NEW YORK STATE
Long Island

1 ·
OLD BETHPAGE VILLAGE RESTORATION

Rural Architecture in Nineteenth-Century Long Island

❀ DIRECTIONS

Take the Long Island Expressway (I-495) to exit 48. Take Round Swamp Road south and look for the entrance almost immediately on your left.

❀ INFORMATION

Open March through December, Wednesday through Friday, 10 A.M. to 4 P.M.; Saturday and Sunday, 10 A.M. to 5 P.M. Closed during January and February. Pick up a self-guided architectural walking tour at the entrance or take a guided tour. There is an entrance fee. (Note: During the school year, you are likely to find groups of schoolchildren on weekdays; if you prefer to visit at a quieter time, plan accordingly.) Telephone: 516-572-8400.

❀ Old Bethpage Village Restoration is an outdoor museum of both historical and architectural interest. A re-creation of a mid-nineteenth-century Long Island village, it includes more than sixty preserved historic structures picturesquely set amid two hundred acres of rolling hills. This collection of assorted buildings—from carriage houses, shops, and cottages to rustic farm structures—features simplified versions of Georgian, Greek Revival, Federal, and Gothic styles that were found in Long Island's countryside from the mid-1700s to the late 1800s.

The Restoration was begun in 1962. Worthy historic structures that were threatened by the region's rapidly growing suburban expansion were brought to this site, once a vast farmland, and restored. Although the majority of these preserved buildings date to the mid-nineteenth century, there are earlier examples, such as the eighteenth-century Shenck House. You are invited to walk from one building to the next, where you will find costumed interpreters assuming the roles of teachers, shopkeepers, blacksmiths, and farmers who typically lived in this kind of rural community. Old Bethpage Village is still expanding, with buildings of historical and architectural merit being added to the site; each is carefully researched and restored and then furnished with authentic pieces.

The following are some buildings that are not to be missed on your architectural tour:

As you leave the Reception Center, you will find the **Shenck House** almost immediately on your left. This distinguished 1765 Dutch farmhouse (one of the oldest still existing in the country) has a side-gabled roof with flared eaves, a massive stone fireplace, and round shingles typical of the Dutch style.

The **Conklin House**, right next to the Shenck House, was restored to 1853. Once a fisherman's cottage, it has touches of Greek Revival (on the porch, windows, and main door), though it is shaped like a saltbox.

If you turn left at the crossroads you'll find **Kirby House** on your left. Once located in Hempstead, this cottage was restored to 1845. It is an example of village architecture with Greek Revival details typical of the period in this region. Note the pillared portico, transom, and entablature over the front porch.

The **Manetto Hill Church** is next on your left. This historic 1857 building was the first structure to be saved and moved here in 1963. Also in the Greek Revival style, it features original detail blocks, a solid frieze, and pilasters.

Turn back and, just past the tiny schoolhouse, you'll find **Benjamin House**. This gambrel-roofed house, originally situated on Long Island's North Fork, displays its date of 1829 on the central chimney. Note its carefully crafted and placed shingles.

Turn left at the main intersection and you'll come to **Noon Inn** on your left. This modified Georgian-style tavern dates to 1850 and is quite large by village standards, including two floors and a center hall.

Two houses away, past the hat shop, is the **Rich House**, a simple cottage built in 1830 by the hatmaker Lewis Ritch. The three-room house is reminiscent of the Cape Cod style.

If you turn right at the next intersection, you come to **Cooper House** (c. 1815), once the home of Peter Cooper, inventor of the steam locomotive. The building has gone through several stylistic changes, from its modest origins (in the mid-1600s) as a one-room dwelling with garret, to its reconstruction as a saltbox in the mid-eighteenth century, to its final remodeling as a Dutch-style house with a roof overhang (as it now appears).

A short walk away, on your left, is the **Powell Farm Barn**, an English-style farm complex dating to the 1850s. This picturesque site is interesting to see, with its displays of hand-hewn beam and wood-peg construction techniques.

Old Bethpage Village Restoration is a much welcome oasis in an otherwise mostly built-up section of this region. We hope you enjoy walking through these pleasant green acres, as you view old structures from Long Island's past.

2·
MELDING EAST AND WEST

The Charles B. Wang Center at
SUNY–Stony Brook

❀ DIRECTIONS

Take the Long Island Expressway (I-495) to exit 62 north. Take Nicolls Road (Route 97) north for nine miles. Turn left into the university's main entrance. There is public parking just across from the Wang Center.

❀ INFORMATION

Telephone: 631-632-4400. Email: WangCenter@stonybrook.edu.

❀ Stony Brook is a contemporary campus, spread out over acres and acres of forests and fields. Most of the buildings (which are in separated clusters across this vast campus) are typical midcentury, functional high-rise structures. But don't miss the Charles B. Wang Center! This building, in the center of the main academic campus, is easily spotted by its bright red entrance pavilion. It should be of particular interest to architecture buffs.

One of the most attractive and imaginative contemporary university buildings we have visited, it was designed by P. H. Tuan. The melding of Eastern and Western traditions into a cohesive design has been tried in many venues, but none more successfully than at the Wang Center. Described as a celebration of Asian and American cultures, it functions as a center for Asian studies at the university. But unlike most such places, its theme is expressed in a variety of aesthetic ways that make it a memorable and eye-catching place to visit. It is open to the public, so walk in and spend some time looking around the main floor.

This is a large three-story building with integrated gardens. It functions as a conference center and space for visiting scholars, as well as a focal point for students in various Asian subjects. The main open lobby space is filled with natural light. Above the main building is a huge (one hundred feet tall)

The Wang Center at SUNY–Stony Brook

octagonal, contemporary pagoda; this tower, which is illuminated at night, is a major part of the overall design.

One of the building's main attractions is its use of water throughout. In front of the structure is the first of a series of ornamental pools. It sits alongside a series of bright red geometric trellises leading to the ceremonial entrance. There are four sixteen-foot columns supporting clerestory windows. These architectural elements are reflected in the water. Inside there are additional pools and much running water, the sound of which is entrancing. One of the major elements, in fact, is the use of fountains; twelve Chinese-zodiac sculptures ornament the south pool in the lobby. Don't miss them.

There are two lovely interior gardens in Asian styles, and the large windows look out on carefully designed outdoor gardens as well. These spaces provide a setting for Asian sculpture, as well as for traditional plantings. If you want more information about this site, visit the building's office on the south side of the lobby.

While you are at the university, you might want to visit one other building of architectural interest. The **Javitz Lecture Center** is in the same part of the campus (walk through the parking garage to its far side, exit, and turn right, past several other buildings to find the light-toned, modernist example).

Designed by Bertrand Goldberg Associates, this 1968–1978 building is composed of two multistoried buildings, each with its own plan, connected by three-tiered walkways high above the ground. It is made of a stark, pale concrete and is almost devoid of windows or ornamentation, in a somewhat Brutalist, abstract, midcentury style. However, the exterior has been softened by gardens all around.

Also in the vicinity is Setauket, Smithtown (see New York State, Long Island, outing 6).

3·
THE GILDED LIFE

Three Glamorous Long Island Estates of the Early Twentieth Century: Eagle's Nest (the Vanderbilt Museum), Centerport; Westbury House, Old Westbury; and Falaise, Sands Point

Long Island has long been known for its Gatsby-like estates and the life styles of a gilded past. Many of its imposing pleasure palaces date to the early twentieth century, an era of opulence, elegance, and excess. A few of these glamorous estates still remain and are open to the public as museums and public gardens. We have chosen three of the most lavish, evocative, and architecturally interesting of these huge homes: Eagle's Nest, now the Vanderbilt Museum; Westbury House and Gardens, once the home of the Phipps family; and Falaise, formerly the estate of Harry F. Guggenheim.

Eagle's Nest: The Vanderbilt Museum

DIRECTIONS: *The Vanderbilt Museum is located at 180 Little Neck Road, Centerport. Take the Long Island Expressway (I-495) to exit 51N (Deer Park Avenue). Take Deer Park Avenue (Route 231) north for six miles to Broadway and across Route 25A, where Broadway becomes Little Neck Road. The estate is on your right, behind white decorative walls, and is clearly marked.*

INFORMATION: The Vanderbilt Museum is open year-round, Tuesday through Friday, noon to 4 P.M.; Saturday, 11:30 A.M. to 5 P.M.; Sunday, noon to 5 P.M. Tours are available of the house, museum, and planetarium. Telephone: 631-854-5555.

When you enter the imposing gates to the Vanderbilt Museum—once the fabled "Eagle's Nest" estate of one of America's most illustrious families —you are transported to an era of glamour, elegance, and privilege in a setting right out of a movie. Located on Long Island's North Shore, where many wealthy families built homes around the turn of the twentieth century, it includes the storybook, fanciful Vanderbilt mansion, a marine museum (housed in the whimsical-looking Hall of Fishes), a planetarium (added much later), six antique marble Corinthian columns in a semicircle near the entrance gate, a charming boathouse, and some forty-three rolling acres overlooking Long Island Sound.

The estate was the home of William Kissam Vanderbilt II (1878–1944), great-grandson of "Commodore" Cornelius Vanderbilt of shipping and railroad fame. What William had begun in 1907 as a relatively modest six-room Japanese cottage was expanded over the years to a much grander twenty-four rooms in elaborate Spanish-Moroccan architectural style, with additional wings, courtyards, arcades, a tall, domed bell tower, a patio with reflecting pool, formal gardens, and a nearby ten-hole golf course and boathouse.

The central building was constructed over some two decades. Whitney Warren, an architect and cousin of Vanderbilt's, was the designer of the building's more modest beginnings, as well as of its grand remodeling, as Vanderbilt's collection grew. Vanderbilt's fascination with Spanish and Mediterranean (Moroccan) architecture became the styles of choice, with extensive remodeling of the main house. Today it features tile roofs, white stucco walls, wrought-iron window grilles, an ornamental Spanish-Colonial-style bell tower, arches and railings, a cloister, and a general Old World ambience. Remodeling and additions to the estate continued through 1935; there are several additional buildings, including a planetarium.

In addition to enjoying the unusual architecture, don't miss the one-of-a-kind collection of thousands of varied items and artifacts collected by Vanderbilt.

The Westbury House and Old Westbury Gardens

DIRECTIONS: *The Westbury House is located at 710 Westbury Road, Old Westbury. Take the Long Island Expressway (I-495) to exit 39 south (Glen Cove Road). Continue east on the service road 1.2 miles to Old Westbury Road.*

INFORMATION: The estate is open from April through October, Wednesday through Monday, 10 A.M. to 5 P.M. (and for special events during November and December). Tours are available for a fee. Telephone: 516-333-0048.

Just a stone's throw from the ultimate contemporary highway landscape, this site is all the more intriguing in its contrast with Long Island sprawl. The estate, built in 1906 by John S. Phipps, a financier and sportsman, is not the only grand house in Old Westbury, where many of the rich and fashionable built their homes at the turn of the twentieth century; nearby are the William C. Whitney Racing Stables, for example.

Phipps hired the London architect George Crawley to construct a Georgian-style "country" mansion, to please his English wife. Westbury House was built atop a hill; its symmetrical elegance is set off by a master plan of landscape design. In fact, the estate is a rare example of landscape and architectural planning that went hand in hand; the complementary designs of the house and its surroundings are worth noting and are of great interest to modern designers.

The interior of the house is elegant and formal. It is open to the public and will appeal to those who enjoy seeing how such country retreats were designed and furnished, from fluted Corinthian columns and French windows to polished antique tables and ormolu clocks. You will also find paintings by John Singer Sargent, George Morland, Joshua Reynolds, and Sir Henry Raeburn.

Don't miss the magnificent gardens, which are a work of art in themselves. In fact, the same architect, George Crawley, along with a French landscape architect named Jacques Greber, created the master plan for the formal, geometrical arrangement of grand allées and romantic English gardens. Clearly based on the layouts of the grounds of great stately homes of England, these gardens are spectacular; they include several structures, such as a Temple of Love, and are an integral part of the overall elegance of the Westbury House.

Falaise (Sands Point)

DIRECTIONS: *Take the Long Island Expressway (I-495) to exit 36. Take Searingtown Road north for six miles to the entrance. (Note that Searingtown Road becomes Port Washington Boulevard, then Middle Neck Road.)*

INFORMATION: Open May through October, Thursday through Sunday. Falaise is located on private property, near the Sands Point Preserve in Port Washington, so you must go there accompanied, via minibus, for your tour of the house. Tours leave at noon, 1, 2, and 3 P.M. Telephone: 516-571-7900. Web site: www.sandspoint preserve.org.

Falaise is one of the last remaining palatial estates that once dotted the "Gold Coast" on the northwest shores of Long Island during the dazzlingly opulent 1920s. Of the many lavish palaces that wealthy New Yorkers built as country houses, the large majority have since been either demolished or converted into housing developments. But, fortunately, Falaise is still with us and is even open to the public.

The mansion was built in 1923 for Harry F. Guggenheim (who years later was to supervise the construction of the Guggenheim Museum with Frank Lloyd Wright), an heir to the illustrious family's mining fortune, and his wife, Caroline. Because Harry greatly admired French architecture (he had spent time in France during World War I), it was designed to replicate a thirteenth-century Norman-style country manor. With its architects—Frederick J. Sterner and the firm of Polhemus & Coffin, who specialized in the French style for American tastes—he created a magnificent example of the so-called French Renaissance style, mixing different architectural elements. Harry and his wife named their new house "Falaise" (French for "cliff") for the dramatic site on which it stood, high above the water.

From Long Island Sound, Falaise appears quite daunting, resembling a mighty fortress, complete with tall foundation walls and steeply pitched heavy tile roofs; but if you approach by minibus or car, the effect is more inviting, softened by the attractive landscaping. There is a narrow front gate, leading to a pretty enclosed cobblestone courtyard and gatehouse. Around the front door is a group of antique columns purchased by the Guggenheims in northern France. In fact, the thirty-room house contains many French and Spanish antique furnishings, mostly from the sixteenth and seventeenth centuries, and architectural pieces found during the couple's extensive travels abroad.

The house and its décor, which remain much as they were during the 1920s and 1930s, are a fascinating mélange. The medieval style is reflected in the way the rooms are positioned—somewhat austerely in a long row—and also in the arches, textured plastered walls, carved stone mantels, and thick wood beams found throughout the house. But there are also Renaissance paintings and sculptures, as well as important examples of modern art. To add to the aura are spacious porches and terraces from which to enjoy the spectacular water views.

After Harry Guggenheim's death in 1971, Falaise and its surrounding acres were left to Nassau County; it is now Sands Point Preserve (where there are beautiful walking trails) and the accompanying manor-museum. If you enjoy fanciful architecture in a very grand setting along with scenic vistas, you won't want to miss this visit. Make sure to call in advance to make your reservation.

4·
A GOTHIC REVIVAL LANDMARK
The Cathedral of the Incarnation, Garden City

❀ DIRECTIONS

Take the Long Island Expressway (I-495) to exit 34. Take New Hyde Park Road south for 3.3 miles and turn left onto Stewart Avenue. Go 2.1 miles and make a right on Cherry Valley Avenue and then a left on Sixth Street (right after the railroad overpass). You will find the cathedral on your right.

❀ INFORMATION

Open Tuesday through Friday, 10 A.M. to 4 P.M.; Saturday, 10 A.M. to noon; Sunday, 8 A.M. to 2 P.M. Telephone: 516-746-2955. Web site: www.incarnationgc.org.

❀ One of the most striking examples of Gothic church architecture in the region has to be the Cathedral of the Incarnation in Garden City. This imposing church—the seat of the Episcopal Diocese of Long Island—is graced with a dramatic spire that soars higher than any other structure within sight. In fact the town's zoning law stipulates that no other building can be taller than the cathedral (208 feet). Clearly this ruling—which has occasionally been bypassed in clever ways—is a testament to the cathedral's historical importance within the community.

The architect of the cathedral was English-born Henry G. Harrison (1813–1895), known for his designs of Episcopal churches. He was most fluent in the Gothic Revival style and built several parish churches and residences in the New York area. For a favorite client, James W. Beekman, a prominent Manhattan philanthropist, legislator, and civic leader, Harrison created row houses and a hospital, as well as "The Cliffs," a Gothic Revival mansion on thirty-seven acres in Oyster Bay that was one of the first grand estates built on Long Island.

But the Cathedral of the Incarnation, representing the "Perpendicular Gothic style"—the favored style of English Gothic architecture in the fourteenth century, characterized by vertical lines in its tracery—was Harrison's greatest achievement. It was built in 1876 as a memorial to the founder of

Cathedral of the Incarnation, Garden City. Photo by John Ellis Kordes.

Garden City, Alexander Stewart. Construction lasted almost eight years, through 1883, and the church was consecrated in 1885.

The stone structure includes the extraordinary tower, which is richly decorated with finials. The tower contains thirteen bells originally cast in 1876 for the U.S. Centennial Exhibition. Within the building are beautiful stained-glass windows, as well as rare examples of marble and hand-carved wood. Not surprisingly, the cathedral is listed on the New York and National Register of Historic Places. As of this writing, it is undergoing substantial renovation and promises to be more resplendent than ever.

5·
BEACHFRONT, DECO-ERA ICON

Jones Beach, Wantagh

❀ DIRECTIONS

Take the Long Island Expressway (I-495) to exit 38 and take the Northern State Parkway to the Meadowbrook State Parkway south. Follow signs to Jones Beach.

❀ INFORMATION

You might want to combine your visit here with a summer day at the great beach, but, of course, it is much less crowded off-season.

❀ Almost eighty years ago, when Art Deco influences in architecture were strong and pervasive, Jones Beach opened to the public. The brainchild of Robert Moses (who was known for thinking big), this oceanfront area became the world's largest public recreational space, and when it opened in 1929, it contained miles and miles of beach and several significant buildings. There were its iconic water tower, two bath pavilions, a swimming pool, restaurants, and even a theater.

Although the credit for the design was mostly given to Moses (who is purported to have done a rough sketch on the back of an envelope), in fact it was an architect named Herbert Magoon who actually designed the buildings. Several were completed with the help of the Works Progress Administration.

The most identifiable building is certainly the water tower (1930), which is a two-hundred-foot-tall, cooper-roofed obelisk. Like the other Jones Beach buildings, it is constructed of sandstone and Barbizon brick in the Art Deco style. Inspired by a Venetian campanile, its height and lights make it visible from afar. Its Deco design elements include its great verticality and elongated proportions, as well as repeated vertical forms at its top and bottom. At its base it is flanked by smaller geometric forms made of stone.

Also worth seeing are the bathhouses. The West Bathhouse also has Deco elements, with its decorative surface of horizontal stripes intersected by columns across the façade. All the buildings have weathered the years remarkably well and are greatly beloved by thousands of visitors every year.

6·
IN SEARCH OF HISTORIC ARCHITECTURE

Stony Brook, Setauket, East Setauket, and Smithtown

❀ **DIRECTIONS**

Take the Long Island Expressway (I-495) to exit 56 and take Route 111 north, which will intersect with Route 25A (Smithtown). Continue on Route 25A (North Country Road) to the villages of Stony Brook and East Setauket. Setauket is reached by Quaker Path, also off Route 25A.

❀ **INFORMATION**

For the **Thompson and Sherwood-Jayne House**, telephone: 631-941-9444. For the **Stony Brook Grist Mill** and the **Brewster House**, telephone: 631-751-2244.

❀ These small villages are very near one another and provide several examples of the Colonial and Federal period of architecture, as well as a charming Stanford White church of the late nineteenth century. You can easily organize a driving tour to visit these sites in one trip, beginning with Smithtown and moving on to Stony Brook and Setauket. Although there are other historic buildings in these villages, we have chosen our favorites, but you can also pick up a local map and tour of additional historic venues at the desks of several of the sites listed below.

Presbyterian Church of Smithtown *(corner of Route 25A and Route 111, Smithtown)*

This is undoubtedly one of the oldest surviving buildings in the area, dating to 1675. This elegantly simple church, now located at a busy intersection, is nonetheless worth seeing. The all-white, high-steepled structure has lovely small-paned, arched windows in what we often think of as the New England Colonial style.

All Souls Episcopal Church, Stony Brook

All Souls Episcopal Church (Main Street, Stony Brook)

A charming, intimate 1889 church, All Souls was designed by Stanford White himself. Its multiple gables, arched dormers, steeply pitched roof, pointed steeple, and dark-brown shingles with white trim make it a precursor to many Arts and Crafts–style buildings. Inside you'll find lots of wood, with exposed rafters and a cozy setting with a few pews on either side of the aisle.

Stony Brook Grist Mill (Harbor Road off Main Street, Stony Brook)

The Stony Brook Grist Mill (1751) is a major attraction, open to the public with many events. It is listed on the National Register of Historic Places and is considered to be a prime example of the early Dutch style of post-and-beam frame construction. Picturesquely set along a riverbank, with its water wheel easily visible, this large brown-shingled building has a gabled roof. It replaced an earlier version that was destroyed by a flood in 1750. You can watch the entire milling process here, in the most complete working gristmill on Long Island.

Thompson House (North Country Road, Setauket)

Also open to visitors, this house is one of the earliest examples of the New England saltbox on Long Island. Dating from 1700, it represents Long Island's "First Period." The saltbox style—in which a frame house has one side of the gabled roof larger and higher than the other, allowing for two stories in the front and only one in the back—was used extensively in colonial times. The Thompson House, which remained in the same family for almost two hundred years, is notable for its corner posts (typical of the period), interesting paneling, unusually high ceilings, and massive fireplaces.

Setauket Presbyterian Church (Caroline Avenue, Setauket)

Of a slightly later historical period, this Federal-style church was dedicated in 1812. Subtle and elegant in style, it features a tall steeple and simple arched, small-paned windows (no stained glass here), and it is surrounded by a historic graveyard.

Sherwood-Jayne House (Old Post Road, East Setauket)

Also open to the public is another example of the traditional saltbox house, this one built in 1730. This house has been somewhat updated during restorations. It has a center chimney and two stories, and it still has its original doors, paneling, and chimney pieces, as well as wall paintings from the early nineteenth century.

Joseph Brewster House (East Main Street, East Setauket)

This is a farmhouse typical of Long Island in the mid-nineteenth century. It actually appears in a painting from 1862 by the artist William Sidney Mount, whose works are displayed at the nearby Stony Brook Museum complex. The house is characterized by its dramatic, pitched saltbox roof, oversized shingles, and double chimneys. It began as a smaller house and over the centuries was slightly enlarged. Today it is open to the public and used for various architectural events.

7 ·
ROSLYN PRESERVES THE PAST

Visiting Cedarmere and Other Pleasures of the Nineteenth Century

❀ DIRECTIONS

To reach Roslyn take the Long Island Expressway (I-495) to exit 37. Turn left at the exit ramp onto Willis Avenue and go straight. Cross the bridge and turn right down the hill, to Bryant Avenue. Continue straight for the center of the village, or turn right if you wish to go first to Cedarmere. Continue on Bryant Avenue for less than a mile and follow signs to Cedarmere. The other sites mentioned are in the center of the village.

❀ INFORMATION

For information on any of the historic/architectural sites contact the Roslyn Landmark Society, located at 36 Main Street, Roslyn. Telephone: 516-625-4365. Cedarmere is open April through November, Saturday and Sunday, 1 to 5 P.M.; the grounds are open daily, year-round. Admission is free. For more information or group reservations call 516-571-8130. Web site: www.nassaucountyny.gov.

❀ Roslyn, a picturesque village on the shores of Long Island Sound, has an usually rich historical and architectural heritage, all concentrated within a relatively small area. There are more than one hundred historic sites within "Greater Roslyn" (which includes both Roslyn and nearby Roslyn Harbor), and many of the structures, including private homes, have been diligently preserved and restored. Some of these sites are open to the public; others, such as the private homes, can be seen just from the street. In any case, there is more to see here than you can possibly do in one day; below we list only a few of the highlights you should not miss.

First, a word about the town's success story as a model of preservation. The admirable commitment shown here is due, first and foremost, to the efforts of Roger and Peggy Gerry, prominent members of the community and activists on behalf of conservation for much of their lifetime. During the 1950s Roslyn, like many other Long Island villages, was being threatened by aggressive developers and city planners; recognizing that its special character and ambience were in real jeopardy, the Gerrys moved quickly to create the Roslyn Landmark Society. This organization, which continues to be active, oversees ongoing efforts to preserve local landmarks. One can only wish that more towns followed their example!

We recommend you begin your historic-architecture tour with a visit to **Cedarmere** and its Gothic Mill. This enchanting estate was the residence of the illustrious nineteenth-century poet, publisher, journalist, and anti-slavery crusader William Cullen Bryant, from 1843 until his death in 1878. It was in this serene rural retreat that Bryant could escape from the pressures of the city, concentrate on his poetry, and indulge his love of nature. You won't find a more romantic site than Cedarmere, picturesquely set over-looking Roslyn Harbor. Among the pleasures included in its seven acres are the house itself, a boathouse, a duck house, a rustic stone bridge, and the Gothic Mill—a watermill built by Bryant to provide his own power. Surrounding these structures are flower gardens (first laid out by Bryant, an avid horticulturalist and supporter of Central Park) and great trees that are reflected in the pond; occasionally ducks make their appearance, adding to the idyllic tableau.

The original house on the site was built by Richard Kirk, a Quaker farmer, in 1787. When Bryant bought the property he embellished the house with a two-story lattice portico. Over the following years he made other substantial changes, adding covered verandas supported by graceful lattice-work columns, bay windows, a third story and attic topped with a gambrel roof, and other architectural features. (He even upgraded the plumbing system, hiring Thomas Wisedell, an English architect and colleague of Calvert Vaux.) Unfortunately a fire in 1902 destroyed much of the house (then owned by Bryant's grandson, Harold Godwin); it was reconstructed in a similar vein but with several modifications, most notably in its exterior building materials. To help prevent fires in the future, the exterior walls of the house were finished in stucco, rather than wood, and a slate roof was installed.

The delightful **Gothic Mill**, right out of a storybook, was built by Bryant in 1860 as a mill and summer cottage. (It replaced an earlier mill that had burned down.) The architect is said to have been Frederick Copley, who built two other cottages elsewhere for Bryant, in a similar style. From this spot you can enjoy some of the prettiest water views on the property.

You are invited to stroll on the property, with a self-guided walking tour in hand (provided at the entrance to the house), which identifies garden structures and noteworthy trees. As of this writing the house is still undergoing further renovation but is open to the public.

The Mill at Cedarmere, Roslyn. Photo by Iris Levin.

After leaving Cedarmere, head back to the center of Roslyn for the continuation of your tour. Drive (or walk) along Main Street, a lovely shaded street with many old (mostly nineteenth-century) houses, off Gerry Park. Though these private residences are not open to the public, you can see them as you go by. The oldest along this stretch is the historic **Van Nostrand Starkins House**, at 221 Main Street (corner of East Broadway). This reddish-brown shingled saltbox (now a museum and open to the public on certain days) dates from around 1680. A small structure, it originally consisted of a single room, measuring about twenty feet by sixteen feet, with a relatively large fireplace. Many changes have been made in subsequent years, including the addition of a lean-to section. Restored during the 1970s by the Roslyn Landmark Society, it contains a collection of locally made period furniture and decorative arts. Another architecturally interesting house is the elegant **Warren S. Wilkey House**, located at 190 Main Street. Dating from 1864, it was built in the Second Empire style, complete with mansard roof, belvedere, and dormer windows. The house was meticulously restored during the 1970s.

The **Ellen E. Wart Memorial Clock Tower**, on the corner of North Main Street and Old Northern Boulevard, is next. This striking landmark is a

Ellen E. Wart Memorial Clock Tower, Roslyn

memorial to a prominent member of the community who devoted much of her time to local charities. Erected in 1895, the granite tower with brownstone trim stands in a small triangle at a busy intersection. (You might find it difficult to approach it on foot, with cars coming by in all directions!) The architects who designed the tower, Lamb & Rich, are the same who built Theodore Roosevelt's Sagamore Hill in Oyster Bay. Somewhat reminiscent of an Egyptian obelisk, the four-story structure has a Spanish-tiled peak. Note the prominent clock, which is still functional. Much of this original structure has been carefully restored.

Finally, visit **Trinity Episcopal Church**, on Church Street and Northern Boulevard. This gracious building was designed by Stanford White; in fact, it was the last church he built. Erected in 1907 as a memorial, its architectural style is fourteenth-century, Norman–Early English, with round-arched windows on the outside. Go inside and look up to see a high, vaulted roof and several beautiful stained-glass Tiffany windows.

❀ IN THE VICINITY

If time allows, we also recommend a stop at the nearby **Nassau County Museum of Art Sculpture Gardens**, in Roslyn Harbor. Though this exceptional site warrants a much more thorough visit—the sculpture garden is one of the largest in the country, and the museum itself offers fine exhibitions of American and European art—we focus here only on the gardens, not with regard to their impressive sculpture but rather to their landscape design, including a particularly delightful trellis gate.

To reach the museum from the center of Roslyn take Northern Boulevard for a couple miles and follow the signs to Museum Drive on your left. Open year-round, Tuesday through Sunday, 11 A.M. to 5 P.M. Telephone: 516-484-9337.

The museum occupies the former Henry Clay Frick mansion. (Frick bought the property from William Cullen Bryant.) It was Frances Dixon Frick, the wife of Henry's son, who, with distinguished landscape architect Marian Cruger Coffin, laid out the gardens. Their inspired design has lasted very well and is kept in pristine condition today. Coffin, who also had an important role in designing Winterthur in Delaware, was one of the first and foremost women in landscape architecture. Her designs show the influence of Gertrude Jekyll.

Within these formal gardens are two central paths that divide four rectangular gardens bordered by low boxwood hedges and narrow brick paths. In the center is a large circular pool with a fountain. On the southern edge, near the rose gardens, is a lacy, dark-green, teak pavilion. This elegant gazebo, designed by the New York architects Milliken & Bevin in 1931, was restored in the early 1990s and is, as of this writing, awaiting further restoration. We find this spot particularly peaceful and appealing in every way.

8·
EXPLORING THE LONG ISLAND LIGHTHOUSE

Eaton's Neck Light, Huntington Harbor Light,
Old Field Light, Stepping Stones Light, and Others

Lighthouses—some of the country earliest and most memorable buildings —are, of course, ubiquitous along the waterfront of Long Island. Varied in design, these practical and evocative buildings are great fun to visit and to climb up in, as well as to examine from an architectural standpoint. How many ways can a single lighted tower on the edge of the sea be designed? A great many, as it turns out; visit a few of those listed below and see for yourself.

Eaton's Neck Lighthouse (Lighthouse Road, Northport)

DIRECTIONS: *Take the Long Island Expressway (I-495) to exit 51. Go north on Route 231 to Route 10 (Deer Park Road, which becomes Ocean Avenue) into Northport. The lighthouse is at the very end of the road, after town of Northport.*

This is an unusual lighthouse, with a hexagonally shaped tower. It was built because of a dangerous reef off Eaton's Neck. The original 1799 tower was rebuilt in 1868 in the same odd shape but taller, with a small cupola and a Fresnel lens. It is the second-oldest light on Long Island and was the first to have a life-saving station.

Huntington Harbor Light

DIRECTIONS: *Take the Long Island Expressway (I-495) to exit 40; take Route 25 east to Route 110 north to the water.*

The unusual element of this lighthouse is its square tower, which is attached to a round foundation. Built of reinforced concrete, it is the oldest such lighthouse on the East Coast, dating to 1857. Its early nickname was "The Castle," and there was no access to the lantern hung in the tower except by climbing up an outdoor ladder and through an upstairs window.

Old Field Light (*near Setauket and Port Jefferson*)

DIRECTIONS: *Take the Long Island Expressway (I-495) to exit 56 and take Route 111 north, which will intersect with Route 25A (Smithtown). Take Route 25A north to Quaker Path Road, then take Quaker Path Road north until you come to Old Field Road. Make a left and go to the end of Old Field Road.*

The original lighthouse here was built in 1823; this solid structure dates to 1868. It is built of granite and has a seventy-foot-high lantern tower. It is now a private home, and the keeper's house has become the Village Hall, but the light is still in use.

Stepping Stones Light (*near King's Point*)

DIRECTIONS: *Take the Triborough Bridge to Northern Boulevard (25A) and make a left on Middle Neck Road. Turn left on Red Brook Road and go to its end at King's Point Road to Steppingstone Park.*

From this park you can see the off-shore tower and house called Stepping Stones Light. The red-brick buildings were established in 1877. The house has a mansard roof. Both house and tower were built some sixteen hundred yards offshore, on nine hundred tons of boulders. The lighthouse still has its original Fresnel light.

Some of the most beloved lighthouses are at the eastern end of Long Island. If you wish to go farther afield, visit the following sites.

Montauk Point Light

DIRECTIONS: *Take the Long Island Expressway (I-495) to exit 71 and take Route 24 to Route 27 to Montauk. (Although this lighthouse is beyond our two-hour limit, it is well worth a visit if you are nearby.)*

INFORMATION: Telephone: 631-668-2544.

This lighthouse at the end of Long Island was first established in 1796 and was commissioned by George Washington. The walls are seven feet thick, and the brightly painted, octagonal sandstone tower is seventy-eight feet high with an iron lantern room on top. The foundation is thirteen feet deep, making it a very sturdy example of lighthouse building, though the constant erosion by the sea of the cliffs beneath it has brought it dangerously close to the shoreline. Efforts are being made to stabilize the cliffs.

The keeper's house was built in 1860. This site was well known to sailors and was a welcome first sight of American shores for thousands of arriving immigrants. Some one hundred thousand people now visit this lighthouse and its museum each year.

Orient Point Light

DIRECTIONS: *Take the Long Island Expressway (I-495) to its end, then take Route 25 to its end, at Orient Point.*

Built in 1899, this is one of the first cast-iron lighthouses, with an iron foundation weighed down with concrete. It was built out of prefab boiler plates. Its strange aspect has given it the nickname of "Old Coffee Pot." Cracks and holes have caused it to tilt slightly, but it is still active and is an interesting site to visit.

Horton Point Light (*near Southold*)

DIRECTIONS: *Take the Long Island Expressway (I-495) to its end, then take Route 25 east to Southold. Turn left on Horton Lane, then right on Soundview Avenue, then left on Lighthouse Road and go to the end.*

INFORMATION: Telephone: 631-321-7028.

This traditional, picturesque lighthouse was built in 1790 and sits 103 feet above the shore of Long Island Sound, overlooking an area known as Dead Man's Cove. Situated on the northeastern shore of Long Island, Horton Point Light has seen its share of action, including functioning during World War II as a lookout for enemy aircraft. There is also a nautical museum here. It is not far from Orient Point Lighthouse.

In addition to these lighthouses, there are several others on the nearby islands of Fire Island and Fishers Island.

9·
LOOKING AT WINDMILLS ON THE EASTERN END OF LONG ISLAND

Water Mill Museum, Beebe Windmill, Hook Windmill, and Pantigo Windmill

❀ DIRECTIONS

Water Mill Museum: *The Water Mill Museum is located at 41 Old Mill Road in the town of Water Mill. From the Long Island Expressway (I-495) take exit 69; go south on Wading River Road to Route 27 east. Continue east until you reach Montauk Highway; continue east until you reach the town of Water Mill.*

Beebe Windmill: *Beebe Windmill is located on Ocean Road in Bridgehampton. From Water Mill continue east on Montauk Highway until you reach Bridgehampton.*

Old Hook Windmill and Pantigo Windmill: *Old Hook Windmill (North Main Street) and Pantigo Windmill (14 James Lane) are both located in East Hampton. From Bridgehampton continue east on Montauk Highway until you reach East Hampton.*

❀ INFORMATION

We realize these sites are beyond the two-hour distance from New York City, but if you are visiting Eastern Long Island, we recommend them.

Water Mill Museum: Open late May through September. Telephone: 631-726-4625.

Beebe Windmill: Open in summer by appointment only; for guided tours call the Bridgehampton Historical Society at 631-537-1088.

Old Hook Windmill: Open in summer and by appointment. Telephone: 631-324-0713.

Pantigo Windmill: Open summer and by appointment. Telephone: 631-324-0713.

❀ Windmills have added architectural and aesthetic appeal to landscapes around the world ever since they first appeared centuries ago. From the earliest wooden, picturesque examples to the slick, contemporary versions, windmills are fascinating structures. These graceful forms in motion appear much more like giant kinetic sculptures than utilitarian machines used to grind grain, to pump water, or—more recently—to generate electricity.

In the seventeenth and eighteenth centuries, eastern Long Island was home to hundreds of windmills, more than anywhere else in this region. Today eleven of these historic mills still exist, of which four are operated as museums and open to the public. You can visit them by guided tour (in season), which we recommend if you are also interested in learning about the inner workings of mills. Off-season you can still walk around the mills and view them from the outside.

Eastern Long Island's earliest windmills (of which none still exist) were simple "post mills" made of wood, like those in England at the time: all machinery was located in a small, enclosed area on top of a large post. As the technology of the windmill developed, so too did its outward appearance. "Smock mills"—such as the existing mills on eastern Long Island—were also made of wood but had a stationary octagonal tower housing the millstones, on which a cap was mounted to hold the sails. Later models had more sophisticated gearing, which eventually was made of cast-iron.

The windmill at **Water Mill** (now the **Water Mill Museum**) is different from the three others we describe here. Built in 1644, it is by far the oldest. It was also Long Island's first water-powered mill, and as such, it had no "sails." The mill passed through many families, from Edward Howell, the original owner, to the Benedicts, who used the building for weaving and spinning, in addition to milling. By the early 1900s the structure was in total disrepair. Finally it underwent a complete restoration, was transformed into a museum, and by the time the 1976 bicentennial came around, was grinding mill once again. On your tour you can still see it in full action.

The **Beebe Windmill** was erected in Sag Harbor in 1820 and moved to Bridgehampton in 1837, in a parklike setting. It was the last mill to be built on Long Island and was functioning until 1911. The mill was constructed with the latest English technology of the time, including a fantail to rotate the cap automatically, cast-iron gearings, and centrifugal devices to make the millstones grind consistently fine flour. This beautiful mill will remind you of those found in Dutch landscape paintings.

The last two mills open to the public, both in East Hampton, are also picture perfect in their traditional appearance. **Old Hook Windmill**, located at the east end of the village, right next to an old graveyard, dates from 1806. Its builder, Nathaniel Dominy, one of the most active millwrights of his time, constructed six wind-powered gristmills and three wind-powered sawmills. A few of these are still standing but are not open to the public: the Gardiner Windmill in East Hampton and mills on both Shelter and Gardiner Islands. Old Hook Windmill, reflecting Dominy's great technical building skills, had (and still has) an elaborate system of wooden gears, as well as some inventive devices to save labor. The mill itself is a quaint wood structure that fits perfectly with its surroundings.

Pantigo Mill, on the other hand, has been moved several times within East Hampton. As of this writing it is located in the gardens of "Home Sweet Home" (named after the author of that song), on the John Howard Payne historic site, where it is expected to remain. It, too, is as picturesque as they come—just what you want on an architecture tour of historic mills!

AND KEEP IN MIND . . .

10 ⋅ First Presbyterian Church, Glen Cove

This fairy-tale-like church, on School Street at North Lane, was built in 1905 in a style described as Tudor Revival. The architect was well known: Oscar S. Teale had a number of important commissions from 1882 to 1927. This church is curiously set at a diagonal to the street, with its entrance on a corner. It has two gables divided by a conical tower; the entire exterior features Tudor-style wood stripes and large, dark-outlined arched windows. The entrance on the street echoes the gables above.

11 ⋅ Brooklyn Waterworks, Freeport

You won't often see another building with the architectural design of this one, located on Sunrise Highway. This large and imposing Romanesque Revival building is surely one of the oldest, and most ambitious, of Long Island's public buildings. The three-story brick structure was created (originally as the Milburn Pumping Station) in the late nineteenth century as part of a system to carry water from Nassau County (Long Island) into Brooklyn. It was decommissioned in the 1920s and eventually sold to private owners. The building is notable for a long diagonal roofline culminating at the top in a tower. At the lower end a huge round arch opens into what seems to be a tunnel. There are many decorative details reminiscent of Romanesque churches. The architect was Frank Freeman, who also designed the Eagle Warehouse in Brooklyn.

12 ⋅ Rock Hall Museum, Lawrence

This old frame house, located at 199 Broadway, is now a museum of Long Island antiquities. Built in 1767 and owned by the same family (the Hewletts) for more than a century, it is thought to be one of the nation's best and most beautiful examples of the Georgian Colonial style. It has a gambrel roof with a lovely balustrade around it, and inside you'll find period furniture.

13 • *Saint George's Episcopal Church, Hempstead*

DIRECTIONS: *From New York City take the Long Island Expressway (I-495) to exit 31S and take the Cross Island Parkway south to exit 26B. Then take Hempstead Avenue east to Hempstead. Take a slight right turn at Front Street (Route 102) and make a U-turn to the front of the church, at 319 Front Street.*

Saint George's Episcopal Church is one of the best examples of Georgian architecture in the region, one not to miss on an architectural tour of the area. The church is beautifully set, surrounded by a picturesque church-yard with a white picket fence, venerable old trees, and eighteenth-century tombstones. You might not expect to find so peaceful an oasis within the bustling and built-up town of Hempstead.

The church was built in 1822, replacing the previous eighteenth-century structure; an extension was added in 1856, and some remodeling was completed later on. The white clapboard building has dark, rounded shutters, a circular tower with an elegant old (1854) clock, and a weather vane that has been perched atop the steeple for over 250 years. We are told that during the Revolutionary War the weathervane was used for target practice, and a few bullet holes are still visible. Inside are grand floor-to-roof columns; shaped from oak trees cut and dragged along the Long Island plains by horse, they

Saint George's Episcopal Church, Hempstead. Photo by Robert L. Harrison.

have stood up remarkably well over the years. There are also a number of stained-glass windows designed by Tiffany Studios.

Saint George's adjoining rectory is a noteworthy piece of early architecture in its own right. Dating from 1793, it precedes the present church by almost twenty years. (The rectory also contains a surprising number of fireplaces, eight in all.) Both the church and its rectory are listed on the National Register of Historic Places.

NEW JERSEY

1 ·
AN EARLY QUAKER COMMUNITY WITH A COLONIAL AND FEDERAL STREETSCAPE

Mount Holly

❁ DIRECTIONS

Take the New Jersey Turnpike south to exit 5 and take Route 541 south to Mount Holly. As you enter town you will be on High Street. Find your way to the library at 307 High Street.

❁ INFORMATION

A self-guided walking tour is available at the library (see below). Tours and open houses are sometimes offered. Call the library at 609-267-7111 for information, or the Mount Holly Historical Society at 609-267-8844. Web site: www.mounthollynjtripod .com.

❁ This town was a surprise to us. We are familiar with the Williamsburg style of colonial towns, where buildings have been moved and restored and residents dress up in colonial clothes and practice colonial arts and crafts for visitors. But how often does one find a town—particularly in busy New Jersey—where the architecture and atmosphere have been preserved with such a delightful combination of history and bustling present-day activity? Mount Holly is a rare treat. If you are interested in lovely early American town architecture, as well as a place with a significant history, be sure to visit here.

Mount Holly welcomes visitors. With a self-guiding map in hand you can find the important historical and architectural sites yourself, or you can take a prearranged guided tour if you prefer. This is a town that apparently understood that it was a treasure to be saved, long before the recent preservationist movement began in the state. No less than thirty-nine historic buildings can be visited here.

Mount Holly was settled in the 1680s by John and Nathaniel Cripps and

159

Edward Gatskill. They chose the site because of its unusual hill (the "Mount" of Mount Holly), which rises 185 feet above the village, and its site on the Rancocas Creek. Originally called Bridgeton because of its many bridges over the creek, the town prospered, with several mills using its waterpower.

Like many other small villages around Burlington, Mount Holly was settled in large part by Quakers, and its history has been tied to Quaker views about independence and abolition. Quakers fleeing persecution in England (and even in the northeastern colonies) arrived in the Burlington area in 1677. When William Penn chose the "middle colonies" as a site for Quaker settlements, the area around Burlington quickly became Quaker country. John Woolman, who later became a leading abolitionist, was a resident of Mount Holly; his *Journal* and "walking journeys" for the cause of the abolition of slavery made Mount Holly a safe haven on the Underground Railroad.

Mount Holly became a center for patriots well before the Revolutionary War. By the time the Revolution began, the British were widely despised by Mount Holly's people, who were forced to feed and quarter them. When the British turned the Quaker meetinghouse into a butcher shop and stable, the residents of Mount Holly were more determined than ever to gain independence. (Visit the meetinghouse to see the cuts in the benches made by meat cleavers in the Britons' ill-conceived use of the building.) One citizen, John Brainerd, preached independence from his pulpit, and consequently his church was burned by the British. Through acts such as these, as well as because of Quaker attitudes about justice and fairness, Mount Holly became a haven for dissenters and outspoken patriots.

During the war itself, in 1776, a violent skirmish with the British took place here. The fierce battle of Iron Works Hill seemed to find the Hessian allies of the British victorious, but the battle was actually a decoy that kept two thousand Hessian soldiers occupied while George Washington was successfully invading nearby Trenton. The Hessians apparently believed they were fighting a much larger force than the small number of Mount Holly patriots who tried to defend their hill. Washington's capture of Trenton at the same time was a significant victory for the Americans.

After the Revolution, Mount Holly took its place as an important New Jersey town; in 1779 it became the temporary capital of the state, and the state legislature met in the town for two sessions in 1779. Its beautiful courthouse (see below) is a testament to its importance in the history of the time.

As slavery became an incredibly volatile subject in the nation, Mount Holly once again played a part in a national debate. Quaker activism on behalf of abolition brought the dissidents of Mount Holly a cause in which

Burlington County Courthouse, Mount Holly

they strongly believed. With John Woolman leading the way, the town became a stop on the Underground Railroad, as did other villages in the Burlington region. A visit to Woolman's house here gives an idea of his importance as a fiery leader of the abolitionist cause. (Several other sites listed below also relate to abolitionism.)

As you undertake the tour of the town, you will see that these dramatic historical events are clearly evoked by Mount Holly's streetscape and setting. Begin your walk at the library at 307 High Street, where you can get your self-guided tour map. (The map contains a great deal more detailed information than we are including in the list below.)

There are a number of colonial examples in the different styles of pre-Revolutionary America. Among these colonial buildings is one of the finest examples of a public building in the country, the Burlington County Court House. Other fine examples of colonial architecture include the Swedish board-and-mortar log house, the early colonial Thomas Budd House (a 265-year-old brick residence), and a colonial inn of 1723 called Three Tuns

Tavern. A student of colonial architecture will find a treasure trove of private and public buildings in this town.

The Federal style is particularly well represented in Mount Holly. Based on the style of the Scottish architect Robert Adams, the Federal design was popular among the nation's leaders and soon was espoused by well-to-do Americans. Featuring a refined multistoried design with arched Palladian windows, low-pitch side-gabled roofs, and decorative balustrades, these buildings were dignified and restrained. Mount Holly has both public buildings and private homes in Federal style.

Robert Mills, the architect of the Washington Monument, built the Burlington County Prison here in Mount Holly; it was one of the first fireproof buildings in the nation. Other examples of Federal architecture include the fine Herald Building of 1820 and the Burlington County Trust Building, built in 1815 with arcaded stained-glass windows, among other elegant features.

The walking or driving tour describes forty-six such architectural sites; the following is a list of some of them, emphasizing those of the earliest periods.

Mount Holly Library, 307 High Street: This wonderful mansion with marble fireplaces is in the Georgian style and dates to 1830. Be sure to see the inside, with its handblown-glass window valances and wonderful pine, random-width floor boards.

Waln House, 301 High Street: This is a red-brick Victorian house with unusual fluted chimneys.

Haines House, 222 High Street: Dating to 1852, this is a great example of a double house of the Federal period.

Read House and office, 204 and 200 High Street: Built in 1770 and 1775, these two Colonial buildings belonged to the distinguished resident Joseph Read, a judge and member of the provincial congress.

Slack House, 211 High Street: Note the herringbone sidewalk and marble steps in front of this Federal-style house.

Burlington County Prison Museum, 128 High Street: You won't miss this great dark-gray prison and workhouse, an imposing presence along the street. Designed by Robert Mills, this massive building can be visited Tuesdays through Saturdays. In the interior you'll see many interesting architectural details, including original iron hardware, high arched ceilings, and foot-thick walls.

Burlington County Court House, 120 High Street: We found this building to be the gem of the entire historic town. What a beautiful courthouse this is! Built in 1796, it is considered to be one of the finest examples of Colonial architecture in the nation. Don't miss it! It has the balanced, symmetrical design typical of the early emphasis on Classicism. And note the two small buildings flanking it; these attractive offices were built in 1807. The three buildings have been in continuous use since the colonial era.

Saint Andrew's Episcopal Church, 121 High Street: This church dates to 1844 and is in a Gothic style; it is a Mount Holly landmark.

Friends Meeting House, corner of High and Garden streets: This colonial meetinghouse was built in 1775. Be sure to go inside to see the results of the British conversion of the building into a butcher shop in 1778. Also visit the adjacent graveyard.

Burlington County Herald, 17 High Street: This Federal-style building was built around 1820. Next, turn onto Garden Street.

Isaac Carr House, 21 Garden Street: This is a late Colonial-style house that was built in 1785. Carr was one of the owners of the ironworks destroyed by the British during the Revolutionary War.

Chapman House, 34 Garden Street: This was a doctor's residence. It is in the Colonial Renaissance style and was built around 1775. Note the evenly spaced up- and downstairs windows.

From Garden Street go to Park Drive to see the **Shinn-Curtis Log House**. It was built circa 1712 but was not discovered until the 1960s within another house. Now the headquarters of the Mount Holly Historical Society, this is a small building made of hand-hewn logs in the style of early Swedish settlers in the colonial era. Next, go back to High Street and turn onto Brainerd Street.

Ridgway House, 10 Brainerd Street: Owned by a bricklayer who built a number of Mount Holly's brick houses, this home was built around 1760.

Cooper and Dobbins houses, 12 and 14 Brainerd Street: These two late Colonial homes were built around 1782. Both have interior chimneys, which was unusual for the time.

Mann House, 20 and 22 Brainerd Street: Dating to around 1785, this building belonged to a Methodist minister.

Thomas House, 34 Brainerd Street: Built in 1813, this house is in the Federal style.

Historic Old Schoolhouse, 35 Brainerd Street: Don't miss this 1759 school building, the oldest in the state at its original site. It can be visited on Wednesdays from 10 A.M. to 4 P.M. or by appointment. Next, turn right onto Buttonwood Street and walk to Mill Street and take a right.

Three Tuns Tavern, 67 Mill Street: This 1723 tavern building—the oldest in Mount Holly—has a long and interesting history. The British were quartered here in 1776.

Burlington County Trust Company, 47 Mill Street: This 1815 Federal-style bank building has stained-glass windows and many other elegant architectural details both inside and out. Next, turn onto Pine Street.

Relief Fire Company, 17 Pine Street: This is the oldest continuously active volunteer fire company in the nation, having been organized in 1752, though this building itself was constructed in 1892. Next, go back to Mill Street, turn left, and then turn right on High Street.

Burlington County Herald, 17 High Street: This building from 1820 is in the Federal style. Next, go back to Mill Street and turn onto White Street.

Earnest House, 14 White Street: Built around 1775, this house is in a typical Colonial style.

Humphries House, corner of White and Church streets: Built around 1747, this house is patterned after an English cottage.

Budd House, 15 White Street: Dating from about 1744, this Colonial is the earliest known house on its original site in the town of Mount Holly.

These are a few of the most interesting historic buildings in Mount Holly, but there are many additional sites not far away, including fine examples of Victorian house architecture. Visit the hill for which Mount Holly is named and also the **John Woolman Memorial** at 99 Branch Street.

2 ·
WHERE THOMAS EDISON LIVED AND WORKED

Glenmont and the Edison National Historic Sites, West Orange

❀ **DIRECTIONS**

Take the New Jersey Turnpike to exit 15W and take I-280 west to West Orange. Take exit 10 and turn right on Northfield Avenue. Then turn left on Main Street toward the center of West Orange. The gatehouse for Llewelyn Park is on your left at the corner of Park Avenue. Edison Laboratory complex is one block farther on Main Street, corner of Lakeside Avenue.

❀ **INFORMATION**

The Edison sites are operated by the National Park Service. Open November through May, Friday to Sunday, noon to 4 P.M., with tours each hour; June through October, Wednesday to Sunday, noon to 4 P.M., tour each hour. Tickets for tours are obtained at the Visitor Center (building number 6) within the Edison Laboratory complex. There is an admission fee. Telephone: 978-324-9973 or 917-785-0550 x42. Web site: www.nps.gov / edis.

❀ Llewelyn Park in West Orange is one of the first gated communities in the United States and is to this day a lovely, bucolic oasis of mansions and woodlands within an urban center. It was designed in 1852 by the noted landscape architect Alexander Jackson Davis with some collaboration by Andrew Jackson Downing and Llewelyn Haskell, for whom it was named.

Davis was the first American architect to focus on the Gothic style. Other famous architects who built houses in Llewelyn Park include Charles McKim, Stanford White, and Calvert Vaux, among others. Unfortunately for architecture buffs, all these estates except for Glenmont Edison's home are not open to the public. So let us focus on Glenmont, a Queen Anne–style Victorian mansion that offers tours to the public as part of the Edison National Historic Sites.

The great inventor lived at Glenmont from 1886 until his death in 1931.

(His wife, Mina, sold it in 1946.) It was built in 1880 by a New York architect named Henry Hudson Holly, in the most fashionable style of the late nineteenth century, the Queen Anne. Like many such mansions, it was built of wood, brick, and stone, with numerous gables and chimneys and porches and other details. It has been painted many different colors over the years; today it is a striking off-red color.

Typical of its interior architecture was its focus on capacious rooms filled with wall and ceiling patterns. Dark wood, stained glass, tile work, painted glazes, major oak stairways, and an emphasis on ornamentation characterize the interior. The tour will take you through the common rooms, each interesting in a different way. Among our favorite highlights in this very elaborately decorated home are the round-walled, glass/screened conservatory, the mantels of oak and mahogany (each room was built with different wood), and the eclectic use of stylistic details and art, ranging from Renaissance Revival to Art Nouveau.

Glenmont's setting consists of fourteen acres of rolling hills, broad lawns, and specimen trees. There are a number of additional buildings: a pump house, a greenhouse, a potting shed, a gardener's cottage, a barn, and a garage, which had room for as many as six of Edison's cars.

Just outside the charming stone Llewelyn Park gatehouse (which was designed by Davis) you'll find the large Edison complex: there are several laboratories, a factory, and the world's first motion-picture studio, known as Black Maria.

This self-contained giant complex was operated by an army of workers (up to seven thousand at one point) and included labs for physics, chemistry, and metallurgy, a machine shop (for Edison's ongoing experiments), a pattern shop, and several factory buildings. Here he also developed the first Vitascope (which evolved into silent movies), the mimeograph, storage battery, and kinetiscope. He was interested in just about anything and everything; in the early 1900s this imaginative pioneer produced *The Great Train Robbery*, a short film that combined narrative with moving images for the first time; it is regarded as a classic by film aficionados.

3·
A COLONIAL STREETSCAPE ON THE DELAWARE

The Well-Preserved Town of Burlington

❀ DIRECTIONS

Take the New Jersey Turnpike south to exit 5 and turn left onto Route 541 and go about three miles. Cross Route 130; you will enter Burlington on High Street.

❀ INFORMATION

The library and the Historical Society both have self-guided walking-tour maps. You'll find the **Historical Society Headquarters** at 12 Smith Lane, near the intersection of High Street and West Broad Street. The **Library Company of Burlington** is at 23 West Union Street, just around the corner from the Historical Society. An audio tape describing historic sites is also available. Telephone: 609-386-0200 or 609-386-4773; for guided tours call 609-386-3993. Web site: www.tourburlington.org.

❀ Burlington is the oldest European settlement in New Jersey. It has managed to preserve a large amount of its heritage: the oldest library, the oldest pharmacy, many of the oldest homes in the state. It was once the capital of New Jersey and was one of the most important Quaker settlements in the region. A variety of events have placed it squarely in the center of many of the state's most historic happenings. Its Historic District encompasses forty sites of colonial interest (one square mile) in an unusually attractive setting for walkers. Burlington sits elegantly along the broad Delaware River, with a walkway along it, parks, and tree-lined, brick-cobbled streets filled with interesting sights. In clear view is Burlington Island, the site of the state's first settlement in 1624. We recommend this outing to any history buff or walker who wishes to get a true sense of what life in New Jersey's long-ago past was like. And even without the touristy addition of costumes and craftspersons dressed in eighteenth-century clothing, Burlington celebrates its past.

Many of the colonial homes have been preserved or restored and cared for lovingly over the centuries, retaining their typical architectural details

Burlington streetscape

such as gambrel gabled roofs, frame and brick walls, and small porches. We know of no other site in New Jersey that gives so complete a feeling of the colonial past in block after block of homes and even in parts of the bustling downtown. And in addition to the over forty colonial sites, there are several nineteenth-century buildings of note in the Gothic Revival style, such as the "new" Saint Mary's Church, designed by the leading midcentury architect Richard Upjohn.

The first recorded settlement in the state was on Burlington Island, where, beginning in 1624, a trading post manned by Belgians bartered with local Native Americans. The earliest record of an African presence in the state is in a Dutch colonial reference to slaves in the mid-seventeenth century. The settlement was passed through the hands of the Dutch, the Swedes, and the Finns, until the English took control in 1664. It became the first permanent settlement for Quakers fleeing persecution in Yorkshire and London; they laid out the town on the riverbank facing Burlington Island, originally calling it Bridlington or New Beverly. It became the leading Quaker settlement in the country, with William Penn visiting frequently from his own settlement just across the river. By the late seventeenth century, it was a flourishing colonial outpost, with its Friends Meeting House completed in 1683. (The present Meeting House dates to 1785, and is still in use; visit the burial ground behind it to see the graves of some of the earliest settlers.) In 1682 Burlington hosted the first meeting of the General Assembly of West Jersey, and five years later the Council of Proprietors met in the town.

It was in Burlington around 1726 that Benjamin Franklin used the first copperplate printing press to print New Jersey's original currency. You can visit the Isaac Collins Print Shop where Franklin and other printers produced the earliest weekly newspaper in the state, almanacs, and Bibles, as well as currency. Burlington also has the first library still in continuous use in the state, the first firehouse in the state, the oldest pharmacy in continuous use in New Jersey, the oldest Episcopal church, and one of the first African American churches in the state.

Burlington became a hotbed of patriot activity during the Revolution, and it was the home of several of the most important figures in the new American government, including Elias Boudinot, the first president of the Continental Congress, whose house can be visited. The grave of Oliver Cromwell, a black Revolutionary soldier, can be seen behind the Methodist church.

During the nineteenth century, Burlington was home to a number of well-known personalities, including Captain James Lawrence, the War of 1812 hero who is famous for his "Don't give up the Ship!" exhortation; President Ulysses S. Grant; author James Fenimore Cooper; and several other illustrious figures. By midcentury, as a Quaker and abolitionist stronghold, Burlington became a major stop on the Underground Railroad; its location on the Delaware enabled fleeing slaves from Southern states to cross the river into several welcoming homes in the village.

Numerous historic buildings remain, and many can be visited inside. There are also several interesting sites, such as churches and the Friends Meeting House, graveyards, the Delaware River walkway, and even the island, where the first Burlington settlement was located. We suggest that you pick up a self-guiding tour map (see Information section above) and note the general layout of the historic district: there are two major streets that intersect and several smaller ones to visit in even the shortest historic walking route. Using your map, be sure to visit High Street, West Broad Street, Union Street, and Riverbank, with its great view of the Delaware and the island.

The first street to visit on this tour is High Street.

Captain James Lawrence House and the attached **James Fenimore Cooper House** at 457–459 High Street: Both houses are brick and covered in cement plaster, a fairly common technique in eighteenth-century America.

The Cooper House (birthplace of the famous author) was built around 1780. The Lawrence House dates to the same year, with the front part remodeled around 1820. You can visit these houses for short guided tours.

The Pearson-How house, at 453 High Street, is now the **Burlington County Historical Society**, a historic-house museum. This house, like many town houses of its time, is brick on the front half and frame with clapboard in the rear part. It was built around 1705.

Also on High Street note the **Hopkins House**, the **Isaac Collins Print Shop**, the **Pugh House** (once called the Counting House), the **Gardiner House**, **Alcazar** (which dates all the way back to 1680), the **Smith House**, and the **Blue Anchor Tavern**, which has been serving guests since 1750.

While you are on High Street, note several later buildings: **Temple B'nai Israel** (1801), the **Burlington Pharmacy**, where runaway slaves were hidden on the Underground Railroad, the **Friends Meeting House** and grounds, and the **Endeavor Fire Company** with its antique spire.

Walk to Union Street and turn left. At 23 Union you'll find the **Library Company of Burlington**. Made of brown sandstone building blocks, it is in Classical Revival style and was built in 1864.

Also on Union Street, on the other side of High Street, is the **Oliver Cromwell House**, at 114 East Union Street. Cromwell was an African American Revolutionary War soldier who crossed the Delaware with General Washington.

Follow High Street, cross the railroad tracks, and you will find the 1839 **Costello-Lyceum Hall** at 432 High Street. Reverse your steps, cross back over the railroad tracks, and look for the **Friends Schoolhouse**, dating to 1792, located between Union and York streets.

On nearby West Broad Street, important sites include the **Surveyor General's Office** of 1676, the 1770 **Kinsey House**, and the Federal-style **McIlvaine House**.

The two **Saint Mary's Churches**, old and "new"—one colonial, the other Upjohn's of the mid-nineteenth century—are both architecturally interesting. The older of the two, on the corner of West Broad and Wood streets, was built in 1703 and enlarged in 1769 and again in 1810–1811. Its architect was Robert Mills; it is thought to be the oldest Episcopal church in the state. Brick covered with stucco, it has a belfry and traditional Colonial proportions. The later Saint Mary's Church was built in the Gothic Revival style by Richard Upjohn in 1846–1854.

Note also **Saint Mary's Guild Hall** and the **Biddle-Pugh House** and **Boudinot-Bradford House** of the early Federal period.

On Wood Street don't miss the **Hutchinson-Revell House**, a brick and frame house with clapboard sides and a gambrel roof. Built in 1685, this is a fine example of colonial-era architecture; it was recently saved from demolition and moved to its present site. You can visit the interior by appointment to see original details, including original paneling, fireplaces, and mantels.

Riverbank, with its lovely view, has several interesting locations to see. Of particular interest is the Victorian-style **Grubb Estate**, facing the river, which reportedly had a tunnel to the river that was used by the Underground Railroad, and the Gothic Revival **Shippen House** and **Riverbank Houses**. Near Riverbank, on Pearl Street, is the **Bethlehem African Methodist Episcopal Church**, founded in 1855. Also on Pearl Street is the 1685 **Revell House**, reportedly the oldest house in this part of the state.

There are other sites of interest here as well. The island where the first settlement in Burlington was located can be reached by boat from the ramp at York Street (off Riverbank). As you will see from the Historical Society map, you can drive to additional sites of interest. But the walking tour, on brick sidewalks, is easily accomplished, and you can leave your car and enjoy the most fascinating of historic-architecture walks in the state.

4·
PRINCETON UNIVERSITY'S STARTLING CONTEMPORARY ADDITIONS TO ITS GOTHIC CAMPUS

Princeton

❀ DIRECTIONS

Take the New Jersey Turnpike south to exit 9. Take Route 1 south toward Princeton, then take Alexander Road toward town. There is a parking garage on your right after Faculty Road.

❀ INFORMATION

You can walk around the campus on your own or take a guided tour. A campus map is available near the main entrance to the university. Telephone 609-258-3603.

❀ Princeton University is not just the prettiest school in our area; it is often called one of the most beautiful in the country. The spacious elegance of the campus—with its great Gothic buildings and archways, geometric pathways, fine modern buildings, grand trees, charming gardens, outdoor sculpture, and lake, and its sense of the gracious past—is easily available to a visiting stroller. The campus provides the visitor with acres to wander through, and the town of Princeton itself includes many wonderful areas. You will have to choose your route by how much time you have, since you could spend several days exploring the many areas here.

The university was founded in 1754; Nassau Hall, at its center, was completed two years later and is still in use. Despite bombardment during the Revolution and two fires, the Continental Congress was able to meet there in 1783, when Princeton served as the nation's capital for four months. The school soon began to add buildings and today is a legendary educational institution, with a fine Gothic chapel (which you should not miss on your walk); the modern Woodrow Wilson School building, designed by Minoru Yamasaki; Maclean House, the home of the university's presidents from 1756 to 1879 and now alumni headquarters; Alexander Hall, a Victorian auditorium; the twin Whig and Clio debating society Greek Revival buildings; the fine art museum; and dozens of other interesting sites. You can walk across the spacious lawns from one building to another, along with students as they stroll to a class or an activity, or you can read in the shadow of the famous Gothic towers or beside a contemporary sculpture. This traditional university is quintessentially "collegiate," and we guarantee you'll enjoy it.

Princeton, the town, faces the campus across the main street, Nassau Street. Shops and restaurants and a bustling atmosphere contrast with the quiet of the campus; you will enjoy visiting Palmer Square in the center of town, as well as several nonuniversity sites. In addition, two other places outside the campus are worth seeing: the Grover Cleveland Tower and Graduate College, with its fine view, and the Institute for Advanced Study, where Albert Einstein and other great thinkers have worked.

Traditional sites naturally include the landmark Nassau Hall, the University Chapel, Prospect House and Garden, the University Art Museum, and the many other fine buildings on your map.

But we are particularly intrigued by the newer additions to this time-honored campus. The university has chosen to enter the new century in several architectural ways, and so our emphasis on this architectural walk is not on the hallowed traditions but on how to combine them with the new. (We will primarily spend our time in the part of the campus that is not along Nassau Street.)

If you parked in the university garage, you will find yourself near **Whitman College**, the first of the new additions. Whitman celebrates the traditional, attempting to re-create the Gothic rhythms and style and even the hand-set stone of an earlier time. Designed by the contemporary architect Demetri Porphyrios, this residential college is his attempt to see Gothic design through a modern lens. Among the highlights are the limestone walls of the Community Hall (set apart from the fieldstone of the dorms) and the trefoils atop the walls. Porphyrios, who has designed buildings for Oxford and Cambridge, sought to make a series of buildings described by the architect as each having its own identity of composition and distinct sense of place. Inside you'll find an extraordinary use of finished oak, with beams forming peaks in gabled ceilings in the dining room, as well as other features reminiscent of a sumptuous past. Whitman shows one direction that contemporary university buildings on a traditional campus can take.

If you walk from Whitman to your right, you'll come to **Wu Hall**, designed by Robert Venturi and dedicated in 1983. This striking low building is a graceful punctuation to its surroundings; it is brick with repeated narrow columns, and it is gently contemporary in style, with a large courtyard of plantings. Its architect said of it, "I have said before that we thought of Wu Hall as a hyphen, since it's a long and narrow building that more or less works to connect the two old buildings the way the hyphen connects two words, often words that are very different in meaning. Wu Hall relates to the old buildings most obviously in terms of material. We made the new building brick, and that in a very clear way promoted unity. We also employed landscape elements to help create a sense of arrival, a sense of place, and a sense of identity when you're here."

With the adjoining area under construction (a new Butler College is under way), we skirt the site to find one of the pièces de résistance of the new-look university.

The **Icahn Lab** is the most recently completed eye-catching building and a major addition to the university. Designed by Rafael Viñoly, a leading contemporary architect, the Icahn Lab is properly named the Lewis-Sigler Institute for Integrated Genomics and the Carl Icahn Laboratory. It is a cutting-edge science center, and its distinctive architecture reinforces its aim to be new and creative. The ninety-eight-thousand-square-foot building, with its thirty-five thousand square feet of labs, forms an L-shape footprint between nearby Washington Road and the adjacent athletic fields. It has a curved wall of glass that is two stories high and a large atrium with curving walls. The building is open to the public, so go inside to see the center, where there are a variety of stunning communal spaces and a dramatic architectural identity.

Among the building's many innovative architectural features are the thirty-one overhead vertical louvered windows looking out to the fields beyond and shading the atrium. These aluminum louvers turn with the sun with a computerized timer. They have white, latticelike bands of aluminum that cast a decorative shadow.

The interior walls of the labs are modular units that can be rearranged; many of the details of the building are designed to foster interaction between different units and disciplines housed here. In the center of the large open area is a most unusual Frank Gehry sculpture, which resembles a small building within the larger space. In fact, it was originally built as a model for a Gehry house.

Princeton University: Lewis Science Library (Frank Gehry) and Richard Serra sculpture

After walking through this striking building, note the ellipse that is created along the edge of the fields, including the contiguous dorm buildings, thus creating an overall design for this new part of the campus.

Walk left on Washington Road to see the brand-new Frank Gehry building that has become the **Lewis Science Library**. When we saw it, it already had the distinctive silhouette of Gehry's dramatic structures, with bold, curving interesting planes that seem to challenge the traditional view of building materials. The exterior was completed first, so we could already see the strong abstract designs of many curving roofs and contrasting angles.

As you leave the Gehry site, be sure to see the Richard Serra sculpture, though it is more of a walk-through monument than a traditional statuary. This two-walled work defines the space much as architecture does, and it fits right in with the nearby Gehry building.

We recommend that you continue your explorations of this wonderful campus, since we have only touched on a few of its many architectural pleasures.

5.
A BAUHAUS-INSPIRED UTOPIAN VILLAGE

Roosevelt

❀ DIRECTIONS

Take the New Jersey Turnpike to exit 8 and take Route 33 west toward Hightstown for a short distance. Take Route 571 south to Roosevelt.

❀ INFORMATION

Roosevelt is a very small village with hardly any public buildings and no town center. There is a post office, however, and you can get local directions there. But many tourists do visit the town, and the school where the artworks are located welcomes visitors. Visit during school hours, and ring the bell for admittance. The school is located on School Lane, just off Pine Drive. Telephone: 609-448-2798. Web site: www.roosevelt.edu.history.

❀ Roosevelt is one of the few communities in the region to retain its original Bauhaus-inspired, modernist image. Designed to be a Utopian settlement during the Depression, it was a project of the Federal Resettlement Administration under Franklin Delano Roosevelt.

The new style broke away from the revivalist aesthetic of the twentieth century, such as classically ornamented skyscrapers and Gothic and High Victorian prototypes. Instead, modernism—sometimes known as the International style—looked to modern life, with its emphasis on technology, for its design ideas. There was almost no ornamentation on modernist buildings, and they were designed to look machine made, with materials that are cold and stark: steel, glass, and concrete. The emphasis was on the horizontal dimension, with rectangular design, flat roofs, geometric patterns of windows, and smooth walls without textures.

The town was laid out by a German-born exponent of the International style, Alfred Kastner, and his assistant, Louis Kahn, who went on to become one of the twentieth century's most illustrious architects. The one-story,

176

white stucco houses were constructed using Bauhaus principles of geometric simplicity and functionalism, in which the cubicle and the rectangular, with repetitive façade, were characteristic. The houses today appear to be the progenitors of the "ranch houses" of the 1950s.

Large areas of green space and forest land were incorporated into the community's design. Each family paid between fourteen and seventeen dollars in rent per month for their corner of what seemed to them like paradise after the crowded ghettos they had left behind in Europe. Between 1935 and 1938 about two hundred houses were built, soon supplemented by a cooperative store, community center, borough hall, school, and synagogue.

The first building constructed was a garment factory. The concept was not without detractors, among them David Dubinsky of the International Ladies' Garment Workers' Union in New York. Albert Einstein, of nearby Princeton, was a major defender of the idea, and he talked to Dubinsky, who finally agreed when it was made clear that workers would turn out clothing only when it was needed and revert to farming when it was not.

A visit to Roosevelt will remind those of us with memories of 1930s America of a time and place filled with both despair and idealism. For younger visitors, it is as close as they can come to seeing a genuine planned community that still functions and endures quite satisfactorily much the way it has for some seventy years. The town of Roosevelt was a Depression-era experiment that brought about two hundred city-dwelling families to remote farmland in Monmouth County. The aim was to start a self-contained, idealistic community. What Roosevelt became is a story in itself, and today occasional busloads of tourists with cameras come from as far away as Japan to see how it worked—and still works. Now, more than half a century later, Roosevelt welcomes visitors as it attempts to live up to the high ideals of a long-ago time, in a contemporary world of commerce and urban sprawl.

The two square miles of Roosevelt were once farmland and forest, and today there is still a great deal of open, preserved space. The concept of the original town of Roosevelt seemed a simple one: to aid city-dwelling immigrants who were without work and who could set up a cooperative village in unused space. Jersey Homesteads was one of the largest and first of the ninety-nine communities that the federal government sponsored in a daring experiment in Depression-era social engineering.

Under the guidance of Benjamin Brown, who was a leader of the Jewish agrarian movement (an idea that dated back to the nineteenth century), immigrants from the city would join him on his New Jersey farm and on additional acreage bought by the government to set up an ideal community. Having convinced the government that his plan would work, Brown went through some 800 family applications and chose just 120. Almost all of them were Jewish garment workers from New York. Each of them contributed five hundred dollars to become settlers. A writer for the Works Progress Administration reported that "Jersey Homesteads is designed to find a simple and happy solution for the complexities of modern industrial life."

The entirely Jewish community was filled with ideologues, Zionists, anarchists, socialists, and artists, but few had farming or industrial experience. Money-making enterprises failed after a few years, but the village continued to thrive. For those who lived there, the community was a philosophical home, a testament to shared values and commitments. In 1945 the village was renamed Roosevelt as a tribute to the president. It had become something of a left-wing artists' community after the arrival of Ben Shahn.

Shahn had been asked to paint a mural depicting the birth of the village. His forty-five-foot-long mural is a masterpiece of 1930s socially conscious art, depicting every element of the founding of the village, from Einstein's intercession to the laying of brickwork and the rows of sewing machines in the original factory. Shahn's brilliant evocation and his support for the village drew numerous other artists to Roosevelt. (The New York Times described Shahn as the nation's "official leftist artist.") "You get a lot of people who felt they didn't fit in anywhere and they came to Roosevelt and they felt welcome here," said the current mayor recently. And many second- and third-generation family members stayed on.

With careful determination, today's Roosevelt citizens are trying to preserve that way of life despite the encroachments of the outside world. When you visit the community you feel you have walked back in time, even though the houses have been added to and decorated and there is now a small restaurant.

The school, where the Shahn mural is now proudly displaced, is a welcoming place, filled with art by esteemed residents. There is an impressive 1936 sculpture of a garment worker by Lenore Thomas. Don't miss a large and fascinating hammered-aluminum wall relief by Otto Wester (1938) depicting garment workers and field workers. There is a series of woodcuts by Gregorio Prestopino and prints by Jacob Landau. You'll find the atmosphere in this place where today's Roosevelt students go to school both historic and artistic.

Walk behind the school to see the fine bust of Franklin D. Roosevelt by Shahn's son, the sculptor Jonathan Shahn, who still lives in the community. And beyond the school grounds is a forest walk, called Roosevelt Woodland Trail. We history lovers and admirers of Bauhaus architecture can only hope (and support) current efforts to keep Roosevelt such a special place.

6·
GUARDIANS OF THE
NEW JERSEY COASTLINE

The Lighthouse as Architecture: Sandy Hook, Barnegat, Navesink, Cape May, Hereford Inlet, East Point, Finn's Point

⚘ DIRECTIONS

Sandy Hook Light: *From the Garden State Parkway take exit 117 to Route 36 toward Highlands and follow signs to Sandy Hook.*

Barnegat Light: *From the Garden State Parkway take exit 63 and take Route 72 over bridge to island; then take Long Beach Boulevard north.*

Navesink Twin Lights: *From the Garden State Parkway take exit 117 to Route 36 toward Highlands. Turn right on Portland Road, just before Highlands Bridge to Sandy Hook; take an immediate right onto Highland Avenue and follow signs.*

Cape May Light: *Take the Garden State Parkway to its end and follow signs to Cape May. Turn right onto Sunset Boulevard (Route 606), and after about two miles turn left onto Light House Avenue. Go less than a mile to Cape May State Park entrance on left.*

Hereford Inlet Light: *Take the Garden State Parkway to exit 6 in North Wildwood. Go right onto Route 147 (North Wildwood Boulevard), make a left at Chestnut Avenue, and go two blocks and make a right on Central Avenue, to number 111.*

East Point Light: *East Point Light is in the town of Heislerville. Take the Garden State Parkway to exit 17 to Route 9 south. Go west on Route 83 to intersection with Route 47 north and turn right. Continue on Route 47 and turn left on Glade Road (just after Moore's Beach Road). Follow signs to Lighthouse Road.*

Finn's Point Rear Range Light: *Take the New Jersey Turnpike to exit 1, then take Route 49 east for about four miles, following signs to Fort Mott State Park. Turn right on Fort Mott Road to Lighthouse Road.*

⚘ INFORMATION

We recommend calling ahead for visiting hours at all these sites.

Sandy Hook Light: 732-872-5970.

Barnegat Light: 609-494-2016.

Navesink Twin Lights: 732-872-1814.

Cape May Light: 609-884-5401.

Hereford Inlet Light: 609-522-4520.

East Point Light: 856-785-1120.

Finn's Point Rear Range Light: 856-935-1487.

Web site: www.njlighthousesociety.

❀ New Jersey's lighthouses guard some three hundred miles of coastline. Most were built in the nineteenth century, and they represent a variety of architectural styles. All of them are fascinating places to visit.

The oldest of these seven lighthouses is Sandy Hook Light (1764); the most recent is the Victorian Hereford Inlet Light. Styles range from the octagonal masonry tower at Sandy Hook to the plain Cape Cod design of East Point Light to the eccentric 1862 Navesink Twin Lights, designed by the architect Joseph Lederle.

Lighthouse designers have faced daunting challenges, since the pounding waves and force of gale winds undermine the structures. Though they are designed for utility, many are beautiful and graceful, as the towers soar high above the ocean coast. In addition to their unusual architectural structures, they are specially colored to stand out clearly from their backgrounds.

Our first visit is to the **Sandy Hook Light**, built in 1764 and the oldest operating lighthouse in the United States. It is one of the first twelve lighthouses established by the colonies. The tower is 103 feet tall, has nine stories, and has brick-lined walls that are seven feet thick at the base. It is white and octagonal and appears stark and austere against the sky. After many years of tidal activity, sands have piled up around it so that it is now a quarter mile away from the coastline. But it is still visible some nineteen miles out to sea. It is the only lighthouse of its era still in service.

Barnegat Light, originally built in 1834, was brought down by the sea and rebuilt in 1858. The original structure was built one mile from the sea, but today it is on the very edge of the water. It was elegantly restored in 1989 and again in 2008 with a new beacon. It is 162 feet tall, with a narrow, tapering tower with red on top and white on the bottom, and it is known

Navesink Twin Lights, Highlands

locally as "Old Barney." You can climb 217 winding steps and look out on the eighteen miles of Long Beach Island.

Though originally built in 1828, the **Navesink Twin Lights** we visit today was constructed in 1862. It is made of local brownstone. Note the decorative stonework in both towers and the connecting structure. Though they are called twin towers, the north tower is octagonal, and the south tower is square; each rises to sixty-four feet. The two side-by-side beacons gave a distinctive signal to ships at sea, identifying immediately their location. The towers were connected by eighteen rooms for the keeper's and crew's housing (today mostly filled by the museum).

By 1883 the first lamps to burn kerosene were installed at Twin Lights. And then in 1898 an enormous (nine feet in diameter) electric light replaced the beehive-type light in the south tower. The Lighthouse Service built a generator to illuminate it. Today you can visit the building at the south of the complex to see the extraordinary light that revolves there. (The light was so bright that the north tower light was discontinued in 1962.)

Another major invention concerned Twin Lights as well. In 1899 Guglielmo Marconi decided to demonstrate his invention of the wireless telegraph at the lighthouse. He placed an antenna and receiving station at the site and reported by telegraph on an America's Cup yacht race at sea. His demonstration proved successful, and the *New York Herald* was able to scoop the outcome before anyone else. After this successful demonstration, Marconi created the nation's first wireless telegraph station at Twin Lights. By the 1920s the U.S. Army was also using the Twin Lights site for experimental electronics, including radar.

Begin your walk at the museum and climb up the north tower. The museum has a large collection of artifacts and documents, in addition to a replica of Marconi's telegraph equipment. The collection of photos and equipment of the U.S. Life Saving Service is one of the best anywhere. Don't miss the Francis Life Car, an iron vessel that was used to bring people ashore from shipwrecks. Climb the north tower, which, though decommissioned, still blinks from dawn to dusk. This is the vertical part of the walk: there are sixty-four narrow, steep steps. The view is, of course, magnificent. Walk around the perimeter of the complex and visit the amazing nine-foot light and the boathouse, with its replica of the lifesaving boats of the past. This site offers a rare combination of electronic invention and maritime history and adventure, brought quite brilliantly to life by the setting and exhibits. The giant light is mesmerizing, particularly for those of us who think of lighthouses as small glowing dots on the horizon.

Cape May Light is similar in style to Barnegat Light. (It is the third lighthouse built on this site.) Its tower rises more than 170 feet and is 27 feet in diameter at the bottom and 15 feet at the top. A white structure with red lantern, it can be seen eighteen miles out to sea. It is listed on the National Register of Historic Places.

Hereford Inlet Light, a few miles north of Cape May, is a tall structure often described as a great Victorian lighthouse. Built of straw-colored wood, it is in the Gothic Victorian style and is surrounded by cottage-style gardens with over one thousand plant varieties. Built in 1874, it is the only one of its kind on the East Coast, and it has steep angles and vertical design that typify so many American Victorian buildings.

East Point Light, on the other hand, resembles an old New England house on a remote bluff. East Point is probably as remote a place as you will find in this populous state. It is presently the only functioning lighthouse on Delaware Bay. A visit here is strangely silent, except for the songs of seabirds (including gulls and herons) and the whistle of the wind through the high reeds and tidal marshes that surround it. History buffs and nature lovers, as well as beachcombers, will relish this unusual spot.

East Point Light is the second-oldest lighthouse in New Jersey (after Sandy Hook). It is a pretty, whitewashed brick structure in a Cape Cod style, with a small tower atop it, and it sits all alone on a bluff above Delaware Bay at its intersection with the Maurice River. The lighthouse was constructed in 1849 to guide oyster boats and other vessels into the mouth of the Maurice River.

Finn's Point Rear Range Light is situated in a remote spot near Fort Mott. This lighthouse consists of a 115-foot wrought-iron tower built in 1876. Its appearance is most unusual, unlike any other lighthouse that we have seen in New Jersey. It has a center column with a superstructure of iron, making it look like a contemporary sculpture with a 119-step spiral staircase. This lighthouse, originally designed to help sailors navigate the difficult Delaware River channel, was built as a military installation, without ever having seen a battle of its own. It is also listed on the National Register of Historic Places.

7·
CRAFTSMAN FARMS
The Arts and Crafts Aesthetic, Morris Plains

❀ DIRECTIONS

Craftsman Farms is located at 2356 Route 10 West, in Parsippany. From I-80 west take I-287 south to exit 39B. Take Route 10 west for about three miles, then turn right onto Manor Lane and watch for the sign to Craftsman Farms. The main entrance is on the right.

❀ INFORMATION

Open April 1 through November 15, Wednesday through Friday, noon to 3 P.M.; Saturday and Sunday, 11 A.M. to 4 P.M. To visit the museum you must take a guided tour, which lasts about one hour. You are welcome to walk around the grounds on your own and visit the gift shop for additional information, as well as for books and objects of relevance to the Arts and Crafts movement. Telephone: 973-540-1165. Web site: www.stickleymuseum.org.

❀ The Stickley Museum at Craftsman Farms was once the home of furniture designer, manufacturer, publisher, philosopher, social critic, and architect Gustav Stickley, America's foremost spokesman for the Arts and Crafts movement of the early twentieth century.

"This is my garden of Eden," he said of what was once a 650-acre tract (now 30 acres) of lush woodlands surrounding the beautifully crafted log house he built in 1911. Stickley's utopian community here at Craftsman Farms embodied the central principles of his movement: the emphasis on crafts and trades (including the teaching of them to young children), the value of country living, and the "simple life."

The Arts and Crafts movement in the United States, culminating in the years between 1910 and 1925, derived from an earlier such movement in England beginning in the 1880s. Both represented a reaction against the excesses and fussiness of the Victorian era, whether in architecture, decorative arts, crafts, or garden design. Fundamental to the Arts and Crafts aesthetic was the notion that beauty does not imply elaboration or ornamentation: it can and should be simple and functional, as well as organic from the earth. The focus was on the master craftsman, who was seen not only as designer of a work but also as producer. Stickley's goal was to create a beautiful house, interior space, furniture, or object by working with his hands at every step of the process, thus taking pride in his handiwork.

Here, at Craftsman Farms, Stickley actually lived his philosophical principles. From 1908 to 1914 he published a journal and designed furniture—sometimes called "Mission" furniture—while overseeing local farm workers who managed his property. He also created a farm-workshop school that offered summer programs in agriculture and handicrafts for children.

The house, which can only be visited by guided tour, is a log "cabin" with a massive stone chimney, rounded ceiling beams, large overhanging eaves, wooden columns, and small diamond-panel windows. The interior woodwork is dark and simple, as is the heavy, wood furniture (Stickley's own). The exterior of the house is typical of the Arts and Crafts style in its emphasis on horizontal lines. Constructed from chestnut logs actually cut from the woods on the property, the house embodies rustic, sheltering simplicity. Its long sloping roofline and wide overhang makes it appear as if it is nestling into the earth.

Other Stickley buildings on this site, which has been designated a National Historic Landmark, include farm structures, stone stables, and three cottages. As with the main house, these all reflect Stickley's philosophy of building in harmony with the environment by using natural materials. You'll find that walking around this fascinating spot with its beautiful woods is an experience not to be missed.

8·
A VICTORIAN VILLAGE ON THE SHORE

The Planned Community of Ocean Grove

❀ DIRECTIONS

Take the Garden State Parkway to exit 100B and take Route 33 east. Follow signs to Ocean Grove.

❀ INFORMATION

Ocean Grove is a bustling summer resort, as well as a continuing Methodist camp destination in August. We recommend visiting in the off-season, if you want to stroll quietly through the village (and along the beach), but there is a lot going on year-round here, including many historical festivals and events. You can pick up a map of the village at any realtor's office and at many of the shops on Main Avenue, as well as at the Chamber of Commerce at 45 Pilgrim Pathway (near the Great Auditorium). Telephone: 800-388-4768; for a walking tour, 732-774-1869. Web site: www.oceangrovenj.com.

❀ The village of Ocean Grove, considered to have the largest collection of Victoriana in the United States, is a one-of-a-kind community. It is a picturesque town with rows of small, well-kept Victorian homes and a vast central architectural wonder: the Great Auditorium. Rows of elegant tents, occupied in season by Methodists, still border the auditorium. Some people say there are more authentic Victorian homes in this town than in any other village in the United States. A fine, wide promenade runs the length of the village along the Atlantic coast.

In a fine example of nineteenth-century urban planning (beginning in 1869), the town was laid out in advance. Houses nearer the ocean were built farther back from the street to create a funnel effect that would bring sea breezes into the center of the town and give ocean views to more people from their porches.

These late-nineteenth-century cottages, unlike the grand houses of the time, are often small and close together; you'll find examples of various Victorian styles, many with mass-produced wooden decorations that can still be seen in porches and balconies. Among the smaller homes are a number of Carpenter Gothic examples, with the requisite gables and decorative details, including small porches, cutout work, and scallops. These homes are sometimes described as looking like dollhouses. The more imposing houses include Gothic Revival and Tuscan-villa styles of Victoriana.

You will not find a similar enclave anywhere else on the Jersey shore. The village is both a scenic delight and a historically well-kept and fascinating reminder of the many religious groups that created lasting communities in the state.

After the Civil War, residents of the growing urban centers of the East were seeking getaway places in the summer. In many cases they were drawn to the idea of a community that had shared beliefs and that was both physically and spiritually healthful. A group of Methodists from Philadelphia was looking for just such a site. Ocean Grove's lovely setting on the ocean —with its high beach and thick groves of pines and hickory, its absence of mosquitoes, and its isolation—appealed to its founders, a group of thirteen Methodist ministers, under the direction of Dr. William B. Osborne, and thirteen laymen.

In 1869, they came in their carriages from Philadelphia to conduct a revival meeting. Methodist camp meetings were usually open-air revivals that drew large crowds and lasted for many days. At Ocean Grove they pitched their tents in this quiet spot, eventually creating a seaside resort in which to pursue annual summer camp meetings in relative isolation. Bounded on three sides by water (there are small lakes both north and south of the village), Ocean Grove provided them with a site that was isolated from the decadence that they associated with popular seaside resorts. They elected a man named Elwood H. Stokes as president of the Ocean Grove Camp Meeting Association. (You will see a statue of him in the village.) By 1874 the tent community, known as "little canvas village," at the height of the season included some two hundred ministers and about seven hundred tents. These semipermanent buildings, which have now lasted more than a century, had their own floors and small kitchens. There are still 114 of them, many having been passed from generation to generation. But many of the nineteenth-century Methodists opted for more permanent homes in the village; soon members were building the hundreds of small, quaint, Victorian-style cottages that make this community a historic architectural treasure.

The Methodist Camp Association, which ran the community, remained a private organization so that it could maintain strict control over its members. Lots were leased for ninety-nine years. Strict rules included no alcohol, smoking, organ grinders, peddlers, vendors, or carriages on the beach; no swearing in the boats or adjacent Lake Wesley; and on Sundays, no wheeled vehicles, newspapers, dancing, or card playing. The gates (through which you will still enter the village) were closed promptly at 10 P.M. and remained tightly shut on Sundays. Visitors on Sundays had to enter over a footbridge from next-door Asbury Park. Trains were not allowed to stop at Ocean Grove on Sundays either. President Ulysses S. Grant, who once visited his mother and sister on a Sunday at their rented Ocean Grove cottage, was obliged to walk into town, like any other pilgrim.

The few recreational activities allowed at Ocean Grove included boating on the sea and lakes and promenading by the shore; the town fathers considered banning swimming because of the immodest disrobing it entailed, but they reluctantly agreed to allow it, except on Sundays.

However, the major activities allowed at Ocean Grove did not involve the seaside and the charming setting. The **Great Auditorium**, the centerpiece of the village, sits in a large, grassy space and is an immense and curious structure. It was built in 1894 in an eclectic, late-Victorian style and is almost the size of a football field. It was designed to accommodate ten thousand people and a choir of five hundred, and it was here that the residents of the community congregated. The auditorium is unusual both in its architectural design and for the fact that it was constructed without nails, in imitation of Solomon's temple. The massive edifice houses a famous organ that is played twice weekly, and many interesting sights are within. Here, during camp meetings, religious services were conducted daily, on a continual basis. Among the numerous illustrious visitors to the building have been seven presidents (Grant, Garfield, Theodore Roosevelt, Taft, Wilson, and Nixon), many governors, opera singers, and public figures. You can find a list of them at the Chamber of Commerce, where you can pick up a map of the village. You will want to walk all around the Great Auditorium to see both the building itself and the rows of tents that surround it. Ocean Grove still holds numerous religious and musical events in the Great Auditorium. Although some of its blue laws have disappeared over time—in 1980 courts ruled that such prohibitions constituted a conflict between church and state —the village retains a quaint, pristine quality that is hard to find elsewhere. Woody Allen set his *Stardust Memories* here.

Great Auditorium, Ocean Grove

Using your walking-tour map, enjoy the architecture between Ocean Avenue and the Great Auditorium. Of particular interest to the architecture buff are **Thornley Chapel** (1889), a simple Methodist frame church; the **Bishop James Tabernacle** (1877), a lovely one-story building with arched windows and the oldest building in continuous use as a house of worship in the village; the **Beersheba Wall** (1870), a High Victorian Artesian well, complete with domed roofs; and **Centennial Cottage** (1874), the prime example of Ocean Grove's Carpenter Gothic style. But of equal interest are the many streets of private homes (many are now bed-and-breakfasts) in the imaginative, picturesque styles of the late Victorian era. Among these quaint streets are Pilgrim Pathway, Central Avenue, and the streets parallel to Ocean Avenue, which is the main thoroughfare along the shore. Don't miss Ocean Pathway, too, a picture-postcard Victorian street lined with trees and park benches. Main Avenue is a bustling street of small shops and restaurants. To re-create the Sunday isolation of Ocean Grove with its original blue laws, walk across the small footbridge over Wesley Lake.

9·

THREE ARCHITECTURAL WONDERS AT LIBERTY STATE PARK

Railroad Terminal, Environmental Center, and Ellis Island

The Railroad Terminal

DIRECTIONS: *Take the New Jersey Turnpike to exit 14B and follow signs to Liberty State Park. The Railroad Terminal building is at the end of Johnston Avenue.*

INFORMATION: The park is open daily from 8 A.M. to 5 P.M. Telephone 201-915-3401 or 201-915-3404.

This very picturesque railroad terminal is typical of many late-nineteenth-century/early-twentieth-century stations in America. But its vast size—it was the terminal for one of the busiest transportation centers in the New York region—makes it even more impressive, because it has the charm and attractive proportions of a much more intimate building.

Constructed between 1912 and 1914, the terminal was for many years both an end and a beginning for its many visitors. Thousands of immigrants took the ferry from Ellis Island to this very building to board trains for their future in the United States. And thousands more arrived and departed from this station as daily commuters to New York City. (Many still do so.)

Attached to the main building is an equally historic edifice: a "train shed" (listed on the National Register of Historic Places), where hundreds of trains pulled in and out; it is the largest of its type ever built. The station has three stories and is built of brick, with a five-part façade of Palladian design. There is a central clock that faces the river, visible to generations of ferry riders from Manhattan. Sets of arched windows—each with its own archway—are ornamented with some thirty different carved faces at the ends. A decorative tower sits atop the many-angled roof.

In the giant interior there are a number semicircular forms making up the design of the hall, along with a balcony supported with iron buttresses and ornamented with wreaths. A skylight and high arched dormer windows bring natural light into the huge interior space. The original glazed-brick walls are still evident. In fact, this beautifully designed building looks (after major renovation in the 1970s) remarkably well cared for and is a fine place to visit for a taste of American / Victorian railroad-station design.

For a complete change of era and design, visit another architectural site not far away: the Environmental Center in the same Liberty State Park.

The Environmental Center

DIRECTIONS: *Take the New Jersey Turnpike to exit 14B and follow signs to Liberty State Park. Take Johnston Avenue to Freedom Way (a right turn before the train station) and follow Freedom Way for less than a mile to the Environmental Center.*

INFORMATION: Telephone: 201-915-3409.

Michael Graves, the well-known postmodern architect, produced the award-winning design of this center in 1980. As in many of his buildings, Graves combined familiar traditional forms of architecture—including columns and gables and imposing entrances—with a contemporary aesthetic. While rejecting the antiornamental ideas of modern architecture, postmodernists have attempted to return these more traditional aspects to their designs. This particular, intimately sized, building is a perfect example of Graves's postmodern style, and it clearly shows how he communicated the purpose of the building through its design.

The center was designed as a "wildlife interpretive center for the study and exhibition of the indigenous wildlife and environmental aspects of the park," as stated in the Environmental Center's brochure. The design of the building—a series of pavilions and paths—reflects the center's efforts to emphasize the important relationship between the landscape and architecture. There are three waterside pavilions containing exhibition rooms and an imposing auditorium, all for disseminating knowledge about the nearby marshy, riverside environment. But it is the design of the complex itself that draws the visitor toward the environment around it. The architecture includes a series of columns suggesting ancient times, as well as wood-framed, shedlike buildings with gabled roofs (relating the building to heavy timber constructions of the American past). The complex can be entered through a monumental gateway bordered by giant columns; you can walk along a pergola that leads to the nature path, and you can spot both an atrium and a basilica inside the building, all suggestive of ancient Rome.

The Environmental Center (Michael Graves), Liberty State Park

Among the many fascinating architectural details are a high "rose window," which actually hides a "multiple bird's nest." The unusual colors and the ingenious spaces throughout the complex are thoroughly contemporary, however, with a formal sense of geometry and balance that permeates the entire design.

(By the way, don't miss spectacular views of the Statue of Liberty, Ellis Island, and New York City from this complex.)

National Historic Site at Ellis Island

DIRECTIONS: *Take the ferry from the Railroad Terminal at Liberty State Park or take the ferry from the New York City Ferry Terminal at the Battery.*

INFORMATION: Telephone: 212-363-3200 for hours. Boat schedule information is available at 212-269-5755 or 201-435-9499. Boat fare is charged, and there is an entrance fee at Ellis Island.

The massive but graceful Ellis Island building, where so many of our ancestors arrived from across the seas, is an appropriately grand edifice in the French Renaissance style. It has been beautifully restored and is now one of the prime tourist spots in the country. You can walk through it and around it, trace your relatives, and soak up the atmosphere, from its graceful architecture to its piles of century-old luggage stacked on the first floor.

A competition was held to design a new structure after the original wooden center burned to the ground in 1897. A massive building was needed to receive the thousands of immigrants whose ships were docking off New York's shores.

A small firm called Boring & Tilton won the assignment, and it is their grand brick building with complex limestone trim that we admire today. Their design has for more than a century been the symbol of America's welcome to the sixteen million people who arrived at this spot.

The brick building was opened in 1900. It has ornate limestone detailing, four brick-and-limestone striped cupolas, and a huge vaulted-ceiling Registry Room on the second floor. In 1918 a beautiful and dramatic ceiling was created by immigrant Spanish tilers. The vaulting uses a complicated plan consisting of three layers of tiles woven together; the effect is both aesthetically pleasing and practical, as the tiles mask the otherwise unsupported vault of the ceiling.

The design of the Ellis Island building is considered one of the premier examples of the grand-scale brick-and-limestone public edifices in the country.

10·
A VICTORIAN STREETSCAPE OF DECORATIVE HOUSES

Belvidere

❀ DIRECTIONS

Take I-80 west through most of the state to exit 12. Go south on Route 519, then make a right on Brass Castle Road and follow signs to Belvidere.

❀ INFORMATION

You can visit the town at any time of year or day, of course. If you would like a guided tour through some of the historic houses, check out the annual event (in September of each year) called "Victorian Days," on which certain private historic houses are open to the public. For further information telephone the Warren County Historic Society (open on Sundays, from 2 to 4 P.M.) at 908-475-4246. Web site: www.belviderenj.com.

❀ Belvidere is aptly named. This scenic river town on the eastern shores of the Delaware River is blessed with beautiful views. A small river, the Pequest, flows right through the heart of town, adding to the picturesque atmosphere. Yet Belvidere is, in fact, an architectural gem boasting more than two hundred structures listed on the National Register of Historic Places.

Here, surrounding a spacious square park dotted with magnificent trees, are streets lined with historic mansions. Though most are from the Victorian era (the town is often referred to as "Victorian Belvidere"), there are also fine examples from the colonial and other periods. Their variety is quite fascinating, including such features as turrets, columns, wraparound porches, and gingerbread and other fanciful details. Shaded by beautiful old oaks, elms, and pines, most of these elegant buildings have been carefully preserved and are proudly maintained. (One definitely senses a proactive community spirit here!) On prominent display in front of the square is the imposing nineteenth-century courthouse, a testament to Belvidere's enduring role as the county seat.

Belvidere streetscape

The nineteenth-century historic district includes Market, Race, Green-wich, and Mansfield streets, from Water Street to Fourth Street.

Like much of New Jersey, this area was once occupied by the Leni-Lenape, whose old village, Pesquase, is said to have been located here. As the Native Americans moved west across the Delaware, this early site evolved from strategic settlement with forts and stockades to farming community. William Penn was one of the first to purchase land here, in the early 1700s.

In 1769, Major Robert Hoops, who eventually gave Belvidere its name and is regarded as the town's founder, purchased from Penn land on both sides of the Pequest River. Hoops sold the south-side parcel to Robert Morris, a prominent financier of the Revolution and signer of the Declaration of Independence, who in turn built a large plantation house for his daughter, Mary Croxall; one of the earliest of Belvidere's grand mansions, it is still standing, at 116 Greenwich Street. Garret Wall, a lawyer and later governor of New Jersey, bought the Croxall property in 1825 and eventually subdivided the land into building lots, thus laying the foundation for the town.

Through the industrial era, Belvidere prospered with its mills powered by the Pequest River. As the town grew in stature (it became the county seat in 1824), more elaborately decorated houses sprang up, mostly on the square and surrounding streets just south of the Pequest. Today a visit to Belvidere is a must for anyone with a special interest in historic architecture. It is best to discover the town's heritage on foot, of course. Some of the buildings are accessible to the public on a regular basis; others are privately owned and can be visited only by special arrangement or through the Victorian Days house tours offered each year on the second or third weekend of September. But you are always free to explore on your own, perhaps by following the suggested route given below, in any order you like.

Park your car on Front Street, at the corner of Greenwich Street. Among the houses to see, as you walk south on Greenwich Street to Fourth Street, are the following:

115 Greenwich: A Victorian built around 1880, this structure, known as the Judge Morrow Law Office (it used to be located right near the courthouse), features molded window hoods and a heavily decorated vergeboard.

116 Greenwich: This Georgian-style house (with a Daughters of the American Revolution historic plaque) from the 1780s is the aforementioned Croxall Mansion and is an important example of Belvidere's colonial period. Inside is an elegant winding staircase of polished walnut leading to bright, airy, spacious rooms. Privately owned, this house is often included on historic-house tours.

220 Greenwich: This highly ornate Victorian, built around 1890, is well endowed with gingerbread decoration surrounding a beautiful round front window.

300 Greenwich: A hard-to-miss Victorian, one of the largest and most elegant in town, this house was built in 1880 by Judge William Morrow, who defended several county officials in the infamous "Ring Trials" of the 1870s. Note the octagonal bay wing, rounded window hoods, and porch.

At Fourth Street turn left and walk to **142 Fourth**, a handsome house built around 1860, with original clapboard exterior.

Turn left on the next block, at Mansfield Street, a street with an eclectic collection of late-Victorian houses, as well as some dating from the 1920s and 1930s. Note especially the following:

424 Mansfield: It might surprise you to learn that this Tudor-style house actually came from a Sears Roebuck catalog in 1930. In fact, between 1908 and 1940, prospective home buyers would contact the company, which would then send them all the necessary supplies and plans. Apparently some 450 such plans were built across the country from these catalogs.

410 Mansfield: This house is a "pseudo-Colonial," which was remodeled from its original Victorian style.

314 Mansfield: Though this house looks authentically Victorian, it was built recently, in 1993.

313 Mansfield: A simple Federal-style townhouse from circa 1845, this is now the home of the Museum of the Warren County Historical and Genealogical Society.

302 Mansfield: A turn-of-the-century Colonial Revival, this house is distinctive for, among other things, its Corinthian capitals.

228 Mansfield: This Victorian, built around 1860 and known as the Hilton House, is a grand Italianate mansion with ornate window hoods, a large decorative front porch, and molded and paneled front doors.

The **Cummins Building**, on the corner of Mansfield and Second Street, is a fine example of Georgian architecture. Built in 1834 from limestone mined in a local quarry, it features an elegant entrance with classical recessed columns.

At 313 Mansfield Street, on the corner of Fourth Street, is **History House** (now a museum focusing on the history of Warren County), built of local brick in the 1850s.

On your right is Belvidere's inviting town square, a focal point of the town. Established in 1840, Garrett Wall Park was named after the town planner who donated this land to remain forever an open public space for walks, picnics, and other leisurely activities. From here you can enjoy nice town views on all four sides surrounding the square.

Leave the square on the south side and walk east (left) on Third Street to Knowlton Street. En route, see the following houses on Third Street:

303 Third: This 1840s house is a combination of Greek Revival (its façade), Victorian (porch's pilaster corner boards, entrance), and Italianate (cornice brackets).

404 and 406 Third: Both of these houses are examples of Greek Revival, with such details as decorative brackets and pedimented window hoods and Ionic recessed columns.

514 Third: This 1897 Queen Anne is one of the grandest on Third Street. Note its turret, second-story porch, and oriel window.

525 Third: A gracious 1870s Italianate example with central gable, round-arched window, ceiling-to-floor windows in front, and a charming carriage house, too.

530 Third: On the corner of Third Street and Knowlton Street, this terrific 1896 Queen Anne Victorian features a decorated wraparound porch, stained-glass sashes, corner tower, and hipped roof. Its interior is quite lavish, with antique wallpapers and furniture.

Turn left on Knowlton, walk one block, and turn left on Second Street.

At 301 Second Street, at the corner of Hardwick Street, is the **Blair Estate**, now home of the Warren County Library. Built in 1865, it is a stuccoed structure with Italianate touches: an elaborate porch, overhanging eaves, and molded window hoods.

The **Warren County Courthouse** dominates all other buildings on Second Street. Erected in 1827, this grand edifice remained unchanged until it was remodeled in 1959. On this site some highly publicized trials took place, especially in the nineteenth century, including the Carter-Parks murder trial in 1844 (with subsequent hanging) and the Ring Trials, involving fraud and embezzlement by local politicians. The view from the courthouse to the square and Garrett Wall Park is spectacular.

Turn right onto Mansfield Street and walk one block north to Front Street. On the way, take a look at the following:

101 Mansfield: Now the United National Bank, this beautiful structure dates from 1929, just before the Great Depression. Note the decorative relief just below the roofline.

On Front Street, don't miss the following:

83 Front: This is a T-shaped Victorian from the 1880s, with wraparound porch and beveled-glass entrance.

87 Front: Also from the 1880s, this Italianate Victorian features a classical columned porch and central gable peak.

312–314 Front: Note the fluted cast-iron columns on both these houses.

329 Front: Dating from around 1840, this house features a front entrance with sidelights and transom, molded door, and window trim.

You should now be near the spot where you parked your car. If you want to explore further, we recommend walking (or driving) to the end of Prospect Street (walk east on Front Street for a couple of blocks, turn left onto Harwich Street, which becomes Prospect after you cross the Pequest River and Water Street). Here you will find the **Robert Hoops House**, home of the town founder. Now housing the Belvidere Rotary Club, this small one-and-a-half-story building dates from the 1760s and is considered to be one of the town's oldest buildings.

11 ·
RURAL VILLAGES OF THE PAST
Walnford, Allaire, Batsto, and Feltville

❀ DIRECTIONS

Walnford: *Historic Walnford is part of Crosswicks Creek Park in Upper Freehold Township. Take the New Jersey Turnpike south to I-195 east (exit 7A) to Route 539 south (exit 8). Make a right on Walnford Road and follow signs.*

Allaire: *Take the New Jersey Turnpike south to the Garden State Parkway south (at exit 11). Go west on I-195 (exit 98) to first exit (exit 31B) and go east on Route 524. The entrance to Allaire State Park will be on your right.*

Batsto: *From the Garden State Parkway take exit 52. Turn right onto East Greenbush Road and then left at Stage Road and left again at Leektown Road, which will take you to Route 542. Make a right on Route 542 and continue to the entrance gates of Batsto.*

Feltville: *Take the New Jersey Turnpike to exit 14; go west on I-78 to exit 44 and turn left onto Glenside Avenue. Feltville Village is less than a block down the road. Note: if you are traveling east on I-78, make a right onto Glenside Avenue from exit 44.*

❀ INFORMATION

Walnford: Open daily 8 A.M. to 4:30 P.M. Telephone: 609-259-6275. Web site: monmouth countyparks.com/parks/walnford.asp.

Allaire: Open year-round, except during January and February, Monday through Saturday, 10 A.M. to 5 P.M.; Sunday, noon to 5 P.M. Telephone: 732-938-2253. Web site: www.allairevillage.org.

Batsto: Visitor Center open daily, 9 A.M. to 4:30 P.M. (self-guided walking tours are available there); grounds are open from dawn to dusk. As of this writing, the mansion is closed for renovation; check for reopening and guided tours. Telephone: 609-561-3262. Web site: www.Batstovillage.org.

Feltville: You can visit at any time of the year; the few existing buildings are not open to the public (except for the renovated Interpretive Center in the church/general store), but you can walk around them. Parking is available on the premises. Telephone: 908-789-3670. Web site: www.ucnj.org.

❀ New Jersey abounds in small, deserted, and restored (but uninhabited) villages from the past. Though they share similarities in their rural simplicity, their architectural styles and histories are distinctive from one another and vary in age from early colonial to nineteenth century. We have picked four of our favorites that make great day outings. In historical order they are Walnford (dating from 1734), Allaire (1763), Batsto (1766), and Feltville (1840s). They are somewhat spread out, so you might not be able to visit more than one or two at one time. Check your map and available time and enjoy the adventure!

Walnford

Unlike most "restored" villages, Historic Walnford does not represent only a particular period. Instead, the decision was made to interpret the site over its long 250-year history, from its beginnings as a colonial farm village to its development as an important gristmill location in the nineteenth century. Located on the banks of Crosswicks Creek, Walnford was a natural spot for a water-driven mill, and much of its history reflects its busy industry. Your walk will bring you past the gristmill on the banks of the creek and past a charming group of cottages, sheds, and barns, as well as many grassy expanses and lovely old trees. A number of buildings have been restored and are open, including the amazing mill itself and Waln House, the mill owner's residence.

What is today Historic Walnford was in colonial times a plantation developed around the original gristmill. The village dates to 1734. At that time its 180 acres contained not only the gristmill but also a sawmill, fulling mill, blacksmith shop, cooper's shop, the fine brick home and five tenant houses, and assorted farm buildings. There were two fruit orchards, one hundred plowed acres, and twenty-five acres of meadowland. In 1772, Richard Waln, an international merchant trader and owner of a commercial wharf in Philadelphia, purchased the entire village, beginning a family ownership that lasted for two centuries.

Today historians speculate that Waln, a Quaker who sympathized with the British, hoped to have his family safely settled in rural Monmouth County before war broke out. He invested heavily in the village, repairing mills and building himself a large and imposing home. Walnford became his commercial base; he shipped flour, lumber, and farm commodities to Philadelphia, New York City, and beyond. Boats carrying goods could navigate Crosswicks Creek to Philadelphia.

In 1799, Waln's son Nicholas and daughter-in-law Sarah took charge of the many enterprises at Walnford. The village's growth reflected the prosperity of the early federal period in the United States. Five nearby farms were acquired during Nicholas Waln's stewardship, and Walnford became a thirteen-hundred-acre site for increased production of grain, milling, and lumber. By 1848, fifty people lived in Walnford.

As the American West opened up to larger farms and railroad transportation at midcentury, grain production and larger farms overtook the small New Jersey industry. At Walnford the various fields and industries were distributed to the wife and many heirs of Nicholas Waln when he died in 1848. Although his widow and children made efforts to keep the town and farms profitable by mortgaging land and industry, economic changes in American life and a disastrous mill fire destroyed Walnford's prosperity. By the end of the nineteenth century, the sawmill, the blacksmith, and the cooper were gone, and the gristmill worked only for local businesses.

The village soon became the idyllic retreat for a Philadelphia family descended from the Walns. The millpond, once the source of power for the mills, became a romantic setting for water lilies and ornamental flower borders. Although a dairy farm and the gristmill still operated, the setting became primarily a country estate.

The entire site was reduced to forty-eight acres by 1954. When it was sold in 1973 to Edward and Jeanne Mullen, the first owners who were not descendants of the Walns, the new owners had it listed on the National Register of Historic Places and subsequently donated the entire village to the Monmouth County Park System.

A walk through the village, using the self-guiding map, will take you from one interesting spot to the next in a short time. But there is a lot more to see than the exteriors of the buildings: there are demonstrations of milling and exhibits of archaeological finds, as well as wonderful hikes throughout the wooded areas and meadowlands of Walnford.

You will begin your walk at the Corn Crib and the many farm buildings that suggest a working farm, from the production of grain and hogs to the stabling of standard-bred horses.

Nearby is the fully restored 1879 carriage house. It was added to the estate by the widow of Nicholas Waln.

The grove of white pines you come to next was planted in the early twentieth century, when being able to view farm operations was no longer considered necessary. By this time Walnford had become more a country estate than a business proposition.

Waln House, the manorlike, Georgian-style family home, is next on your walk. Note the various changes that have been made over the centuries to the house, including the picket fence and front porch. Nearby, alongside the creek, is the formal garden.

Next is the great gristmill, built in 1872 after fire destroyed the earlier building. Go inside for a careful and fascinating look at how a stone mill operated. You'll also see traces of the original mill, which stood on the opposite side of the creek.

Nearby are a few remains of the eighteenth-century tenant houses that once dotted the area next to the mill. Foundations of the smokehouse and blacksmith shop are in the same vicinity.

From here you will enter the meadows and farm lanes of Walnford, as well as the cow pasture and the cow barn, built in the early twentieth century and now housing a variety of programs and events. From this spot we recommend that you take advantage of the picturesque scenery to walk through the landscape that surrounds the village.

Walnford's history can be seen as typical of the small family-owned American villages that dotted the area beginning in the colonial era, adapting to the changing economic and cultural movements of the times. Fortunately, a few of them, such as Walnford, were saved for us to experience.

Allaire

Allaire, which was originally built around a bustling iron forge called the Williamsburg Forge, has a long history beginning around 1763. By 1814 this picturesque spot in Monmouth County had become a vibrant and very busy bog-iron center, producing iron cauldrons, pots, pipes, stoves, and other objects.

By 1822 a man named Benjamin Howell joined forces with a brass founder named James Allaire to establish the Howell Works on the site. They employed some four hundred people in bog-iron mining and refining. (Bog iron is produced by decaying vegetation.) By 1837 the community contained about sixty buildings. The village was a thriving success until the opening of the American West introduced higher-grade iron ore and improved smelting systems. By midcentury Allaire's forge was closed down, and shortly thereafter the village was abandoned.

Through the generosity of the twentieth-century owner, Mrs. Arthur Brisbane, and the help of the Boy Scouts and other local organizations, the empty village and its surrounding woodlands and marshes were saved.

Strolling among the well-tended buildings and green lawns of the empty village we feel as though we have jumped back in time to the mid-nineteenth century. But as we walk through the bucolic and picturesque village today, we have to imagine the incredible noise (the iron smelter roared day and night) and the overwhelming odor and heavy, acrid smoke caused by the charcoal pits that made the fuel for the furnace. Also in operation, and providing both noise and pollution, were a sawmill, a gristmill, a blacksmith shop, and a screw factory, which employed the children of the village. Many of the workers toiling at these hard and grimy jobs were paid only in scrip, which they then spent in the several company stores of the village.

Though it is difficult to imagine these hard conditions, a visit to Allaire creates an unusually accurate sense of a nineteenth-century company town. There is also a narrow-gauge steam train, the Pine Creek Railroad, running at Allaire; its desolate whistle adds to the ambience of the past.

You will find the buildings at Allaire surprisingly far apart. Only about twenty of the original sixty structures still exist. Their restoration is not in the least hokey: each building has been carefully refurbished. Most are closed, though the General Store is open for visitors when the village itself is open. If you call for information you will find that many events are scheduled that demonstrate crafts and material culture of the past, such as cider making, candle dipping, and quilting. Also, the steam train takes riders on a brief trip.

Begin your walk at the entrance to Allaire. You'll find a two-story brick building, now the Information Center. This has the distinction of being the last remaining of the row houses built by Allaire for his workers in the 1830s. Here you can pick up a self-guiding map or take an official tour if you prefer.

The next building is the tiny foreman's cottage, dating to 1827. Note its simple and charming style. It was the first brick structure built in the village. With just one room on each of its one and a half stories, it is now furnished with vintage country pieces.

Nearby is the entrance to the adjacent woodlands, with the site of the original sawmill. In the grinding mill and screw factory, the iron items produced in the village were ground and polished. Note the gristmill and blacksmith shop, which date to the 1830s. Continue on your walk and you'll find the old bakery; the upstairs of this building housed the village schoolroom. James Allaire paid for the school from his own pocket, we are told.

Perhaps the oldest building of all is the manager's house (circa 1750). This farmhouse is a mustard-colored frame house standing also at one and a half stories. Recently restored, it houses early American antiques.

The one business that is functioning whenever the village is open to visitors is the General Store. Filled with all kinds of items and goodies, this emporium reminds us of the importance of the old-fashioned community store. The carpentry shop and enameling building are next along the path. In the enameling building you'll find exhibits of the various crafts practiced in Allaire's heyday.

Soon you'll come to the furnace stack, the most historically important of the sites at Allaire, as this is the last remaining iron furnace in the state. The furnace was powered by a waterwheel, but today only the stack remains. The dormitory for the ironworkers (one of the original buildings at the site) is nearby. Mr. Allaire himself lived there with his workers—certainly an unlikely situation for a factory owner today. The carriage house, hay barn, and cattle barns are next as you continue on the path through the village.

And finally you will come to the charming Christ Church, an Episcopalian church built in the 1830s. (Some of the timber used in its construction dates back to an even earlier structure.)

There are foundations and remains of other buildings at Allaire, and the interested walker can delve more deeply into the history and architecture of this quintessentially American small town by visiting the library and exhibits.

Batsto

The Historic Museum Village of Batsto comes as somewhat of a surprise. Set in the deeply wooded Wharton State Park of the Pine Barrens, it is thoroughly unlike the tourist attractions that pervade the region at the nearby coastline. The state has done a fine job of retaining and protecting the village's rustic charm, the wide-open spaces, and the Mullica River that rushes over the dam that powered the forge. It is also a surprise to find, in the midst of this country village of the past, an imposing Victorian mansion. Once the home of the ironmaster William Richards, and later of Joseph Wharton, an industrialist from Philadelphia who owned almost all the area in the 1870s, it is an unexpectedly grand house, complete with a fanciful tower.

Batsto was founded in 1766 by Charles Read of Burlington, New Jersey. It was Read who envisaged a thriving industry developing from the chunks of bog iron that were accessible in the wetlands and creek beds of the area. The reddish material had been used only for face paint by the Leni-Lenape Indians, who had hunted and fished in the area even after European colonists

Batsto Village

built small settlements along the rivers. Read recognized the deposits and decided to try smelting them at a forge to make iron.

The ironworks thrived, and by the time of the Revolutionary War, Batsto had become a major arsenal and supplier of iron for the Continental Army.

Batsto changed hands several times over the following years. In 1786 it was sold yet again, this time to William Richards, whose family continued to own it for a century. It was the Richards family who constructed most of the village buildings we see today, as well as the original mansion that is still the centerpiece of the village.

Batsto's heyday was soon to end, however, as coal was discovered in nearby Pennsylvania, making the bog-iron industry obsolete. In 1876 Joseph Wharton purchased the remains of the then-deserted village and surroundings for fourteen thousand dollars. One of his main accomplishments was refurbishing and expanding the mansion. (He also added several outbuildings in the village.)

In 1954 the state acquired the Wharton tract (about one hundred thousand acres) and began the village's restoration as a historic site. Today this unusually well kept lakeside village gives the walker a realistic picture of life in a nineteenth-century rural town. You can see and hear the water rushing over the dam as you cross the little bridge in the center of the village. The interiors of several of the buildings are open to the public, including the great mansion (though, as of this writing, it is temporarily closed for restoration).

Batsto's many historic buildings and sites offer an intimate glimpse at life in the region from the 1760s to the mid- to late nineteenth century. You can visit the general store and post office (c. 1847), gristmill (c. 1828), blacksmith shop (c. 1850), and sawmill (c. 1882).

The mansion, of course, is the town's most glamorous structure. The building that you see today bears little resemblance to the earlier, more rugged residence of the Richards family. Wharton changed its appearance to the Italianate architectural style, which was popular at the time. He remodeled the interior and added porches, a new façade, and the four-storied tower. (The tower was not only decorative; it served as a fire lookout and housed a water cistern to be used, just in case.)

The guided tour, which lasts about an hour, takes you through the thirty-two-room mansion (don't miss the unusual fireback, which dates to colonial times), as well as the carriage house, blacksmith shop, and gristmill. On your own you can visit several other sites including craft cottages (recently restored), the sawmill, the post office, and the ruins of the iron furnace.

Feltville

There is much more to discover in the vast Watchung Reservation than you might expect. In fact, within these two thousand acres of woodlands, trails, and wildflowers is an intriguing and little-known site, the remains of an abandoned mid-nineteenth-century village known as Feltville. When we first came here we were surprised to find—tucked away amid the trees on a bluff overlooking a brook—a handful of houses that still looked habitable. Scattered along a winding stretch of road, they seemed to us mostly discarded and forlorn. Some had rustic Adirondack-style porches, appearing almost resortlike. We knew at once there had to be an interesting story behind these façades.

Feltville was apparently founded on utopian principles: to provide an ideal and self-sufficient and controlled environment for the improvement of the lives of its inhabitants. What makes this abandoned village especially interesting to us today is that it is one of the only (and the only one we could find) nineteenth-century utopian communities still standing in New Jersey. The better-known Phalanx, near Red Hook, for example, has completely vanished.

In 1845 David Felt, a successful printer and stationery dealer from New York City, bought 760 acres of land in this secluded area. Here "the King" (as he was known by his employees) established the mill town of Feltville for the manufacture of paper and books. Wishing to create a contained community where his workers would both work and live, he built—in addition to the paper mill and a gristmill—cottages and dormitories, a school, a church, several stores, and even a circulating library ("to improve their minds," he said). Concerned about the workers' spiritual well-being, he even hired an outside Unitarian minister, a man named Austin Craig, who later founded Antioch College in Ohio. For all Felt's lofty ideals and apparent benevolence, he ruled with an iron hand: he absolutely required that his workers live on the premises, where he could control their daily routines —even sounding a bell when he felt they should retire for the evening!

For fifteen years Feltville thrived, until for reasons still unclear Felt sold the community and left town forever. After several takeovers from one owner to the next, including a manufacturer of patent medicines known as the "Sasparilla King," the town was transformed into a summer resort and more attractively renamed Glenside Park. It was at this point, in the 1880s, that porches and dormer roofs were added to existing dwellings, changing their simple Colonial look into something more fanciful and Victorian.

The property was eventually bought by the county for parkland. Today its 120 acres have become the site of something called "Operation Archaeology," a Union County program that introduces historical archaeology to young students, giving them hands-on field experience. Montclair University has also been carrying out on-site excavations to examine the life of the town and its inhabitants.

Though Feltville once had as many as thirty-five houses and structures, only ten survive; of these, three are presently occupied. Because the structures are fragile, visitors are not allowed to walk up onto porches, except in the case of the recently refurbished Interpretive Center in the Church/ Store Building. Further restoration of existing buildings in the park is now under way.

The park offers a self-guided walking tour and descriptive brochure (available at the Interpretive Center); the recommended one-mile walk begins and ends at the parking lot off Glenside Avenue. (Note that a one-room schoolhouse once stood where you now park your car.) As you walk through this now-quiet site, you can try to imagine its past, when it was a lively and industrious place, bustling with activity.

From the parking lot walk down Cataract Hollow Road; if you want to visit the village cemetery first (as suggested in the brochure), make a left at the first trail crossing and wind your way down the ravine, following the signs. (You can also save exploring the cemetery until the end of your walk.) Here members of the Willcocks family are buried. Peter Willcocks, the area's first European settler, came here before the Revolutionary War and built a dam across Blue Brook and a sawmill; Felt bought his land from Willcocks's descendants. Of the five tombstones still standing, only one (at the far right) is original.

Retrace your steps up to Cataract Hollow Road, turn left, and walk to the first house. This rather large building (it was originally much smaller) served as Felt's business office. Walk to the next building down the road. Recently restored, this was once the general store and church and now serves as the Interpretive Center. We are told that the steeple was added well after the building was used as a church.

Continue along the road as it winds around, and you'll come upon a group of four houses. These were used by the workers and their families. Each house was divided up to accommodate as many as four families, with separate entrances. After the village became a resort, the houses were converted into single units.

Walk farther along the road until you see a bridle trail, along a stone wall; go down the trail until you reach Blue Brook, the site of the former mill and the center of activity in Feltville. (In the era of Glenside Park, the mill was used as a stable for cattle.) Go back up to the road, turn left, and you'll see three little cottages. Apparently these smaller dwellings accommodated couples who had no children.

Your last stop is Masker's Barn, at the end of Cataract Hollow Road. This building, dating from the 1880s, was used as a barn for the horses that transported resort guests; today it houses Operation Archeology (whose dig site is nearby). Retrace your steps and walk back to the parking lot.

12·
A FANCIFUL VICTORIAN SEASIDE RESORT

Cape May

❀ DIRECTIONS

Take the Garden State Parkway to its end and follow signs.

❀ INFORMATION

Visit in the off-season if you can, as Cape May is crowded in warm weather. Pick up a map at the Welcome Center (407 Lafayette Street). A map is also available at the head of Washington Street at an information booth. Telephone the Welcome Center for information and events: 609-884-5404. Web site: www.capemaymac.org.

❀ Cape May is a Victorian resort that is well known to tourists and vacationers. It is filled with charming homes, historic buildings, horse-drawn vehicles, gaslights, and other accoutrements of the successful resort. In the off-season, you will find it a delight, despite a few too many wreaths on doors and other twenty-first-century ideas of Victoriana. But don't be put off; the town is actually a treasure trove of true nineteenth-century gingerbread architectural pleasures and is a great place to walk from street to street to ocean. Not far from the town itself are a number of additional sites of historical and architectural interest, so a visit to Cape May can include a variety of experiences, including two terrific lighthouses and a reconstructed village.

It is an interesting fact that Cape May was one of our nation's first resorts; it became a summer getaway before the Revolutionary War. (A newspaper ad in 1766 recommends it.) By 1819, when the first steamship connection from Philadelphia was inaugurated, it was already a fashionable place to vacation. Train service began in 1830. By the 1840s daily ships were arriving. People flocked to the seaside village with its charming streets and beaches. Many stayed in private homes and boardinghouses,

Cape May

but by the mid-nineteenth century great hotels were built, including the three-thousand-room Mount Vernon (then the world's largest hotel), which burned down in 1856. Fires have played a continuing role of destruction in Cape May; most of the buildings were built in 1878, following another major conflagration.

Cape May became known as the "playground of presidents," including Abraham Lincoln (still a congressman in 1849), Franklin Pierce in 1855, James Buchanan in 1858, Ulysses S. Grant in 1873, and Chester A. Arthur in 1893. President Benjamin Harrison used Cape May's Congress Hall Hotel as his summer White House in 1890 and 1891. Other illustrious visitors included Senator Henry Clay (1847) and John Philip Sousa, whose "Congress Hall March" paid tribute to the big hotel. Among the many highlights of a vacation in fashionable Cape May was an auto race early in the twentieth century between Henry Ford, Louis Chevrolet, and Alexander Christy. (A wave broke over Ford's car, ruining his chances.) Curiously, Cape May owes its architectural preservation to the growth of Atlantic City; the new resort cast Cape May into decline, luring visitors and money to the more northern town. Cape May was left to its Victorian charm and in the last decades has become almost overwhelmed by its own popularity. Numerous events are held here, including Civil War reenactments; telephone the Welcome Center for dates.

Wherever you choose to walk in Cape May, you'll find houses and hotels of architectural interest. You can get a self-guided-tour map at the Welcome Center, which will point you in the direction of notable buildings, including the following:

Allen Victorian House (1863), 720 Washington Street, an imposing Italianate villa. This elegant frame building, with cupola and extended one-story porch, is among the state's most impressive nineteenth-century seaside houses.

The **Chalfonte Hotel** (1875), on the northwest corner of Howard and Sewell streets, is a three-storied structure with belvedere and elaborate two-story porches. It is the oldest and most decorative existing hotel in town. Originally built as a private residence, it was later converted to a hotel.

The **Emlen Physick House** (1879), 1048 Washington Street, is a stick-style house designed by the architect Frank Furness. (Stick-style houses have irregular shapes, porches, and high, steep roofs.) A fine example of Victoriana, it features dormers, gables, mansards, and a one-story arcaded porch. It is now a museum. Telephone: 609-894-5404.

Cook's Villa (1879), 9 Perry Street, was also designed by Frank Furness, as well as by George Hewitt. This frame Victorian includes a mansard roof, dormers, and two-story porches decorated with tiles.

Congress Hall Hotel (1879), on Beach Drive between Congress Place and Perry Street, was built by architect J. F. Meyer in a brick L shape. It features a three-story verandah, a mansard roof, and many bays. President Benjamin Harrison had his executive offices here in 1891.

Stockton Cottage (1872), 26 Gurrey Street, is the best preserved of eight identical cottages designed by Stephen Button. Here you'll see a gable roof, elaborate porch, and balustraded deck.

The **Windward House**, 24 Jackson Street, is a lovely Edwardian home known for its stained and beveled glass.

The Abbey, at Columbia Avenue and Gurney Street, is a 1869 Gothic Revival mansion with stained glass and a sixty-foot tower.

And don't miss the myriad gingerbread houses along practically every street in town.

Just outside town are several additional sites of historical and architectural interest.

❈ IN THE VICINITY

Historic Cold Spring Village

DIRECTIONS: *From Cape May take Route 109 north to Route 9.*

INFORMATION: Telephone: 609-898-2300. Web site: www.hesv.org.

Historic Cold Spring Village is an outdoor living-history museum that interprets farm and domestic life of the nineteenth century. It is a particularly good place to take children, as there are twenty-five restored historic buildings and all kinds of crafts, animals, horses, and buggies, as well as a full-costumed cast of characters to bring the place to life. If reconstructed historic sites appeal to you and your family, this is a very complete and interesting one. Among its many enterprises are a blacksmith at work, a leather shop, a jail, a bookbinder, and a cobbler. Here, too, you can get a self-guiding map.

13·
AN EIGHTEENTH-CENTURY MORAVIAN VILLAGE BUILT OF STONE

Hope

❀ **DIRECTIONS**

Take I-80 west to Route 521 south (exit 12) and follow signs for about two miles.

❀ **INFORMATION**

Although you can visit Hope year-round, it is especially inviting in spring and autumn—the fall colors of the surrounding countryside can be truly magnificent. You can take your own self-guided tour (a brochure with complete listings and map is available at the Inn at Millrace Pond, the former Moravian gristmill). Guided tours are also offered from April through November, on the first and second Saturday of the month. Telephone: 908-459-9177 or 908-459-4884.

❀ The town and architecture of Hope, with its Moravian heritage, has an intriguing history and is still a vibrant community. Little has changed since its Moravian beginnings in the mid-eighteenth century, and the explorer can still visit many of the same buildings, as well as the gristmill and cemetery.

As you will note on your walk through Hope, Moravian architecture featured simplicity in both style and structure. Limestone, readily available in the area, was the most common building material, with cut stone used only in corners and around doors and windows. Red-brick and stone arches over windows and doors were characteristic adornments, as were herringbone doors and red-brick interior chimneys. The steeply pitched roofs, which had been made of tiles or wood shingle in earlier days, appeared in slate during the eighteenth century, at the time Hope was founded.

The Moravians were a pious, hardworking religious sect from Moravia and Bohemia in Central Europe. Their roots date to the fifteenth century, well before Martin Luther, when the followers of John Hus of Moravia (leader of a revolt against the Catholic Church) had to flee to the mountains; there they created their sect. Groups of Moravians arrived in America beginning around 1735 to escape persecution. In 1768, after moving to different locations, they were offered one thousand acres by Samuel Green in western New Jersey, for which they paid one thousand pounds sterling.

A few years later the community was fully developed, becoming one of the first planned communities in America. It included a large, stone gristmill (at the foot of High Street and one of the town's earliest structures); the limestone Gemeinhaus (on the corner of Union and High streets), which started as a community center and later served as a church, a courthouse, and finally a bank; residences; a tavern; a school; a distillery; and numerous other structures. Some 150 people lived here, in log cabins, stone houses, and communal arrangements.

During the Revolutionary War, the Moravians, who were conscientious objectors, did not serve but provided nursing care for wounded American soldiers. A severe epidemic of smallpox virtually destroyed the thriving community in 1799, reducing its population by half. The Moravians who were left sold the community of Hope for forty-eight thousand dollars and moved west to Bethlehem, Pennsylvania. Hope then became a village of farmers; no industry came here, due to the town's remoteness and lack of transportation facilities. In 1973 Hope was entered into the State and National Register of Historic Places to preserve its historical integrity.

A walk through this uncommercial historic village is a treat for architecture buffs, too. Note some of the features typical of Moravian architecture: red-brick window arches and chimneys, limestone window arches, economical use of cut stone, deeply pitched roofs, and two-story attics.

Although Hope is a small village within just a few blocks, there are more than thirty sites to see, all clearly indicated in the village brochure. In case you cannot see every one of them, here are some highlights not to be missed:

Begin your circular walk at the foot of High Street, where you'll find the gristmill, now the **Inn at Millrace Pond**. Dating from 1769–1770, the gristmill is the oldest building in the village; it was used during the Revolutionary War to grind grain for Washington's troops.

The **Moravian Distillery** (Millbrook Road), built in 1775, was the site of rye-whiskey and beer production, with the brewmaster and his family occupying the second floor.

The oldest remaining stone residence (1775–1776) is the quaint **Farm Manager's House and Barn** on Walnut Street. The barn is one of two original Moravian barns to be found here, the other being Nicolaus Barn, on the corner of Cedar and Hickory streets. Look for the sites of two log cabins on Walnut Street once occupied by two early settlers in Hope, Peter Worbass (first manager of the community) and Samuel Green. It is presumed that the cellar of the present house was part of Worbass's 1769 cabin.

The old **Moravian Log Tavern** on Walnut Street is where George Washington apparently dined with his troops in 1782. In the mid-1800s a church was built here. The present building was restored in the 1950s as a community center.

The **Stephen Nicolaus House** on Hickory Street, built in 1775–1776, was the second-oldest stone house of the village. Notice the original double-herringbone doors and latches, a typical feature of Moravian architecture. The basement of this house became Hope's first public school in the early 1800s.

Around the corner on High Street are a 1780 Moravian house and the 1832 **Canal Era House**, now a conference center.

Next to the Canal Era House is **Saint John's United Methodist Church**, dating from 1876, well after the Moravian era. (The original, built in 1832, had to be replaced when the congregation outgrew it.) Note the foyer with its decorative fleur-de-lis pattern stencil.

Behind the church is the 1773 **Moravian Cemetery**, which contains sixty-two graves, all very simple and plain. On each rectangular stone slab you can read the deceased's name, birth and death dates, and a number that corresponds to the list of burials in the Moravian Archives at Bethlehem. Those buried here all died between 1773 and 1808.

Saint Luke's Episcopal Church on Hickory Street was built in 1832 of native limestone. Gothic Revival in style, it features an interior spiral staircase, which is said to have been based on a design by Sir Christopher Wren.

The **Gemeinhaus** on the corner of High Street and Route 519, dating from 1781, was certainly one of the most important structures in the early history of Hope. Here the Moravian community worshiped. Men and women used separate staircases that led to the church room on the second floor. On the first floor were the pastor's living quarters, as well as a small school for boys. Later, in 1824, the building was used as the county courthouse, then as an inn and, since 1911, as a bank.

Next to the Gemeinhaus, farther down the road, are more Moravian houses dating from 1780 to 1800. Across the street is the **Single Sisters School**, dating from 1803. The last structure built by the Moravians in Hope, it housed the colony's unmarried women, then became a girls' school, a florist shop, and finally an office building.

The **Long House**, near corner of High and Walnut streets, is an original Moravian stone structure dating from about 1777 (some parts were added later on). Over the years, it, too, has been used for many different things: confectionary stores, butcher shop, and post office. Today it contains shops, offices, and exhibition space. Right next to it is the **Hope Historical Society Museum**, a building that dates from the early 1800s and was probably the bridge tollhouse. The museum is open on weekends during the summer.

Finally, don't miss the so-called **Moravian Bridge** across High Street, a stone bridge actually built after the Moravians left, between 1810 and 1820.

14 ·
ARCHITECTURAL PLEASURES
IN A HISTORIC TOWN SETTING

Perth Amboy

✿ DIRECTIONS

*Take the New Jersey Turnpike south to the Garden State Parkway south (exit 11) to exit 129
and New Brunswick Avenue. Make a left on New Brunswick into the center of town. Turn
right on State Street and then left on Market Street to get to the town square.*

✿ This historic town is at the mouth of the Raritan River just across Arthur
Kill from Staten Island. Founded in 1683, its name honors the Earl of Perth;
it was settled by Scots and served as capital of East Jersey from 1686 to 1702.
In 1718 it became the first incorporated municipality in the colony. In the
early nineteenth century Perth Amboy was a fashionable resort, as well as a
center for the oyster industry and, subsequently, a busy center of manufacture for copper, bricks, and terra-cotta. (The Raritan Copper Works building on Elm and Market streets is listed on the Historic Register of the state
of New Jersey.)

Today Perth Amboy is a bustling commercial hub with a multicultural
population. A number of historic buildings have been preserved from its
more glamorous past, and we found them well worth a visit.

At the town square at the intersection of Market Street and High Street
some of the architecturally interesting sites to see are the following:

City Hall, the oldest public building in continuous use in the nation, and the
small **Surveyor's Office** next door: Here at the City Hall the Bill of Rights
was ratified for the first time. Built in 1713, the whitewashed brick building is
an imposing edifice in Colonial style.

The **First Presbyterian Church** (also on the square) was built in 1900. It is
an interesting Gothic Revival structure with surprising stepped rooflines.
Houses around the square also date to the eighteenth and nineteenth centuries. Many of them have been updated.

Walk south on High Street, turn right at Harrison Place, and then left at Kearny Avenue. **Proprietary House** at 149 Kearny Avenue is an imposing official royal governor's house built in the 1760s. This is a white-brick Georgian mansion, which has had an eclectic past (as a rooming house, a resort hotel, a retirement home, etc.) in addition to its illustrious beginnings. But it is being renovated as a historic site and museum, and nowadays it even offers candle-lit teas on some afternoons. Its style is known today as Palladian Villa (or High Georgian), and it an example of colonial architecture at its most imposing. If you visit, you will see original decorative moldings and a few carefully reconstructed interiors.

Additional sites in Perth Amboy include the tiny four-room house called **Kearny Cottage** (63 Catalpa Street), which dates to 1780; the cantilevered **Outerbridge Crossing** to Staten Island (a graceful 1928 construction); **Saint Peter's Episcopal Church** (at Rector and Gordon streets), an 1849 Gothic Revival structure; and down on the picturesque waterfront the old **United States Naval Armory Building** of 1929.

15·
SKYLANDS

A Deliberately "Aged" Mansion by
John Russell Pope, Ringwood

❀ DIRECTIONS

Take I-287 to exit 57, then take Skyland Drive north to Ringwood State Park. Follow signs to Skylands on Morris Road.

❀ INFORMATION

Open May through October, Tuesday through Sunday, 10 A.M. to 4 P.M. Telephone: 973-962-9534. Web site: www.njbg.org.

❀ Skylands is a forty-four-room mansion built as a summer home for Clarence McKenzie Lewis. It sits near the entrance to one of the most beautiful botanical and formal gardens in the state. Of particular interest to architecture buffs is the English manor house in the Jacobean style, designed by the architect John Russell Pope in 1924.

John Russell Pope (1874–1937) was an American architect of both public and private buildings. From his establishment of an architectural firm in New York City in 1900, he was a leading professional of classical taste and elegance. Among his celebrated designs were the Lincoln Memorial and the National Gallery of Art in Washington, D.C. But he also designed many country residences.

Skylands was deliberately built to look "aged." Thus, we see a sagging roof, weathered stone façade, and metal drainpipes that have been aged to look like old copper. It has stained-glass windows and unusual interior wood paneling—all imported from Europe—and it has a glorious garden setting.

AND KEEP IN MIND . . .

16 • Dickinson House: A Patterned Brick House in Alloway Township

DIRECTIONS: *Take the New Jersey Turnpike to exit 2A, then go south on Route 540 to Alloway. Dickinson House is on Brickyard Road at the junction of Route 45 and Bassett Road.*

Patterned brick was a style used on houses in the colonial era in certain sections of the state. These dwellings were typical of Salem County and generally date to the 1790s, but the origins of the style are even older. Many Quakers came to this region in the 1670s, bringing with them their brick-building traditions. And the clay soil was ideal for brick making here.

The Quakers' tall, narrow buildings had few windows, steep gabled roofs, and austere design, which suited the Quaker taste for simplicity. But one aspect of the style was strikingly decorative: colored bricks in often zigzagging patterns (sometimes including the owner's initials and the date of the house) adorned the windowless, gabled side façades. The builders also created a checkerboard pattern, combining blue bricks (made by longer burning) with traditional red bricks in geometric patterns. Dickinson house is a typically decorative example of the style; there are several others in the same region.

17 • A Picturesque Railroad Station, Tenafly

DIRECTIONS: *From New York City take the George Washington Bridge to the Palisades Parkway north to exit 1. Turn right onto Route 9W (north), then turn left at Clinton Avenue (Tenafly) and go all the way down the hill to the center of town. Turn right on West Railroad Avenue. The station will be on your right.*

INFORMATION: The station is, as of this writing, a restaurant called Cafe Angelique. Telephone: 201-541-1010.

One of the most delightful buildings we've discovered in suburban Bergen County is the Tenafly Railroad Station right in the center of town. This local landmark is in the decorative High Victorian Gothic Revival style and dates to the 1870s. It was designed by a local architect named Daniel T. Atwood and largely financed by local citizens, who wanted a "suitable gateway" for their community. The fanciful stone structure has a steeply pitched roof, as well as eaves and gables and a weather vane on top of its steeple. In the time since it served as a railroad station (many years ago), it has housed a series of shops and restaurants. Be sure to check out the interior too, whether or not you plan to eat in the cafe.

18 • Buccleigh: A Georgian Mansion, New Brunswick

DIRECTIONS: *Buccleigh is inside the Rutgers University Campus, New Brunswick. Take the New Jersey Turnpike south to exit 9 and take Route 18 west to Route 27 west into New Brunswick. Make a right on Easton Avenue. The mansion is set in Buccleigh Park.*

INFORMATION: Telephone: 732-745-5094.

Buccleigh is an elegant Georgian mansion in a lovely garden within the Rutgers University campus. Originally known as White House Farm, it was built in 1774, confiscated by the Americans in 1776, occupied by the British in 1777, and then visited and slept in by George Washington, as well as John Hancock and Alexander Hamilton, among other famous patriots. An excellent example of Georgian elegance, it has a great fan window on the top floor.

19 • The Ruins of Undercliff: "Bloomer's Beach," Englewood

DIRECTIONS: *From New York City take the George Washington Bridge to the Palisades Parkway north to exit 1. Bear left after the exit ramp and go down the steep (but wide) Henry Hudson Drive. Follow the signs to the Englewood Boat Basin, where you can park your car, preferably at the northern end of the huge parking lot, past playgrounds, picnic areas, and fishing docks. Walk north (with the river on your right) to find the footpath along the water. Undercliff was located in this area.*

Here, just beyond the Englewood Boat Basin (walking north), are the ruins of a once-bustling 1930s bathhouse. Take the shore path to find "Bloomer's Beach." These roofless stone ruins are the remains of a grand structure (which can be seen in old photographs) with repeated arched windows and doorways and imposing steps up from the shoreline. It is hard to imagine

Ruins of Undercliff on the Hudson, Englewood Cliffs

that the Hudson River was once a popular bathing destination, but these rather extensive ruins are evocative of a glamorous era.

20 • The Ruins of Long Pond, Hewitt

DIRECTIONS: *The ruins of Long Pond are located on Route 511, two miles east of Greenwood Lake, in the hamlet of Hewitt. Take I-287 to exit 57 and follow Skyline Drive to its end. At the intersection of Route 511 (Greenwood Lake Turnpike) turn right (onto 511) and go about six or seven miles (around Wanaque Reservoir and Monksville Reservoir dam). After Monksville Reservoir causeway you'll find the Long Pond Ironworks Visitor Center on your right.*

If ruins intrigue you, this National Historic Landmark is a fascinating place to visit. When you reach the tiny hamlet of Old Hewitt, look for the Visitor Center/Museum (formerly the Olde Country Store) right by the side of Route 511. It lies directly across the street from the Hewitt Methodist Church, a picturesque structure dating from 1895. Here you can pick up the walking guide to the 175-acre Long Pond Ironworks Historic District, which includes a recommended one-mile loop with stops along the way. (Since several of the structures shown on that map are now gone—or have yet to be unearthed—you will have to use your imagination.) You'll follow a rustic trail, not always clearly marked, as you wind your way through somewhat rugged, hilly, woodsy terrain dotted with ruins still being excavated and restored. This is a fascinating archeological site, where you can wander freely about the grounds to discover crumbling foundations of cold cellars and the remains of old furnaces and dilapidated stores, houses, and dormitories that once housed workers.

In its heyday, Long Pond included the workers' village as well as the ironworks themselves—furnaces, waterwheel, and forges, strategically placed near the Wanaque River. Note that some of the houses now found in the village were brought in from other locations, after the Monksville Reservoir was flooded in the 1980s. An early-twentieth-century sawmill and ice house were added after the iron industry gave way to other enterprises such as ice harvesting, lumbering, and farming.

From the Visitor Center you can follow a wood-chip path that leads you to the first group of historic houses, including two old farmhouses. Continue to the large brook-side Stone Double House, perhaps the oldest in the village, dating from 1760; if you look to your left you can see ruins of an ice-pond dam. Take the wooden bridge across the river to the central section of the village. If you pursue the trail on your left, you'll see a variety of ruins

Ruins of Long Pond, Hewitt

and foundations; straight ahead at the crossroads is the Manager's House, clearly a more upscale dwelling than most.

If you turn right at the crossroads and follow Furnace Road, you'll come to the most interesting section of this walk. Here beyond an open grassy area are the remains of three iron furnaces built between 1766 and 1865. The oldest was about twenty-five feet high and produced iron during the Revolution; the stone walls you see are the foundations for the furnace's casting and wheelhouse. The other two were built during the Civil War; apparently reaching a height of sixty-five feet, the one to the north, oddly known as "Lucy" by the workers, was the last of the Long Pond furnaces to shut down, in 1882.

Continue past this last furnace to two waterwheels that harnessed the river to power the furnaces; follow the short uphill trail to the stone raceway that conducted the water to the waterwheel. A dirt road takes you from here to the remains of the Company Store, from which you follow Furnace Road back to the Visitor Center to complete your loop. Before leaving Long Pond don't miss the museum, with its various artifacts and displays of life here.

21 • A Riverside Mill and Historic Village, Clinton

DIRECTIONS: *The Red Mill (the centerpiece of the Red Mill Museum Village) is located on Main Street, in downtown Clinton. Take I-78 west to exit 15 and follow signs to Clinton. Turn right onto West Main Street, then left at Clinton House. Just beyond you'll see the entrance to the Museum Village and the unmistakable Red Mill.*

The Red Mill, in the heart of Historic Clinton, is like no other mill we've come across. Set in idyllic splendor along a rushing waterfall on the banks of the Raritan River, it is delightfully asymmetrical in shape and brilliant in color. Its one-of-a-kind, eclectic look evolved over many years and under many owners, with parts being added and reconfigured, from the time it was originally built as a much smaller and simpler—and probably not even red—structure in 1810.

The mill is part of a ten-acre stretch along the river known as the Red Mill Museum Village, and it is listed on the National Register of Historic Places. The village, created around the mill in the early 1960s, also includes towering limestone cliffs and a quarry, as well as several structures—among them, a blacksmith shop, schoolhouse, and log cabin—scattered about the

The Red Mill, Clinton

grassy expanse. Some of the buildings were brought here from other locations; others—the more recent ones—were actually built on-site.

In its early days the mill was used only for processing wool. Over the following one hundred years it was used in a variety of ways, including grist milling, plaster grinding, graphite processing, pumping water, and generating electricity. As its functions expanded, the mill's architectural appearance inevitably changed. For example, the eye-catching roofline that makes this structure so special was extended in 1908, no doubt for practical reasons, to accommodate some equipment or machinery.

Today the mill functions as a museum exhibiting everything from farm equipment and tools to antique quilts. We especially enjoyed looking at its waterwheel as it churned away, making its inimitable creaking sounds. And, of course, the view of the dramatic waterfall is irresistible.

We recommend a walk through the village (a self-guided tour is available at the entrance to the mill), to explore the various structures, which are interesting historically and also architecturally. Walk on and you'll come to a picturesque iron bridge (built in 1870); it connects to a second mill, a large building made of limestone from the quarry. Dating from the 1830s, it also operated in various ways—at one point, even as a sausage factory!

At present it houses the Hunterdon Museum of Art, and it has also been placed on the National Register of Historic Places.

22 • A Louis Kahn Icon: The "Trenton" Bathhouse, Ewing

DIRECTIONS: *Take the New Jersey Turnpike south to I-195 west (exit 7A) to Route 29, turning right (toward New Hope). Turn right off Route 29 at West Upper Ferry Road. Continue through the town of Ewing to the corner of Parkway Avenue. Turn right and you'll see a sign on the right for the Jewish Community Center.*

INFORMATION: If you want to see the interior, ask the staff at the Community Center. Telephone: 609-989-6545. Web site: http://home.mindspring.com/~kahnpage/bathhouse/.

Louis Kahn designed this unusual structure in the middle of his illustrious career. Kahn said, "From this came a generative force which is recognizable in every building which I have done since." He was talking about the "Trenton" bathhouse, a cruciform-shaped concrete-block group of four separate windowless pavilions surrounding an open atrium. Each of the four sections is topped by a raised, wooden, truncated pyramid-shaped roof, which appears to float above the walls, allowing natural light to illuminate the interior. Built in 1955, this complex was supposed to be part of a much larger project (never realized), and it represents Kahn's exploration of geometric forms and proportional relationships, as well as his interest in the design of ancient ruins.

You can visit this unusual building, which is in need of renovation due to the use of substandard materials, invading moisture, and the passage of time. However, for anyone who is interested in the history of twentieth-century American architecture, it is worth seeing. If you go in the summer, you'll find a day camp with a pool at the site, and you can easily see the interior.

DELAWARE AND PENNSYLVANIA

1·
FROM GEORGIAN BRICK
TO GOTHIC REVIVAL

The Historic River Town of New Castle, Delaware

❀ DIRECTIONS

New Castle is six miles from Wilmington and about three miles from exit 1 on the New Jersey Turnpike. From New Jersey cross the Delaware Memorial Bridge and exit onto Route 9 south; stay in the leftmost lane, which will take you straight into the Historic District.

❀ INFORMATION

For information concerning times that various houses are open, tours, fees, or other information telephone the New Castle Historic Society: 302-322-2794. George Read House (where you can also pick up a self-guided walking tour and map) is located on The Strand. Open Tuesday through Friday and Sunday, 11 A.M. to 4 P.M.; Saturday, 10 A.M. to 4 P.M.; closed on Monday. Telephone: 302-322-8411. Web site: www.hsd.org.

❀ A visit to New Castle, Delaware, is a step into a genteel world of eighteenth-century grace. This rare historic village of mostly red-brick Georgian houses on quiet tree-lined streets combines architectural charm with an enchanting setting along the shores of the Delaware River. One of the oldest settlements in the Delaware Valley, New Castle offers an impressive number of public buildings and homes of architectural interest, spanning some two hundred years. You will see many houses in the dignified Georgian style, but you'll also find Colonial, Federal, Queen Anne, Victorian, and Gothic Revival examples. A visit to this historic spot provides a delightful sampling of American architecture.

Fortunately New Castle has not been commercialized or otherwise spoiled by the onslaught of tourism. There are few shops and commercial establishments within the historic district, and those we saw seemed tasteful and discreet. You are left to enjoy the quiet atmosphere of a well-kept secret. New Castle remains a carefully preserved yet vibrant living community

Sites in New Castle

with none of the contrived atmosphere of some historic places, where people might parade about in colonial garb for the gratification of visitors. The majority of historic houses continue to be lived in and have not been converted to museums or other establishments. Much of New Castle's healthy state of affairs is due to its active preservation society, which has seen to it that buildings retain their historic character and that they are tended carefully in old age. But the village's odd history has also conspired to keep it intact, with few new buildings replacing earlier sites.

New Castle (originally called Fort Casimir) was founded in 1651 by Peter Stuyvesant of Manhattan fame, then governor of the Dutch West India Company's American enterprise. The fort's strategic setting gave the Dutch an advantage in Delaware River traffic until 1664, when the fort was captured by the English. New Castle's importance culminated in the early eighteenth century, when it was made the colonial capital of Delaware and then briefly the state capital. The town enjoyed its role as a transfer point for those traveling to and from Washington, D.C., Baltimore, and other spots along the coast. But it eventually was bypassed, as development of modern transportation by rail and highway made its harbor outmoded. Its neighbors, Wilmington and Philadelphia, grew to become large cities, but New Castle remained a small town with no need to expand or replace its old buildings.

The houses, churches, and other public buildings reflect the styles of the past two hundred years—and even earlier, as there are quite a number of pre-Revolutionary buildings. Some of the early houses have been added on to, and it is sometimes difficult to determine an exact date. The overall effect is one of architectural harmony, as even the nineteenth- and twentieth-century buildings and additions blend in well with the old.

You will probably want to wander around on your own to explore the several blocks that make up the historic district, although there are weekly guided tours for those so inclined. You can start your tour by visiting the **Court House** on Delaware Street, one of the must-see spots. This fine Georgian building (1732), surrounded by the historic green, was built on the burned remains of an earlier seventeenth-century courthouse. It was the meeting place of the Colonial Assembly for many years before the Revolution, and then it was the site of the drafting of the Constitution of Delaware. It became a county courthouse and later was even used for commercial activities, eventually falling into some disrepair. Restoration since the late 1950s has brought it back to its earlier appearance. You'll want to linger in the wonderful courtroom, refurbished in the style of Delaware's colonial days.

Now, with walking map in hand, you can begin your exploration of the town. There are over ninety historic houses, buildings, and other sites of interest within this small area (described in a booklet available at the Court House). Though many are private and can only be seen from the outside, they help create the rare architectural harmony of New Castle.

The **Immanuel Episcopal Church** on the green near the Court House is one of the oldest and most august buildings in New Castle. Begun in 1703, it was partially damaged by fire and later rebuilt; but the walls and tower fortunately survived, and the rest of the structure has been carefully restored. The old churchyard will please those of you who like to wander around such places; it is filled with eighteenth- and nineteenth-century markers, including those of signers of the Declaration of Independence, framers of the Constitution, judges of the Supreme Court, and Delaware governors. As you walk around and read the epitaphs you feel like a witness to an important period in American history.

On the south side of the green you'll find the **New Castle Presbyterian Church** (at 25 Second Street); built in 1707, it is one of the oldest buildings in town.

Facing the church is the **Old Library Museum** at 40 East Third Street, an unusual hexagonal building dating only from 1892. In the past it has had a variety of uses—once even as a sculpture studio—but it is now a museum that displays historical memorabilia concerning New Castle and surroundings.

Along Third Street, facing the green, is a charming row of eighteenth- and nineteenth-century brick houses. Among them is the **Old Dutch House** (at 32 East Third Street), which fortunately can be visited inside and out. Built in the early eighteenth century, it has the deeply pitched roof and overhanging eaves typical of the Dutch style. It is now also a museum, in this case of early-eighteenth-century Dutch furnishings and artifacts. Surrounding it is a little garden that has recently been restored.

The **Amstel House** on the corner of Fourth and Delaware streets is a wonderful eighteenth-century Georgian house that is also open to visitors. Built in 1738, it was (or so it is claimed) the site of a wedding attended by the ubiquitous George Washington. Not to be missed are its carved cornices and other special architectural details.

The **George Read II House** and garden on The Strand is no doubt New Castle's most elegant house. It was built between 1797 and 1804 by George Read II, the son of a signer of the Declaration of Independence. He wanted it to be a proper Philadelphia-style house, with high ceilings, marble fireplaces, plaster ornamentation, finely carved woodwork, and gilded fanlights. The result is a grand house with an appropriately stately garden, both of which can be visited.

The George Read II House is only a block from the Delaware River, so you must not miss a walk to the banks to enjoy the view. Unfortunately, the once-bustling wharf is no more, but you'll find the river setting charming.

2·
GREY TOWERS

A French-Style Château in Rural Pennsylvania, Milford

✿ DIRECTIONS

From I-84 take Route 6 east toward Milford (exit 46). Turn right onto Old Owego Turnpike and follow signs. Grey Towers is on the left. Additional driving directions can be found on the Web site (see Information section).

✿ INFORMATION

Open Memorial Day to the end of October, weekdays, 11 A.M. to 4 P.M.; weekends, 10 A.M. to 4 P.M. Tours, which are required to see the interior of house, are offered hourly. Telephone: 570-296-9630. Web site: www.fs.fed.us/na/gt.

✿ In a rural, off-the-beaten-track area of eastern Pennsylvania you'll find this castle and its one hundred acres of grounds beautifully situated on a wooden hill beyond the small town of Milford (just a few miles from the much-traveled I-84). Like the mansion, the complex garden structures, walls, patios, pergolas, and the many outbuildings are all made of native bluestone, a picturesque and evocative material. The design of the entire estate creates a romantic sense of faraway times and places.

Grey Towers was constructed in 1886 by the Pinchot family, long residents of the area. The first Pinchot emigrated from France in 1816 (his charming house in Milford is now the Community House and public library). James Pinchot was a prosperous manufacturer; his son, Gifford, was a prominent environmentalist who was appointed by President Teddy Roosevelt to head the U.S. Forest Service. Gifford Pinchot became governor of Pennsylvania in 1927 and lived at Grey Towers until his death in 1946. The site was designated a National Historic Landmark (with President John F. Kennedy in attendance) in 1963. Pinchot's lifelong interest in conservation continues at Grey Towers today, where environmentalists still use the estate for conferences.

And what an estate it is! The forty-one-room mansion with its three great stone towers is a cross between French medieval design (and furnishings) and affluent nineteenth-century taste. Its architect, Richard Morris Hunt (who designed the Metropolitan Museum of Art in New York City, among other grand buildings) created an American castle curiously set just outside a thoroughly ungrand village. (The house is open for public tours in summer.)

Around the castle are many small buildings and the garden area. These constructions have such intriguing names as the Finger Bowl, the Baitbox, and the Letter Box, as well as the more familiar moat, icehouse, and pergola. Pinchot's ideas for the grounds were the result of extensive travels, apparently both to foreign countries and into the past of his imagination.

Immediately beyond the dining room's French doors, for example, is the Finger Bowl, a raised pool surrounded by a mosaic terrace and tanks for aquatic plants. The "bowl," a unique table with water in the center, was created after the Pinchots returned from the South Sea Islands. Here the family occasionally dined by candlelight, sitting round the pool's table edges and eating from Polynesian serving bowls that floated in the water.

Steps lead from this terrace to another enclosed stone-walled area that was once the family's swimming pool and is now beautifully landscaped with wisteria vines and gardens. Surrounding the mansion is a complex set of gardens on different terraced levels—all of them created by the use of bluestone paths and walls and steps—as well as ancient-seeming pergolas and trellises. Many of the terraces contain gargoyles: turkeys and eagles, among other beasts, appear in small niches and atop marble columns. And numerous statues decorate the place, including a bust of the Marquis de Lafayette in a niche on the second story of the house. There are vined gazebos, a rock garden, a water-lily pond, benches, fountains, mosaics, a reflecting pool, and an amphitheater (used by the family for theatricals and campaign gatherings). At the far end of the reflecting pool is the Bait Box, built as a playhouse. Millstones taken from local gristmills also adorn the gardens. In among these many man-made divisions and artistic ornaments are luxuriant flowers and other plants. Grey Towers is an example of architecture being enhanced and complemented by its gardens.

3·
PYRAMIDS, GOTHIC ARCHES, AND CLASSICAL TEMPLES

West Laurel Hill Cemetery, Bala Cynwyd, Pennsylvania

❀ DIRECTIONS

Take the New Jersey Turnpike south to the Pennsylvania Turnpike to the third exit, Route 611 south (marked Willow Grove). Take Route 611 to Route 1 west, then take the exit for I-76 west and exit at City Avenue. Go to Belmont Avenue and turn right. The entrance is on your right after the second intersection.

❀ INFORMATION

Open Monday through Saturday, 8 A.M. to 4:30 P.M.; Sunday and holidays, 9 A.M. to 4:30 P.M. Telephone: 610-664-1591. Web site: www.westlaurelhill.com.

❀ It may surprise you to find a cemetery as a site for an architecture walk, but this is not an ordinary cemetery. A walk through West Laurel Hill, in Bala Cynwyd, near South Philadelphia, is like a fantastic tour through the history of architecture. Not only is the natural scenery spectacular—there are more than 150 species of trees, many of which blossom in season—but there are mausoleums in styles ranging from Egyptian pyramids to Greek temples to miniature Gothic chapels.

A walk around this very large area is filled with intriguing sights, beautiful views, and food for thought: Who were these people who were buried like kings in nineteenth-century America? Where did they get such curious ideas of art and architecture, combining Egyptian or classical Greek tomb styles with the brilliant colors of Art Nouveau stained glass or the whimsical design of Moorish ironwork? (Postmodernism seems to have been preinvented at West Laurel Hill!) Why does the ornamentation include so many references to ancient Egyptian and classical myth in these nominally Christian tombs?

Many of the mausoleums are dramatic, imposing, and grand, yet they are still miniatures; two of them are replicas of the Parthenon. As you walk through the graceful landscape you feel almost as though you are Gulliver in a small mythical city.

In fact, the sense of being in another time and place is pervasive: there are few visitors (we were there on weekdays) and nothing to read—there are almost no inscriptions beyond the names of the honored dead—and the stillness is broken only by the sound of the wind in the giant old trees. You can walk up to the "entrances" of many of the tombs (which, of course, are never entered) and peer into their empty interiors to see the colorful stained-glass light, or you can sit on one of the numerous walls or stone stairways to draw or contemplate your surroundings without interruption.

West Laurel Hill Cemetery was originally a country estate on the outskirts of Philadelphia, about four miles from the city. In 1869 the hilly spot was purchased by some leading citizens for use as a cemetery; it was to provide a safely removed and inspirational spot for contemplation of nature and God. (Cemeteries such as West Laurel Hill became models—with their design of pathways, plantings, and open space—for the great public parks that appeared in the nation's cities in the nineteenth century.)

Because of the cemetery's situation beyond the city's limits, transportation there was difficult in the early days. Funerals took all day, with excursions by steamboat on the Schuylkill River or by carriage up to the high bluffs of the cemetery. Eventually railway cars were employed to carry funeral corteges. As you will see from the names on the tombs, leading citizens of Philadelphia's business and social world chose this cemetery as their last resting place. By the turn of the century it had become a testament not only to worldly success but also to the Victorian fascination with grandeur —both in art and nature.

A walk through the grounds poses some problems. The area is very large, and you will necessarily have to leave out some of the walkways unless you have a great deal of time. The old carriage roads cover more than one hundred acres of hill and dale. It is possible to drive through most of the cemetery if you wish, but you will be unable to leave your car along the way, so we recommend parking at the office lot in the center of the grounds. You can then follow our route to see the tombs we think most interesting, or if you prefer, you can wander at random.

As you walk, you may note—in addition to the particular sites described —some sixty-two obelisks, numerous marble statues and urns covered with ivy, several sets of classical columns unattached to buildings, and a recurrent, architectural detail at the top of the façade of many temples: the Egyptian winged sun disk or Winged Ba (representing the soul), occasionally inter-twined with snakes. You will also spot Doric, Ionic, and Corinthian columns, Gothic arches and spires, and a marvelous collection of doors. These portals to the tombs are in every conceivable style, some echoing the design of the windows within, others in ironwork of Moorish or Art Deco design. Be sure to go up the steps to look in beyond the doors at the vast variety of stained glass within many of the mausoleums. Although most of the tombs are built of marble, you will also find sandstone and granite; the overall impression is of sparkling white buildings set against an extraordinarily green landscape.

One additional note before you begin: don't overlook the trees and shrub-bery. The natural beauty of the 187 acres is astounding. Many of the trees were planted more than one hundred years ago. Among the 150 species is a sixty-five-foot-tall magnolia shadowing a grave marked "Carpenter," flower-ing dogwood, cherry, weeping beech, sweet gum, oak, birch, euonymus, sugar maple, fern maple, and copper beech; you'll also find flowering shrubs in season, from mauve hydrangea, azalea, and rhododendron to (of course) a profusion of laurel. Colors are particularly grand in spring and fall.

As you drive into the gate you will see painted arrows on the roadway directing you to the office. Follow them by car and park in the lot in front of the beautiful ivied tower and the brick office building. At the office you can buy a history of the famous people buried in the cemetery and pick up a detailed map (which, however, includes no names or guide points). As you park you will be facing the first stop on this tour.

Directly bordering the parking area are two side-by-side graves marked "Soulas" and "Pidgeon." We begin with these two graves because they typ-ify the Neoclassical style, an emphasis that you will see time and again on this walk. Each of these graves is distinctive for the classical mourning fe-male figures behind glass-topped graves. (The tombs appear empty when you look into their fifteen-foot depth.)

Turn to your left to find the first large mausoleum of this walk. This is a monument to Frederick August Poth, a very successful German-born brewer. This Classical Revival structure is marble with symmetrical Corinthian col-umns, flanges, and urns. It is massive and impressive and dates to 1905.

If you continue on the pathway to the left of the Poth tomb, you will come to a row of some of the most interesting mausoleums. Here you'll find the Greek Revival style in a number of forms, most including stained glass in an Art Nouveau mode. Be sure to go up the steps of each and peek in to see the widely divergent styles of the glass and the doorways.

In addition to the Greek Revival designs along this row, there are also two interesting mausoleums showing Moorish influence. One of them is the John Lang monument, a curious blend of Moorish and classical design; note the carved decoration. Across from it (and slightly farther along) is the Coane monument. This one, which contrasts with its Neoclassical neighbors, looks rather like a beehive.

Just behind the Coane monument is a grave marked "Stetson." Though it is not of particular architectural interest, you may like to see where the founder of Stetson hats is buried!

Also on the right side of this roadway—but somewhat behind this row— is a very distinctive tomb for Matthew Simpson (1811–1884). He was a bishop of the Methodist Episcopal Church. His mausoleum is a replica of a Gothic chapel complete with a Gothic arch, trefoil (intersecting circles symbolizing the Trinity), and Latin cross. Note the fine stained-glass windows, which include a New Testament scene, a fleur-de-lis, and a Star of David.

If you return to the same pathway, opposite and somewhat farther along, you'll find the Eisenlohr monument, one of the finest of the Greek Revival examples. It is not only distinguished in its architectural detail; it also has unusually nice stained glass in the Art Nouveau style within.

At the end of this section of roadway is a major monument marked "Harrah." Charles J. Harrah (1817–1890) was a steel and railway magnate and humanitarian who personified the successful nineteenth-century industrialist. His career took him to Brazil, where he developed railways and shipyards, as well as the first public school. His mausoleum is appropriately grand, with its Victorian Gothic spires and ornamentation. Its design is based on a series of rounded and pointed arches culminating in a spire with a cross at the top. It has been likened to the Prince Albert Memorial in London and is what used to be known as an "architectural confection."

Returning to the intersecting paths at the Harrah memorial, take the narrow path and climb up the hill. At the top, to your right, you'll come to several interesting mausoleums overlooking lower areas of the cemetery. First, you'll see the Alter monument, whose unusual stained-glass windows pick up the intricate Moorish design of the wrought-iron door.

Surrounding this tomb are two oddities: large, white marble chairs that look like bizarre monuments themselves. They were placed on private lots by some long-forgotten gravesite owners to provide a view of the hillside and, presumably, a place for meditation and prayer. In their peculiar juxtaposition with the varied tombs and monuments, however, they seem like works of art placed by some twentieth-century sculptor in an unlikely place. There are several other such monuments at West Laurel Hill.

On the same path is a distinctive and very ornate Art Nouveau tomb dedicated to John P. Mathieu. Note the Saint John the Baptist windows, the curlicues on the roof, the stylish arched door, and the matching decorative flowerpots.

Go back to the intersection and continue in the same direction until you come to the Berwind memorial. Another well-known capitalist, Edward J. Berwind was a naval aide to President U. S. Grant and became one of the largest individual owners of coal mines in the country. Berwind's mausoleum is noteworthy; it was designed by the famous architect Horace Trumbauer (who is also buried at West Laurel Hill). It is a striking, tall, octagonal tower, with Neoclassical winged figures in a bas-relief circling the eight sides.

In a parallel row nearby is one of two monuments to the Pew family. The mausoleum of Joseph Newton Pew, the founder of the Sun Company, resembles a large Neoclassical temple, with graceful proportions and elegant surfaces.

Just around the bend is another Pew monument, and though there is no miniature temple here, this one is nevertheless another evocation of ancient Greece. It consists of linked marble columns set in a lovely site, surrounded with greenery.

Following the map, climb to one of the highest and most beautiful spots at West Laurel Hill. Here the founder of the Campbell Soup Company, John T. Dorrance, is honored with a Neoclassical temple of Ionic columns and a flat roof. Its imposing entranceway between the columns was placed on the long side of its oblong shape, giving it a massive façade. Dorrance, one of the world's richest people during his lifetime (1919–1989), was a patron of the Philadelphia Museum of Art and an art collector himself. Next to the Dorrance mausoleum on the hilltop is another tomb belonging to the same family.

Continue along this roadway to get a quick glimpse of one of the largest (but not particularly interesting architecturally) tombs on the tour. This huge building honors a public-utility magnate named Clarence H. Geist. His mausoleum is a massive, white, austere cube.

Beyond the Geist memorial, on a pathway to your left, is a row with three tombs of interest. The first (on your right) is an Ionic-style temple that is a miniature replica of the Parthenon, though it is hardly miniature. This grand mausoleum is dedicated to Edward M. Story.

A bit farther along, on your left, is the J. Howell Cummings mausoleum, a particularly nice example of stylish 1920s architecture with its soft peach and gray façade and elegant doors decorated with sheaves of wheat.

Next you'll come to a curiosity: Algernon Sidney Logan's obelisk and temple. Logan was a poet and novelist (1849–1925), and the titles of his books are carved into the side of the marble obelisk, along with a clock face, whose hands are set at three o'clock, the time he died. This is one of many obelisks throughout the cemetery. Note the variety of styles, particularly at the topmost points.

Finally in this region you'll come to a sandstone castle-style mausoleum with a wrought-iron gate. This is quite unlike the pale-toned tombs that fill most of the grounds. Instead, this one—dedicated to George Miller—is distinctive for its deep sand color and its somewhat medieval appearance.

From here walk up to the left path to a three-way intersection. Here you'll come to one of our favorite architectural examples: the Henry M. Schadewald mausoleum on the left. This unusual building is a Moorish design that seems to have been inspired by the *Arabian Nights*. Its beautiful doorway is a series of Art Deco arabesques made of iron. Don't miss this one.

Opposite, just across the intersection, is one of the most intriguing of all the mausoleums at West Laurel Hill Cemetery. The Drake family, two of whose members survived the sinking of the *Titanic*, are interred here in an Egyptian-style temple set on a small knoll. This strange structure boasts a number of apparent Egyptian symbols, including the four statues at the corners of the roof, lotus flowers carved into the façade, and the winged sun disk over the entrance. In addition to the Egyptian theme, the architect added some ancient Greek symbols for good measure; the four statues that seem to be Egyptian sphinxes (male lions with human heads) are, in fact, winged female lionesses, a Greek adaptation of a Near Eastern motif. This odd mausoleum was moved from the city cemetery, bodies and all, and reconstructed at its present site.

On the same side of the roadway, on your left, is another Egyptian-influenced mausoleum, this one dedicated to John Kenworthy. It also bears Egyptian symbols and ornamentation.

A bit farther on the same path is one of the oddest of all the mausoleums at West Laurel Hill. This Theban-style tomb is in the shape of a flat-topped pyramid, a rather ungainly curiosity. It bears the name Charles E. Ellis, a streetcar tycoon.

Follow the curving path to a curious mausoleum just down some little stone steps from the Harrah monument. Here you'll find an eccentric tomb with the name Avery D. Harrington. This little building bears medieval symbols in an almost modernistic setting. The geometric, horizontal pattern of the door is reflected in the design of the stained-glass window within.

Following this path you will head back toward the office complex. But shortly before you reach it, stop to see the Dingee tomb, an extremely graceful Neoclassical example; it is another replica of the Parthenon.

From here turn right at the next intersection, toward the giant green-domed mausoleum dominating the vista just ahead. One of the largest and most imposing mausoleums of the entire cemetery, this is the tomb of John F. Betz, a beer-company magnate. It is a beautifully proportioned and massive building in the grand nineteenth-century French style. It reminds us of the wonderful buildings in Paris on the Boulevard Haussmann—in miniature, of course—with its solemn symmetry, Neoclassical columns, and lovely domed roof topped with a winged figure. Be sure to walk all the way around it.

Not far from it you'll spot two curiosities, a pair of graves marked "Jones" and "Platt." Both are stone markers in the shape of tree trunks and are quite realistically carved and surrounded by smaller stones. Another such tree monument is the Kugler monument, a large granite tree trunk fronted with four granite logs. All these markers strike us as very odd and rather modern in concept, though we understand that there is an old tradition of using tree-trunk forms as memorials.

Nearby and slightly up the hill is another peculiar tomb, also reminiscent of France. This is the Cornelius Harrigan monument. It is a tomb in the French Empire style, shaped like Napoleon's in the Hôtel des Invalides in Paris.

Returning to the pathway, continue toward the office (which can be seen in the distance), but take the road that goes behind it. Go down the hill to spot an interesting monument to a family of sculptors. Slightly off the path is a Celtic cross honoring the Calder family. Though the mobile maker Alexander Calder is not buried here, both his father, Alexander Sterling Calder, and his grandfather, Alexander Milne Calder, are. They were well-known artists whose works grace both Philadelphia's and New York City's public spaces. The cross, which bears the names of various other Calders as well, is notable for the carving in its Scottish granite. The cross has a distinctive intertwined pattern of rosettes, as well as the traditional circle intersecting the arms of the cross. Be sure to walk fully around this monument and not to miss the Celtic writing on the front.

4 ·
MODERNISM MEETS SYMBOLISM

Frank Lloyd Wright's Beth Sholom Synagogue, Elkins Park, Pennsylvania

✤ DIRECTIONS

Take the New Jersey Turnpike south to the Pennsylvania Turnpike to the third exit, Route 611 south (marked Willow Grove). Go south on Route 611 for more than five miles, through the town of Willow Grove, crossing railroad tracks. After Abingdon Hospital on your right and the intersection with Route 73, go two more blocks and you'll see the synagogue on your left, at the corner of Foxcroft Road. The street you're on will now be called Old York Road, and the synagogue's address is 8231 Old York Road.

✤ INFORMATION

Tours of the synagogue are offered Sunday through Thursday. Telephone: 215-887-1888 or 215-887-1342.

✤ America's most famous architect designed only one synagogue, and it is well worth a visit. Frank Lloyd Wright, the icon of American architecture, created the most curious of designs: an amalgam of his characteristic modernism and the symbolism of Judaism. Located in the northern suburbs of Philadelphia, the building stands out among the rectangles of a busy commercial area: it is an eye-catching, soaring structure that is unlike any other building around it—indeed, unlike any building anywhere. (It most resembles an ancient ziggurat.) A visit here will astonish the viewer, not only for the building's unlikely overall design but also for the wonderful Wrightian details throughout.

Wright was asked to design the synagogue in 1953. He completed the building but didn't live to see it dedicated. His work—in conjunction with the congregation's first rabbi, Mortimer J. Cohen—is a powerful symbolic statement (unlike most other Wright buildings). It is obvious that the architect and the religious leader worked closely together to incorporate

Beth Sholom Synagogue, Elkins Park

elements of traditional Jewish teaching into this very modernist, untraditional design.

The building, as you will see when you approach, is a towering, mountainlike edifice, with a twelve-sided shape signifying Mount Sinai. (The twelve sides represent the Bible's twelve tribes of Israel.) Made of concrete, aluminum, and glass, this rising shape tapers to a flat top (like Mount Sinai). Light, which pours through the entire mountain shape, is of particular significance. The "mountain" sits on a sort of hexagon, representing two hands together with their thumbs rising on either side. As Wright himself said, "When one enters a place of worship, he should feel as if he were resting in the hands of God." In front of the building is a fountain that spills into a small pool, a symbol of the Laver, the basin used in a ritual of washing and purity.

When you enter the building, you are unprepared for the extraordinary sanctuary, though the lovely Wright details, such as the angular divisions of space and the wonderful modernist iron door handles, remind you that a master was at work. But on going up the stairs and into the sanctuary you will be amazed by the light, the vast space, the soaring tower, the tipped floor, and the accoutrements, including stained glass. Unlike many Wright buildings that have a certain intimacy to them, this one is characterized by giant space (it seats 1,020 worshipers), and its height gives it an even larger feel.

There is quite a bit of color throughout: carpets are a deep Indian red, suggesting the desert, and the centerpiece is a brilliant stained-glass and aluminum triangle (also designed by Wright). It is suspended over the Ark and signifies wings (and the sixth chapter of Isaiah) and uses symbolic colors and designs. The fine walnut Ark at the center is visible from all around the sanctuary and is bathed in light.

The interior of the rising glass structure is covered in fiberglass. Like many Wright innovations, the fiberglass is problematic in a practical sense; we were told that the synagogue is hard to heat and cool. But it enables the changing light to fill the vast space at all times of day. Congregation Beth Sholom was recently named a National Historic Landmark.

5 ·

HENRY CHAPMAN MERCER LEAVES HIS "ARTS AND CRAFTS" MARK ON A SMALL TOWN

Doylestown, Pennsylvania

❀ **DIRECTIONS**

Fonthill and the Moravian Pottery and Tile Works: *To get to Fonthill and the Moravian Pottery and Tile Works take the New Jersey Turnpike to I-287 west (exit 10). Go fifteen miles to exit 14B, then west on Route 22 for 3.5 miles to sign for Route 202 (toward Flemington and Princeton). Take Route 202 to Doylestown and turn right on Swamp Road to the intersection with East Court Street; access to the Moravian Pottery and Tile Works is off East Court Street; access to Fonthill is around the corner, off East Court Street. (Note: because these sites are right next to each other, you can park in either place and walk to the other.)*

The Mercer Museum: *The Mercer Museum is at 84 South Pine Street. To get there continue on East Court Street for several blocks and turn right at Pine Street. The museum is located at the intersection of Pine and Ashland streets.*

❀ **INFORMATION**

Fonthill, the Moravian Pottery and Tile Works, and the Mercer Museum are all part of the "Mercer Mile" and are close to one another.

Fonthill: Open Monday through Saturday, 10 A.M. to 5 P.M.; Sunday, noon to 5 P.M. Guided tours only (last tour leaves at 4 P.M.). Telephone: 215-348-9461. Web site: www.fonthillmuseum.org.

Moravian Pottery and Tile Works: Open daily, 10 A.M. to 4:45 P.M. Self-guided tours every half hour (last tour at 4 P.M.). Telephone: 215-345-6722. Web site: www.buckscountry.org.

Mercer Museum: Open Monday through Saturday, 10 A.M. to 5 P.M.; Tuesday night until 9 P.M.; Sunday, noon to 5 P.M. Telephone: 215-345-0210. Web site: www.mercermuseum.org.

❀ Doylestown, in the heart of Bucks County, is a delightful place to visit, with a wonderfully old-fashioned downtown filled with intriguing little shops and eateries. But what makes it of particular interest are three most unusual sites: Fonthill, the Moravian Pottery and Tile Works, and the Mercer Museum. These structures together make up the so-called Mercer Mile, named for their creator, Henry Chapman Mercer. A true Renaissance man, Mercer (1856–1930) was an archaeologist, historian, architect, engineer, and avid collector of early American tiles, German pottery, and tools. Influenced by the American Arts and Crafts movement, he believed that American society was being destroyed by industrialism and proceeded to do something about it—at least on the local level (he was born and died in Doylestown). He remains one of Doylestown's most eminent native sons.

The three distinctive buildings he designed and constructed here in the early 1900s are a testament to his passion for craft, and for tile in particular. All three buildings are made of the same material—hand-poured concrete —but they vary somewhat in their architectural styles.

We begin with **Fonthill**, where Mercer lived for many years until his death. This "concrete castle for the New World," as he called it, was built between 1908 and 1910. The imposing structure is an eccentric architectural wonder, which reportedly took 106 men to build. It has everything—columns, towers, arches, and balconies—and is one of those American fantasies that fascinate (or horrify) today's more staid designers.

Fonthill is of very grand proportions, with forty-four rooms, eighteen fireplaces, thirty-two stairwells, and at least two hundred windows of various sizes and shapes. Not surprisingly, practically everything within the lavish interior is decorated with tiles (Mercer's own designs, of course), from ceilings to stairways to tables and headboards. Adorning the interior spaces are also some nine hundred prints and art objects from around the world. You can only visit the mansion by guided tour, so plan accordingly (see the Information section for hours).

You can easily walk to our next site, the **Moravian Pottery and Tile Works**, where Mercer's tiles were actually made. This exotic-looking factory complex looks like none other we've seen. Considered to be a "living history museum," it is vaguely reminiscent of a Moorish castle, with rounded archways and cupolas. Mercer built this Mission-style structure in 1912, soon after Fonthill. Here his handcrafted tiles and floor and wall mosaics were created, using local materials. These decorative designs, mostly of whimsical animals and plants, are still being reproduced in the tiles made

Moravian Pottery and Tile Works, Doylestown

here today, using more or less the same methods; you can purchase these contemporary versions at the gift shop.

After seeing where Mercer lived and worked, you will want to visit the **Mercer Museum**, which houses his monumental and impressive collection. (It is only a short drive away; see the Directions section.) Mercer built this massive granite structure to contain thousands of ancient artifacts—some Native American implements are said to date as far back as 8000 B.C.—as well as early American farm and household objects. The collection reflects Mercer's fascination with tools used in metallurgy, textile weaving, woodworking, and agriculture.

The imposing seven-story building was completed around 1916. Much like Fonthill in its castlelike austerity, it is an eclectic jumble of turrets, gables, and parapets. Surrounding the building is a rustic, grassy area with farm sheds displaying additional outdoor tools. The entire complex is a curious combination of grandeur and farmlike simplicity.

6·
A WALKING TOUR THROUGH
A TREASURE TROVE OF
HISTORIC HOUSES

Doylestown, Pennsylvania

❀ DIRECTIONS

Take the New Jersey Turnpike to I-287 west (exit 10). Go fifteen miles to exit 10, then west on Route 202 to Doylestown. Head for the center of town, to the courthouse.

❀ INFORMATION

Park in the courthouse parking lot and begin your walk there. You can get a walking tour and map at the Michener Art Museum (138 South Pine Street) or use our somewhat more abbreviated listings below.

❀ Set on a hilltop in a picturesque part of eastern Pennsylvania, Doylestown has been a bustling town for centuries, and its polyglot architecture shows its continual evolution. From a colonial village at the crossroads of two major routes to Philadelphia and New York City, to the site of two Revolutionary War encampments, to its burgeoning growth in the first half of the nineteenth century (it became the county seat in 1813), to a Victorian era of elegance, Doylestown has a storied history—and it has the architecture of each period to show for it.

In addition to the major landmarks of the courthouse and the museum complex, there are a few main streets of architectural interest: Broad, Main, Court, State, and Pine streets.

East Court Street's proximity to the courthouse, once Doylestown became the county seat, led to the construction of many fine buildings, including a row of attorneys' houses (known as Lawyer's Row). We recommend the following buildings on East Court Street:

The **Doylestown Presbyterian Church,** corner East Court Street and Church Street: This 1871 edifice has Gothic features (arched windows and buttresses) and was designed by an eminent Philadelphia architect named Addison Hutton. (He also designed Lenape Hall in town.)

Former **Melinda Cox Free Library,** corner of East Court and Broad streets: Originally built as a bank in 1886, this formal design incorporates elements of various historical styles, including decorative roof battlements.

Old Intelligencer Building, 10 East Court Street: This is an unusual and fanciful site, built to house the oldest newspaper in Bucks County still in existence today. Dating to around 1876, the former headquarters of the newspaper has a delightful tower, a mansard roof, and an overall Second Empire style. The architect was Thomas Cernea, who designed several other buildings in town.

Charles DuBois House, 60 East Court Street: Once part of a block of fine late Federal houses, this one (built for an attorney) has survived since its construction in about 1833. The elegant brick building has an elliptical fan window, double connecting chimneys, and a side entranceway.

Dr. Hugh Meredith House, 68 East Court Street: Built to house Dr. Meredith's residence and office, this 1833 house was redone in the 1870s. It has Federal elements (including adjoining frame office section), as well as later additions, such as the decorative windows and mansard roof.

On West Court Street:

Pugh Dungan House, 33 West Court Street: This symmetrical Georgian-style house was built around 1832, during Doylestown's first building boom. The house was once considered one of the most desirable in town.

Lunn Hatter's Shop, 45 West Court Street: A fine example of Second Empire architecture, with French mansard roof and wrought-iron cresting, this house was originally built in 1839 and then rebuilt in 1874. Originally it housed a hat shop, hence its name.

Eugene Schuman House, 204 West Court Street: Here is a Queen Anne–style house, one of many in Doylestown. Among its features are a square tower with carved wood panels, windows with tiny panes, and shingled gables. The house dates from about 1885.

Connard House, 210 West Court Street: This delightful "gingerbread" Victorian was built around 1871. Note the many decorations and ornamentations typical of this style.

Summers Smith House, 255 West Court and South West streets: Dating from around 1870, this house is an early example of Gothic Revival style. Everything here is on a vertical plane, from the steeply pitched roof to the tall windows.

On North Main Street:

Jonathan Brock Building, 10 North Main Street: Originally constructed as a hardware store around 1837, this building was redone in the Colonial Revival style in 1900, when there was a movement to celebrate the earlier styles of American architecture.

Josiah Hart Bank, 21 North Main Street: Built around 1858, this is one of Doylestown's most distinctive sites: a Greek Revival bank building, complete with projecting pediments and columns in the style of a classical Greek temple. It was designed by Thomas Cernea.

Charles Meredith House, 90 North Main Street: Dr. Hugh Meredith was an ancestor of Henry Chapman Mercer, whose contributions to Doylestown's history and architecture can be found in the preceding outing. Meredith was the town's first doctor; he built this house for his son around 1805. It is a fine example of Georgian architecture, with its five symmetrical bays and elegant proportions.

Nathan James House, 110 North Main Street: Built around 1888, this imposing mansion is in the late-Victorian shingle style, characterized by its gambrel roof and shingle work.

James Lorah House, 132 North Main Street: This house, also built by a member of the Mercer family, dates to around 1884 and is an example of the changing and eclectic architectural styles of the fine houses of Doylestown at that time. It has Federal elements (such as the connecting double chimneys), Greek Revival elements (the eyebrow windows), and even Italianate elements (the window hood moldings).

Titus-Chapman House, corner of North Main Street and Broad Street: An eclectic architectural design, this house built around 1807 belonged to a prominent attorney. An addition was designed by Thomas Cernea in 1874 in the Gothic Revival style (note its steeply pitched roof).

On South Main Street:

Shaw-Swartzlander House, corner of South Main Street and East Oakland Avenue: One of the earliest of the houses on this tour, this Federal-style home was built around 1801. Shaw was a justice of the peace. Behind the house is a Shingle-style building that was erected in 1894 as a veterinary hospital for horses.

Lenape Hall, 1 South Main Street and East State Street: This imposing building was designed by the Philadelphia architects Addison Hutton and Thomas Cernea; it dates to about 1874. It is a large, brick corner building that housed a theater, shops, and offices, behind a grand Victorian façade with a typically eclectic mix of historical elements. Arches can be seen throughout: on the corner of the roof is a rounded Romanesque arch, and the windows are arched as well. Notice also the horizontal-striped divisions and the suggestions of columns.

On South Pine Street:

Saint Paul's Episcopal Church, corner South Pine and East Oakland Avenue: Built around 1846, this church is in the Gothic Revival style, characterized by pointed Gothic arches reminiscent of medieval European churches.

John Livezey House, 72 East Oakland Avenue at South Pine Street: This is another example of historical styles meeting in a Doylestown house. Originally built around 1827, it was a comparatively simple stone building that was renovated in the late nineteenth century: additions included an octagonal tower and Queen Anne–style windows.

Samuel DuBois House, 19 South Pine Street: This house is typical of the mid-nineteenth-century row house; it belonged to the town's first portraitist and photographer.

G. T. Harvey House, 104 East Ashland, corner of South Pine Street: Generally considered the finest example of Italianate architecture in Doylestown, this imposing house built around 1871 features a flat roof, square proportions, a square cupola, and bracketed eaves; it was an elegant addition to Doylestown's architectural pleasures.

On State Street:

Masonic Hall, 55 East State Street: This Greek Revival structure dates from about 1844. Though it has undergone some alterations over the years, it still stands as one of only two such examples in the town.

Dr. James Rich House, 100 East State Street: This 1824 house is an elegant combination of early-nineteenth-century design. Its double chimneys and semicircular fanlight reflect the Federal style, and its symmetrical façade is Georgian.

John Barclay House, 140 East State Street: The home of a prominent citizen (he was once mayor of Philadelphia, as well as chief judge of the Bucks County Court), this house is an excellent example of Federal-style architecture. It dates from about 1814.

Fountain House, corner of West State and North Main streets: At this important crossroads once stood a colonial roadhouse (c. 1758) that served as an inn and stagecoach stop. Later, a Second Empire–style mansard roof was added, as was a fountain (you can still see its foundation near the entrance).

Hannah Green House, 54 West State Street: This late-nineteenth-century example of Queen Anne–style architecture stands out for its gracious details; notice especially its many gables and its flat-roofed tower.

James Snodgrass House, 253 West State Street: This mid-nineteenth-century house (c. 1850) underwent a substantial renovation in the late nineteenth century. Note the Greek Revival–style upper-story eyebrow windows, the generous-size porch with pediment and attached gazebo, and the various Queen Anne windows.

On Broad Street:

Charles Myers House, 77–79 North Broad Street: If you like the Queen Anne style, you won't want to miss this fine example—perhaps the best in town. Dating from about 1887, it features an imposing multilevel roof profile, recessed porches on the top floor with bays, a lovely circular verandah, and an interesting variety of wall surfaces featuring different textures. The windows on the tower are pure Queen Anne, with their small panes.

W. H. Kirk House, 87–89 North Broad Street: In this house built around 1888 you see a combination of two popular nineteenth-century styles. The Shingle style is reflected in the gambrel roof and shingled upper story; the Queen Anne style is seen in the ornamented chimney, which emphasizes verticality (note its height). Look for a whimsical griffin at the top of the gable.

Ross Law Office, 29 South Broad Street: This small building was moved to this location in 1960, when it was about to be demolished to make way for the present (rather unattractive, we think) courthouse. It once was located on East Court Street, along with the other Federal-style structures of Lawyer's Row.

7·

A NINETEENTH-CENTURY RAILROAD VIADUCT BALANCING PROGRESS AND NATURAL BEAUTY

Starrucca Viaduct, Susquehanna, Pennsylvania

❀ **DIRECTIONS**

From New York City take I-80 west to I-380 north to I-81 north. Exit at Route 171 for the town of Susquehanna.

❀ The Starrucca Viaduct is still a sight to see. In the mid-nineteenth century it was an icon of progress, with its eighteen graceful arches spanning a beautiful landscape. Built of bluestone, it carried railroad cars filled with lumber over the valley below. It was the combination of progress and aesthetic beauty that captivated painters and poets at that time in America.

In particular, the Hudson River School painters brought the beauty of the American landscape to the attention of a nation that had greatly overlooked it. In the rush to build and develop the country, Americans had paid little attention to their native scenery. The first Hudson River painters spoke of "God's hand" in the American landscape and of the duty of everyone to preserve it. They were, of course, talking about the rivers and hillsides and forests unspoiled by human hands. Their paintings of these glorious views became the first "native" style of painting.

It was one such painter, Jasper Cropsey, who painted this very viaduct, thus combining natural scenery with the beauty and celebration of progress represented by the viaduct. Cropsey's painting of Starrucca Viaduct (now in the Toledo Museum of Art) shows us that little has changed in this landscape almost a century and a half later.

The Starrucca Viaduct was a widely heralded achievement in American engineering. Constructed in 1847–1848 by the Erie Railroad, it is the oldest stone railroad bridge still in use in Pennsylvania and is a monumental sight to see. It is 1,040 feet long, 100 feet high, and 25 feet wide; its massive but artistically arched design is still striking today.

Fortunately for walkers, there is an uncommonly lovely way to see the viaduct and to spot the very site of Cropsey's painting. (Keep in mind that in those days artists often worked—or at least sketched—out of doors.) We believe that this walk will take you to the view that the artist saw along Susquehanna's charming banks. The walk there, which is less than a mile long, is in itself a delight, and the sighting of the viaduct is both romantic and dramatic.

Begin your walk by leaving your car in the small shopping center behind the First Methodist Church at the intersection of Route 92, Route 171, and Erie Street in the town of Susquehanna. (Cropsey's painting is subtitled *In the Susquehanna Valley near Lanesboro, Pennsylvania*; you will be walking toward Lanesboro.)

Walk through the parking lot behind the stores. You will see the river and the railroad tracks. Cross the tracks carefully (they are occasionally still in use), where you will find a wonderful riverside path heading to the right (as you face the river). We took this walk in the dead of winter, and it was glorious. If you prefer, you can drive along Route 171 for a view of the viaduct, and if you continue for a mile or two, you can ride under its massive arches.

AND KEEP IN MIND . . .

8· An Architectural Drive through Northeastern Pennsylvania: From Milford to Cortez

The northeast corner of Pennsylvania provides a lovely driving trip for architecture buffs. This is a rural area of small villages and unspoiled countryside. (If you visit Grey Towers in Milford you'll be very nearby.)

From Milford take Route 6 north to Honesdale, then Route 191 to Bethany. In this small village you'll find the Presbyterian church; dating from 1836, its architecture was influenced by the London churches designed by Sir Christopher Wren. Note, too, the particularly charming collection of nineteenth-century houses surrounding the town green.

Return to Honesdale and take Route 6 west to Route 296 south to South Canaan. Just south of this village is the Saint Tikhon Monastery and Seminary. The quintessential onion domes of Eastern European churches are well represented here. This delightful setting is always visible. Inside are painted icons, wood carvings, and other decorations. Telephone: 570-937-4144.

Continue south on Route 296 toward Cortez. On the way, look for a rare octagonal schoolhouse made of big blocks and locally mined stone.

9· A Historic Village and William Penn's Estate: Fallsington and Morrisville, Pennsylvania

These two sites are very close to each other (five miles apart) and are historically related. William Penn lived in Pennsbury Manor and worshiped in Fallsington.

Fallsington

DIRECTIONS: *Take the New Jersey Turnpike south to I-195 west (exit 7A) to Route 29. Take Route 1 south to Route 13 south and exit onto Tyburn Road.*

Fallsington has twenty-five extant buildings from the seventeenth and eighteenth centuries. You will enjoy this streetscape; note particularly the 1685

Moon-Williamson House (a traditional log cabin), the 1789 Burges-Lippincott House (notice the elegant doorway), and the stone Stage Coach Tavern (late eighteenth century). This town is thought to represent historic preservation at its best; in fact it offers a three-hundred-year survey of American architecture from its log cabins to its Victorian homes.

Pennsbury Manor, Morrisville

DIRECTIONS: *Pennsbury Manor is located at 400 Pennsbury Memorial Road in Morrisville. From Fallsington take Tyburn Road east and make a right on New Ford Mill Road. Then make a slight right on Turkey Hill Road, a right on Bordentown Road, and a left at Pennsbury Road.*

INFORMATION: Telephone: 215-946-0400. Web site: www.pennsburymanor.org.

Pennsbury Manor, a forty-three-acre country estate dating from the late seventeenth century, was once the home of William Penn. A beautifully kept reconstructed colonial manor house with a number of outbuildings is an example of the Pennsylvania Quaker style, simple and functional.

10 · An Early Roebling Suspension Bridge, Lackawaxen, Pennsylvania

DIRECTIONS: *From I-84 take exit 46 onto Route 6 north; follow signs for Greeley and then take Route 590 to Lackawaxen.*

This precursor of the famed Brooklyn Bridge sits in rural northeastern Pennsylvania, on the Delaware River. Known as the Delaware Aqueduct, Roebling Bridge, or Roebling's Delaware Aqueduct, after its creator, John A. Roebling, it dates from 1847—well before his masterpiece in 1883. Considered to be the oldest surviving wire suspension bridge in the country, it connects Lackawaxen to Minisink Ford, New York, a span of about 535 feet. The bridge represents a true engineering feat for its time and has been designated a National Civil Engineering Landmark, as well as a National Historic Landmark.

Roebling Bridge was built during the height of the Canal Era, to speed up canal traffic and ease the inevitable bottlenecks that occurred along the route. Roebling's remarkable suspension design enabled vessels to move with greater fluidity, significantly reducing canal traveling time. It was so successful that it was soon replicated in other bridges in the area: a sister bridge nearby and two aqueducts in New York State, all of which were eventually dismantled.

Restored in the 1980s, the bridge is now one lane, serving vehicular traffic; what were towpaths have become sidewalks. But don't expect to see anything resembling the extraordinary Brooklyn Bridge with its iconic Gothic towers. What you see here is a simple horizontal structure without frills, one that speaks of strength and quiet dignity—and an important history.

GLOSSARY OF ARCHITECTURAL STYLES IN THE REGION

Colonial (1620–1740)

The New England Colonial style, which can be seen throughout the area, features simple, boxlike houses, occasionally with a saltbox roof (one side lower than the other) or overhanging second story. These houses are generally modestly sized, built of wood, with shingled or clapboard sides, tall chimneys, lean-to additions, small casement windows with diamond-shaped panes upstairs, and very little ornament. Churches of the period are also wood-framed, elegantly proportioned, with tall steeples and high, arched, many-paned windows.

Dutch and Huguenot Colonial styles of the seventeenth and eighteenth centuries (found primarily in New York and New Jersey) feature stone, brick, and wood construction. In this region many are built of pinkish sandstone. Some have the stepped roofs typical of Dutch houses; others have steeply pitched, flared, gambrel roofs (with two slopes on each side). Homes often have horizontally divided front doors, raised porches, and end chimneys. Public buildings feature linear designs with each room having access to the outdoors.

Quaker Colonial style is characterized by unusual brick patterns on the exterior walls, and Moravian Colonial style features cut-stone common buildings with steeply pitched roofs.

Georgian (1700–1776)

Following a style developed in England (often based on the works of Christopher Wren, who was an admirer of Renaissance styles), Georgian architecture aims for symmetry, elegance, and a dignified sense of order. As the colonies became more prosperous, builders favored grander designs; Georgian architecture features larger, symmetrical, horizontal-focused two-story buildings with flat or hip roofs, often with classical details, such as cupolas and balconies to ornament façades of brick or clapboard. Other characteristics are elaborate portico entrances and Palladian central windows. Many public buildings were built in this gracious style.

Federal (1780–1820)

Favored by leaders of the new American nation, the post-Revolutionary Federal style was based on the designs of the Scottish architect Robert Adam. More refined and dignified than Georgian designs, large Federal houses in this region feature a vertical focus, symmetrical frame and clapboard construction with central chimneys, Palladian windows (and occasional round and semicircular windows), wrought-iron balustrades and railings, decorative lintels above the windows, and elaborate doorways with fan-shaped windows above. Sometimes patriotic symbols such as eagles and stars are part of the surface ornamentation.

Classical and Greek Revival (1820–1850)

The popularity of classical Greek design can be seen in the design of many public buildings from this period, as well as in elegant private homes. From state capitol buildings to banks to classical-style churches, the Greek Revival design is characterized by series of Doric and Ionic columns, strong and symmetrical proportions, low roof slopes, heavy cornices, an off-central entrance, and gabled porticos—all suggesting the classical Greek temple.

Roman Revival (1820–1850)

The domes of ancient Rome are the most characteristic element of the Roman Revival style. Following Thomas Jefferson's Monticello, which was based on Roman design, the centralized dome and the classical porticos, columns, and roof balustrades all refer to ancient architecture.

Gothic Revival (1830–1870)

A major architectural style in nineteenth-century America, the Gothic building is still in evidence throughout this region, from numerous churches to whole villages of decorative Gothic design to ornate country houses and many college campuses. An eclectic style loosely based on the picturesque medieval architectural designs of Europe, it features steep gables and towers (some crenellated like castles), sharply pitched roofs, asymmetrical forms, arched and pointed windows and doors, dormer windows, high chimneys, and decoration of all sorts.

The Carpenter Gothic style is picturesque, with lacy cutout ornamentation, and Gothic Revival churches are known for their tapering, pointed steeples. Color is a central element in building exteriors.

Italianate (1840–1880)

Based on the design of northern Italian villas and palazzos, this style became popular with designers of palatial country houses. Following the prototype of the elegant villa, these homes often have Tuscan towers or cupolas, arcaded porches, flat or low roofs, overhanging eaves supported by brackets or narrow columns, and round-headed windows with eyebrow or hooded moldings. Country houses are painted in different colors, and city buildings sometimes have cast-iron exteriors.

Second Empire (1855–1885)

This French-influenced style was based on Parisian design, and it became popular in the construction of grand public buildings, as well as large private homes. Tall, stately buildings, some with domes or low symmetrical towers, are distinguished by their mansard roofs, as well as ironwork and elaborate exterior decoration, including pilasters, pediments, and columns. Varied textures on the exterior are common, with wall surfaces that project and recede, and arched windows are often set into pavilion-like sections of the façade.

Queen Anne (1870–1900)

This is another Victorian style that originated in England. It emphasizes contrasts of form, color, and texture, with a variety of building materials used in the same house for different floors. Stained glass and bay windows, steep gabled roofs, and large encircling verandas are other characteristics of these irregularly planned buildings.

Victorian Eclectic (1880–1900)

The Victorian Eclectic style designates complicated, inventive buildings with features of many different styles and eras and nationalities. It is sometimes referred to as "romantic, picturesque irregularity," for its imaginative, eclectic elements. (Such elaborate concoctions have only recently been considered worth saving.)

Beaux Arts (1880–1920)

Mostly used in the United States for public buildings and palaces for the very wealthy, this grand style is based on French designs. Used in the United States for stations, museums, libraries, and private estates (such as the mansions of Newport, Rhode Island), Beaux Arts buildings are characterized by massive size, classical details, columns, and statuary and by design that incorporates into the overall plan the layout of outdoor areas around the building, with gardens, fountains, and sculpture.

Arts and Crafts (1895–1920)

An emphasis on simplicity and the hand-made characterize the Arts and Crafts movement (in contrast to the fussiness of late Victorianism and the impersonality of a machine-oriented culture). Following the strictures of John Ruskin and William Morris in England, the American movement focused on both buildings and furniture. Architectural emphasis is on low, dark-wood horizontal houses; they feature gabled roofs with projecting eaves, elaborately jointed and hand-cut overhanging beams (sometimes logs), shingled exteriors, and an overall rustic appearance.

Prairie (1900–1920)

Frank Lloyd Wright was the architect who introduced Prairie-style houses, a response to the low, flat plains of his native Midwest. The houses are modern and geometric in their design of space; they are low and horizontal with broad, sheltering, overhanging roofs and little exterior ornament. There are balconies and porches at different levels, a central chimney, and occasional patterned stained-glass windows; the overall effect is of low, geometric forms softened by large glass windows integrating architecture and nature.

Art Deco (1925–1940)

This fashionable style affected every aspect of design after the trend-setting Expo in Paris in 1925; in the United States it can be seen in major public buildings, skyscrapers, movie theaters, and aspects of fashion and interior design. Larger private homes in certain areas also adhere to Art Deco's brilliant combinations of pattern and architectural line. Art Deco's characteristics involve a combination of horizontal, vertical, and curving lines and repetitive geometric forms, augmented with embellishments of all kinds. Materials for detailing include stainless steel, glass brick, and tile, and ornamentation includes floral, animal, and natural images. In the 1930s, with a nod to the new age, Art Deco integrated "Streamline" design with machine imagery.

Modernism (1922–1940) and Mid-Century Modernism (1945–1975)

In the period after World War I, as "modern" architecture appeared in Europe in the International style and the Bauhaus style, American architects sought new styles as well. Influenced by leading European architects (some living in the United States), Modernism took hold in the form of simple, functional, geometric buildings. Undecorated boxlike forms with flat roofs, Modernist buildings are clad in glass or reinforced concrete; these designs became central to tall buildings in cities across the country. Houses from the period emphasize open space in the interior.

Mid-Century Modernism softened the rigorous boxlike outlines of the earlier period. This turn to more graceful homes emphasized many of the Prairie school's designs, with houses nestled into—and relating to—the landscape and the use of as many natural materials as possible.

Postmodern (1965–)

As a reaction to the undecorated and rigorous modernist styles, Postmodernism attempted to mix in styles from the past. Thus, a Postmodern building may have classical columns, a Tuscan tower, Victorian arched windows, or even elements of Asian architecture, all set within a contemporary framework.

Contemporary

Today's architecture has moved into brand new territory, using sculptural and high-tech designs. With silhouettes that soar and swoop, with dramatic, overhanging shapes and all kinds of original lines and forms, new buildings (particularly large public buildings, such as campus structures) explore some of the most original concepts of architecture. Although many houses are still built in traditional styles (Neocolonial, for example), architects are using high-tech engineering and sculptural form to create a new style for the twenty-first century.

CHOOSING AN OUTING

Examples of Architectural Styles

COLONIAL

GEORGIAN

ABOUT THE AUTHORS

Lucy D. Rosenfeld and Marina Harrison are the coauthors of eight guide-books, including *A Guide to Green New Jersey*. Among their books are walk-ing tours of gardens, historic sites, public art, and nature preserves. They are lifelong friends who enjoy exploring new places and introducing them to their readers. Lucy D. Rosenfeld is also the author of more than twenty books on art and architecture. Marina Harrison, in addition to writing guidebooks, worked for many years in publishing.